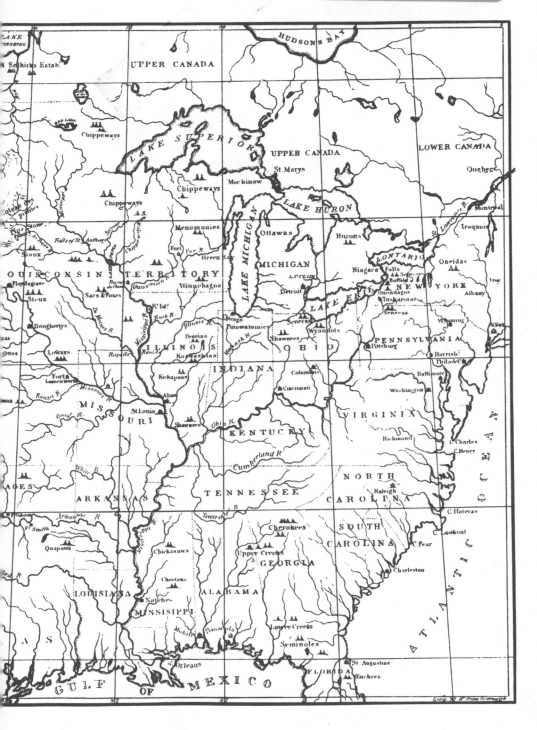

WHITE SAVAGE

The drawing of John Dunn Hunter by Charles R. Leslie appeared as the frontispiece of his own *Memoirs of a Captivity among the Indians of North America* in the London edition of 1824. (Reproduced courtesy of the American History Division, The New York Public Library, Astor, Lenox and Tilden Foundations.)

Drawn by C. R. Leslie

Printed by C. Hullmandel

.JOHN.D.HUNTER.

WHITE SAVAGE
THE CASE OF
JOHN DUNN HUNTER

Richard Drinnon

SCHOCKEN BOOKS / NEW YORK

FOR

the Children of
Tecumseh
and Richard Fields

Acknowledgments

I have long been of the opinion that reference librarians are probably the finest people in the scholarly world. Over the past several years my search for fugitive materials on a forgotten man has hardened this opinion into an unshakable conviction. In Britain and from coast to coast in North America I have repeatedly received help which was breathtaking, so far did it go beyond the usual definitions of professional responsibility. Assuredly without what I was pointed toward or had turned up for me, this essay could not have existed. In the footnotes below I try to express my appreciation to some individuals. A list of all the others who merit mention would be impossibly long and would read almost like a staff directory of the major research centers in this country and abroad—most recently, for instance, threescore and more librarians enthusiastically joined in my search for Thomas Jefferson's copy of Hunter's narrative. But perhaps they and all the others will accept this note addressed to them collectively: I salute you, benefactors, and thank you for your uncommon generosity.

Since a Faculty Research Fellowship financed the beginnings of the larger study from which this book stems, I may appropriately express my gratitude here to the Social Science Research Council. I am also grateful to the Trustees of Bucknell University for summer grants which helped in the research and writing.

Old intellectual debts are never really repaid and new ones add obligations of their own. Of them all, I want merely to mention now, once again, my indebtedness to Mulford Q. Sibley and to Henry Nash Smith: *White Savage*, I like to think, happily reveals the joint influence of the former's preoccupation with the libertarian tradition in politics and the latter's lifelong quest for the meaning of the West. Alix Shulman and Jack Cook, personal friends, read the study in an earlier version and offered their encouragement, for which they have my warm thanks. Mark Neuman, fellow historian, read Part One and made some valuable suggestions. Roger Shugg, an old publishing associate, helped it get into print in ways unforeseen by either of us at the time. Judy Poust's cheerful competence in handling clerical chores and her thoughtful advice have helped immeasurably. I am grateful to John F. Thornton of Schocken Books for his faith in the work and for his courteous editorial assistance. Finally, I am much obliged to Native American friends for giving me passing insights into their life worlds. The Mohawk White Roots of Peace group, in particular, has given me some sense of what was lost and of the magnitude of the tragedy acted out in our heedless Winning of the West.

Contents

List of Maps

Introduction

Who was John Dunn Hunter? No one ever knew—not even Hunter, if he spoke the truth—who his parents were and what his real name was. And this unknown is merely a particular aspect of the larger mystery called American history: "What are you? What am I?" asks a shadowy figure in Melville's *Confidence Man* (1857). "Nobody knows who anybody is." This study attempts to respond to the question both in its particularity and in its generality.

Nowadays literally nobody knows who Hunter was and that in itself is significant. Why have we forgotten him? The time was when a writer could assume his readers knew of the romantic life of the celebrated white captive. In the 1840s, for instance, Henry Stuart Foote could suppose in his history of Texas,

> that most of those who may chance to honour these pages with a perusal, will have heard, at least, if they shall not have read much of this extraordinary person; since he was, many years ago, the writer of his own strange life and adventures, and, at one time, was an object of such uncommon curiosity, both in England and the United States, that all his movements were minutely observed upon in the gazettes of either country; and his most trivial remarks were deemed worthy of elaborate scrutiny and solemn criticism.[1]

By the end of the century Hunter had dropped out of the public consciousness. His life and adventures simply had no place in the expansive destiny of the United States. In 1905 a leading western historian had to identify Hunter in a footnote, in which he reflected a professional verdict not effectively challenged since:

> The career of John Dunn Hunter was a remarkable one, even if he be considered an impostor. According to his own statements, he was

1. Foote, *Texas and the Texans* (Philadelphia: Thomas Cowperthwait, 1841), I, 240.

of white parentage, but captured when a child by the Indians, among whom he grew to manhood. Abandoning his tribe in 1816, he went to New Orleans, placed himself in school, and acquired sufficient command of English to edit a book concerning his adventures. This was published under the title, *Manners and Customs of Several Indian Tribes located West of the Mississippi* (Philadelphia, 1823). . . . About this time Hunter went to Europe, and was lionized and praised in both London and Paris. He gave it to be understood that his life work was to ameliorate the condition of the North American Indians, and about 1824 went to Texas and joined the band of Cherokees located near Nacogdoches. He remained true to his engagements with the Fredonians [revolutionaries who tried to establish a Red and White republic so named], even after their cause began to decline, and was therefore shot by a renegade Indian, under circumstances of considerable barbarity. American pioneers pronounced Hunter an impostor, and his book a forgery. The evidence to that effect by Lewis Cass, William Clark, and Auguste Chouteau seems conclusive.[2]

In truth a remarkable career: How many real impostors would risk their lives remaining "true to their engagements"? But, such questions aside, this was an able summary of the little that could be recalled about Hunter.

I confess I had not even heard of the man before a chance encounter in the course of other research. Perhaps if I explain how this came about, the reader will more readily grasp the themes and organization of the chapters which follow.

A few years ago, before the topic became so fashionable, I received a grant from the Social Science Research Foundation to pursue an inquiry into patterns of American violence. In the summer of 1967, still working on this larger undertaking, I was gathering materials in the British Museum for a chapter to be entitled "Transatlantic Images of Violence." One day I wandered off on a side trail which took me to Hoxie Fairchild's *Noble Savage* (1928), where I amused myself reading Felicia Hemans' sweet verse warnings to someone named Hunter, "the child of the forests," not to heed a Buck-like call of the wild. I lingered to note Fairchild's explanation that Hunter's narrative "is one of the best known of the numerous 'captivity' chronicles. . . . He gives a favorable, but not a sentimental, picture of Indian life." Already this far afield, I decided to venture a little farther and seek Hunter out. Perhaps he could help

2. Reuben Gold Thwaites, ed., *Early Western Travels, 1748–1846* (Cleveland: Arthur H. Clark, 1905), XVIII, 368n.

me resolve my perplexity over the origin and extent of the fears in the settlements whenever the issue of captives came up.

A first reading of Hunter's narrative persuaded me that it was an important document, perhaps a minor classic in the American literature of self-discovery. Like the much more impressive works in this tradition —Thoreau's *Walden* (1854) and Whitman's *Leaves of Grass* (1855) —come to mind—it seemed to have grown up outdoors someplace, perhaps at the edge of the woods like a sumac bush or a wild grapevine. Since the narrative had last been published in 1824 (as I then thought), I decided to devote a few weeks to the research which would enable me to edit a modern edition. My first find was a pamphlet defending Hunter against charges of imposture. When I followed up these charges to an American periodical, I found that their anonymous author was in fact Lewis Cass, Governor of the Michigan Territory. I knew Cass had later become Andrew Jackson's Secretary of War and therefore had something to do with the removal of the Cherokees and their Trail of Tears. I seemed to remember him also as the harsh critic of Cooper's Indians in the Leatherstocking Tales. Now well into the underbrush of charges and denunciations, I stumbled across a campaign biography of 1848, when Cass was the presidential nominee of the Democratic party, and read there, as one of the candidate's claims for political preferment, the fact that he had exposed Hunter's book as "a palpable forgery." This was unsettling: if the forgery were really that *palpable,* what had happened to my, not to mention Hoxie Fairchild's, capacity for critical reading?

So did Hunter rise up out of my other research and take over my waking hours. Still, how this happened can perhaps best be explained not by listing the sources which led him to me but by invoking D. H. Lawrence's prophetic discovery of "terrible spirits, ghosts, in the air of America": one of these unappeased demons thrust through my topic on international projections of violence to demand my undivided attention. All the same, it still strikes me as a bit odd for him to have shown up in the Reading Room of the British Museum with orders which sent me running off for answers to such questions as whether there was ever "a grain of wild rice" in the Osage country.

The sidetrip of a few weeks became an expedition of four years. In Parts One and Three of the book I begin and end with the strange life and adventures of John Dunn Hunter. I may fairly observe here that for some good while I seriously entertained the possibility that he was an impostor. In some ways this made him still more intriguing: imagine someone so internalizing the idea of a New Man being born out of the encounter of European stock and the American wilderness, with Indians acting as midwives, that he commenced to live this fantasy even to the point of death! But I had to give up this fascinating prospect and conclude that he was authentic. As always, the critical reader will reach his own conclusions.

Hunter was a remarkable man, even if he not "be considered an impostor." He was distinguished by his friends and enemies alike. The latter included Cass, of course; Jared Sparks, the editor of the *North American Review;* Henry Rowe Schoolcraft, the Indian agent and explorer; John Neal, the American novelist; Peter Stephen Duponceau, the pioneer linguist; Joel R. Poinsett, the American minister to Mexico and future Secretary of War; Stephen F. Austin, the famous *empresario;* Colonel Peter Ellis Bean, the soldier of fortune; Manuel Lisa and Pierre Chouteau, the merchants and fur-trade barons; and William Clark, the explorer, along with practically all the agents and army officers associated with Clark's St. Louis Superintendency of Indian Affairs. Hunter's friends ranged from an obscure young English journalist named Elias Norgate, who wrote the pamphlet in his defense, to the Duke of Sussex and included Thomas William Coke, the agriculturist and Whig statesman; Sir James Smith, the botanist; Cyrus Redding, the editor of the *New Monthly Magazine;* John Halkett, the pioneer historian of Indian–white relations; Chester Harding, the American portraitist; Thomas Jefferson; Sir Henry George Ward, the English chargé d'affaires in the City of Mexico; Richard Fields, the Cherokee chief; Herman Mayo, the Texas rebel and Mississippi newspaper editor; and George Catlin, the great Indian painter and ethnologist.

In his close and friendly relationship with Robert Owen, who founded the communal societies of New Lanark and New Harmony, Hunter served as a link between Indian tribalism and the modern cooperative and communitarian movements: he thus has immediate relevance today both for Red Power advocates and for those radicals seeking communal solutions. As a former captive who came back with news that Indian life was good, Hunter served, or more accurately, might have served, as a link between the white and red worlds and, by extension, to the great majority of mankind in the rest of the nonwhite world. In his proposed Indian country, he offered an alternative to extermination; in their rejection of him, white Americans rejected their humanity. Implicit in his life and writings was the promise of a new consciousness, of new ways of looking at and defining "civilization" and "savagery," or, better, of new ways of thinking of brotherhood and of being at home in nature.

On one level this study is simply an attempt to pull the man and his book out of an undeserved oblivion. But even on this plane of biography, with all its attention to individual particularity, I soon had to bring history and anthropology together to gain some understanding of the Indian and white cultures which Hunter internalized and then externalized in his writings and actions. This necessity soon made me keenly aware of just how stubbornly ignorant American historians have remained of the body of knowledge and techniques built up by ethnologists. It is as though, as spokesmen for the victors and worshipers of success, we have impatiently rejected any responsibility for taking the victims seriously as persons who had—and have—manners and customs which merit our respect and careful study. If I have successfully worked past some of my own deficiencies in these matters, this study may be a presentable essay in ethnohistory. And I may as well admit here that it is still more interdisciplinary in fact, especially in my handling of the catalog of charges discussed in Part Two. I draw on psychoanalysis, I hope not heavy-handedly, to deal with some of the irrational dimensions of white racism. I depend on literary history and criticism for help in dealing with the captivity chronicles as a genre and as means of understanding myths, including that of the noble savage. There is even a smattering of anthropological linguistics, along with traces of archeology and botany. If for no other reason, this study is slightly eccentric in the range of materials it draws on.

The biographical treatment of the subject stands in a dialectical, back-and-forth relationship with a more ambitious undertaking, a comprehensive overview: a nation is known by its victims. An inquiry into what made Hunter a victim quickly takes us into the mystifications of the real confidence men and of what Melville called "the metaphysics of Indian-hating." Winning the West meant murdering, looting, and uprooting. And those who vanished did so with hardly a sound. As a writer in the *Cincinnati Literary Gazette* sadly observed after reading Hunter's narrative, the Indians "have had no poet and are dead"; in the course of his review he did take some comfort that they were at last finding a voice through Hunter. But the official outriders of the conquering civilization understandably preferred to have their victims "melt away" noiselessly—to go quietly, as we say—and they moved to still Hunter's voice. A study of him and of the response to him takes us inside the colonial mentality in America. It opens up possibilities of tracing a few of the complex inter-relationships of racism, nationalism, and expansionism. Hunter's experiences in the City of Mexico and in East Texas lay bare some of the connections between domestic racism and imperialism and even offer insights into the thinking of those modern Americans who have made the passage to Indochina. Understanding why Minister Poinsett opposed Hunter's Indian project in Texas, for instance, puts in clearer perspective what the Monroe Doctrine was all about. And there are other incidental gains, not the least of which is a chance to compare the attitudes of Englishmen and Americans toward the Indians, progress, civilization—indeed toward a number of the leading questions of the day. The enthusiasm with which Hunter was received by the English derived in part, of course, from the fact that the Indians he presumed to speak for were not those of Asia but of America. Still, this is only at best an incomplete explanation.

An illustration may serve to bring the considerably more complex problem into focus: At a Paris soirée in the 1820s, Sir John Franklin jumped to Hunter's defense against the attacks of an American. "I am aware, Sir," asserted the famous Arctic explorer, "of all that has been objected to Hunter's narrative, as I have both perused the work and conversed with the writer or author; and I do not hesitate to declare that he has given the best account of the manners and customs of any author I have ever read. And," he added with emphasis, "allow me to be something of a judge!" When the American informed Lewis Cass of this conversation, the general expressed surprise "that Sir John Franklin should have given credit to this fabricated book, called Hunter's narrative. It is only another evidence of the facility with which the most intelligent men often surrender their convictions to circumstances unworthy of their consideration." Was it? Why were Franklin and other members of the Royal Society willing to consider Hunter one of the wonders of the age? Why were Cass and many of his compatriots determined to expose him as one of its most dangerous frauds?

My study of Hunter had thus ironically led me back to the transatlantic theme and to the realization that the sharply opposed responses to him had to do with national patterns of violence. The research which started in London took Anna Maria Drinnon and me to Coke's estate in Norfolk, to various historical societies in England and the United States, to Office of Indian Affairs and State Department files in the National Archives, to the Jefferson Papers in the Library of Congress, back to the Public Record Office in London, to other depositories and archives, and, last of all, to Thoreau's copy of Hunter's narrative in the Concord Free Public Library. I suppose I should have known that the research itself was likely to bring me back round to the writer who has been one of my enduring interests; as in the Indian Round Dance, I seem always to be coming back to where I started, to be ending where I began. By this point I was not too surprised to discover that I was doing a part of what Thoreau would have done so well had he lived to write his masterwork on the American Indian. He knew better than anyone how deep our need has been for a history with "some copper tints and reflections at least."

RICHARD DRINNON

Milton, Pennsylvania
Weekapaug, Rhode Island

PART ONE

SAVAGE CELEBRITY

During this winter, 1823–4, Hunter was the *Lion* of the fashionable world in London. He was freely admitted at Almacks, and was pressed with multitudes of invitations to routs and balls, and parties, from ladies of the highest rank and fashion. Such was the strife for his society, that he had often several engagements in the same evening, and happy was the lady whose party was distinguished by his presence.

Natchitoches *Courier,* March 20, 1827

Memoirs of a Captivity

1

> People are ready to run wild into the woods again and to
> be as Heathenish as ever, if you do not prevent it.
>
> INCREASE MATHER,
> A *Discourse Concerning the Danger of Apostacy,* 1679

From mythological times into modern, the European imagination has been captivated by the prospect of discovering somewhere a pure, living example of "natural man." Daniel Defoe's justly famous Footstep in the Sand was only a relatively recent expression of this ancient, tantalizing quest. Early in the nineteenth century the capture of the "savage of Aveyron," a boy of about fifteen found in the French forest of that name, pushed forth a new wave of curiosity about "wolf children" living "in a state of nature." And in the spring of 1823 English reviewers began to take notice of a "striking and singular" new book which seemed to speak to the question.

On April 19 the *Literary Gazette* led off by announcing the publication of *Memoirs of a Captivity among the Indians of North America, from Childhood to the Age of Nineteen.* . . . In this and the issue of April 26 the *Gazette* carried lengthy extracts from the narrative, and their reviewer predicted for its author, John Dunn Hunter, an interest like that aroused by Robinson Crusoe.

This prophecy may not have been entirely disinterested, however, for it appeared in what was in some measure a house organ of Hunter's publisher: Longman, Hurst, Rees, Orme, and Brown, as the firm was then constituted, owned a one-third interest in the *Gazette.*[1] The connection with the house of Longman may also have had something to do with the reviewer's contempt for the Philadelphia edition of the narrative. Previously, he explained, the book "was wretchedly got up and published in America, so interlarded and *mended* by some editor who could not appreciate its value as it came untouched from the lips of its author, with

---

1. William Jerdan, *Autobiography* (London: Arthur Hall, Virtue, 1852), III, 216. Jerdan was editor of the *Literary Gazette* from 1817 to 1850.

all its original characters, mode of expression, style, and native thought about it, that its restoration to what it ought always to have been is not only a service to literature, but to philosophy [as well]." The role of Hunter's editor was a real problem, but it was not resolved by the new edition. Longman took over the book, published in Philadelphia earlier in the year by J. Maxwell under the title *Manners and Customs of Several Indian Tribes Located West of the Mississippi* . . . , and brought it out virtually unchanged, except for the new title and three additional chapters.[2]

Still, the reviewer may have come to a quite genuine enthusiasm for Hunter's narrative on his own. Others without ulterior motives did so quickly. Only a few months later I. J. Chapman, a traveler in the United States, wrote Thomas Jefferson about a letter he had received from Joseph Sabine in England: "Mr. Hunter, about whom I spoke to you when at Monticello, is mentioned as having been received in the best literary society in London, in a manner in which no foreigner (to use Sabine's own expression, if we may call an American so) has previously been received—that he has already sold one Edition of 1500 copies of his work, and is now sitting to Leslie for his portrait, to be prefixed to the second Edition." [3] Across the Atlantic, according to the *Saturday Evening Post* of August 16, 1823, there was an unusually rapid sale of the English edition in Philadelphia. "I understand that this work is in the hands of the principal Booksellers of this City," the writer added, "and is offered to the public at a price corresponding with that of other American publications. The price first fixed was certainly too high, and the reduction, though late, is judicious, and places the work within the reach of readers generally."

Moving to take advantage of the keen interest on both sides of the Atlantic, Longman brought out a second edition in the summer of 1823 and a third in 1824. As Hunter's fame spread to the Continent, his *Memoirs* were quickly translated into other languages: Dutch and German editions were published in 1824 and a Swedish edition in 1826.

2. See the Bibliographical Essay, pp. 260–61, for the full titles and publishing details on the American, English, and Continental editions.

3. Chapman to Jefferson, July 20, 1823, Jefferson Papers, Library of Congress. Joseph Sabine was a leading figure in the Horticultural Society and a Fellow of the Royal Society. Charles Robert Leslie was an American portraitist who had taken up residence in London over a decade earlier. His drawing of Hunter was prefixed to the second and third London editions. The side-view in the second edition was dated July 1823.

2

Had Romulus published an account of his experiences with the she-wolf, it would have struck many as only a bit more extraordinary than Hunter's story of his life with the wild men of North America. Though much had been heard about the Indians "and the wild regions which they inhabit—the country rude as the savage, and the savage rude as the country," observed a writer in the *Monthly Review*—little or nothing had been heard from the Indians themselves. Yet here was an account "from the pen of an individual who has been for years one of themselves, and, in everything but his actual birth and parentage, an Indian, imbibing their feelings, practising their manners, and living their life."

What was striking and singular about it, the *Monthly Review* writer insisted, was the fact that a man avowedly ignorant of the art of book-making and imperfectly acquainted with the English language should still undertake to be "the memorialist of his own captivity by the Indians of North America, and of his residence among several of their tribes, from the period of his infancy to his assumption of the habits of civilized life at the age of manhood." The details of his expeditions, in the battle and the chase, with the Pawnees and the Kansas, the Kickapoos, the Shawnees, and the Osages, had so romantic an air as to make the reader incredulous:

> It may well excite astonishment, indeed, that a person kidnapped in his infancy; torn away from all civilized society before he could lisp his mother's tongue or articulate his mother's name; plunged into the deep forests of America by a tribe of savages, and learning no other than their barbarous and imperfect language; following for nearly twenty years the wandering life which they passed, roots and wild buffalo his food, and the skins of hunted animals his clothing;—it must excite astonishment, we say, that a person so brought up should, in the short space of a few years from his escape, have been able to compose a volume in the English language, in which terms of art and science are frequently and appropriately used, and subjects relating to physics, morals, juris-prudence, natural history, commerce, manufactures, &c. are introduced as occasion requires.

Little wonder, then, that when the book was announced, "it was suspected to be a fabrication of some ingenious impostor."

Hunter appeared, however, with letters of introduction "from gentlemen of the highest character and station in the United States" and

> happening to know persons who have become well acquainted with him in this country, we learn on their indisputable authority that none who have passed a single afternoon in his company, whatever might have been their previous impressions, have any longer had the slightest doubt that he is exactly what he represents himself to be: or that his story, recorded as it is entirely from memory, the savages among whom he lived having no written language, is perfectly faithful.[4]

Other commentators agreed. After meeting Hunter in company, the *Literary Gazette* reviewer had found it "impossible but to entertain a deep interest" in him.[5] A writer in the evangelical *Eclectic Review*, without the advantage of such a meeting, nevertheless concluded that "the internal marks of authenticity are so strong, that we entertain no suspicion whatever of its substantial genuineness and accuracy." [6]

Putting behind them their initial suspicions, reviewers treated their readers to some of the exotic details of Hunter's life and samples from his discussion of Indian manners and customs. In the course of presenting one of the more able digests, the writer in the *Monthly Review* commenced with a discussion of the circumstances that led to the author's captivity.[7]

"I was taken prisoner at a very early period of my life," Hunter had related, "by a party of Indians who, from the train of events that followed, belonged to, or were in alliance with, the Kickapoo nation. At the same time, two other white children, a boy and a small girl, were also made prisoners." Since Hunter had also reported that he left the Indians in 1816, when he had reason to believe he was nineteen or twenty years old, he must have been born in 1796 or 1797. It was probable that his parents were settlers on the frontier, perhaps somewhere in the Old Northwest. And, since he had some "indelible impressions" going back to that time, "while others not so strikingly characterized" crossed his memory "like

---

4. *Monthly Review*, CII (November 1823), 243, 244.
5. *Literary Gazette*, April 19, 1823, p. 242; the extracts from the *Memoirs* in its issue of April 19 were on pp. 242–44 and of April 26 on pp. 260–62; in the issue of May 3, 1823, it published a communication from Hunter on his name in various Indian languages on pp. 278–79.
6. *Eclectic Review*, XX (July–December 1823), 173–81.
7. *Monthly Review*, CII (November and December 1823), 234–56, 368–81.

the imperfect recollection of a dream," very possibly he was captured as an infant of two or three, i.e., in 1799 or 1800. But all of this was most uncertain:

> I have too imperfect a recollection of the circumstances connected with this capture, to attempt any account of them; although I have reflected on the subject so often, and with so great interest and intensity, under the knowledge I have since acquired of the Indian modes of warfare, as nearly to establish at times a conviction in my mind of a perfect remembrance. There are moments when I see the rush of the Indians, hear their war-whoops and terrific yells, and witness the massacre of my parents and connections, the pillage of their property, and the incendious destruction of their dwellings. But the first incident that made an actual and prominent impression on me happened while the party were somewhere encamped, no doubt shortly after my capture; it was as follows: The little girl whom I before mentioned, beginning to cry, was immediately dispatched with the blow of a tomahawk from one of the warriors: the circumstance terrified me very much, more particularly as it was followed with very menacing motions of the same instrument, directed to me, and then pointed to the slaughtered infant, by the same warrior, which I then interpreted to signify, that if I cried, he would serve me in the same manner. From this period till the apprehension of personal danger had subsided, I recollect many of the occurrences which took place.

Though he was adopted into the family of one of the principal warriors, he was taunted by the Indian boys "with being *white,* and with the whites all being *squaws,* a reproachful term used generally among the Indians, in contradistinction to that of *warrior*. This often involved me in boyish conflicts, from which I sometimes came off victorious." He was taken from the Kickapoos by a roving band of Pawnees and from the latter, after a skirmish, by a victorious party of Kansas Indians. Among the latter, "I was adopted into the family of Kee-nees-tah by his squaw, who had lost a son in one of their recent engagements with the Pawnees. I was exceedingly fortunate from this election, and not only the chiefs and squaws, but the whole tribe treated me with regard." After some years with the Kansas, when he was "a lad of ten or twelve years of age," his foster mother drowned during a flood. He felt sharp grief, for she "had treated me with great tenderness and affection."

A short while later the band of Kansas he was with found themselves cut off from the rest of their tribe during a time of war with the Osages;

unable to return to their people safely, they went to the Osages and
successfully claimed "the rights of hospitality":

> I had not been long with the Osages before I was received into the
> family of Shen-thweeh, a warrior distinguished among his people for
> his wisdom and bravery, at the instance of Hunk-hah, his wife, who had
> recently lost a son, in an engagement with some of the neighbouring
> tribes. This good woman, whose family now consisted of herself, her
> husband, a daughter almost grown, and myself, took every opportunity
> and used every means which kindness and benevolence could suggest,
> to engage my affections and esteem. She used to weep over me, tell me
> how good her son had been, how much she loved him, and how
> much she mourned his loss. "You must be good," she would say,
> "and you shall be my son, and I will be your mother."

About a year after he arrived among the Osages, when he was fourteen
or fifteen, the tribe bartered furs for rifles with some visiting traders and
presented one to each of the boys who had been on a recent hunt: "I soon
learned the use of my rifle in the chace, and used it with great success,
in consequence of which, the Indians gave me the name of the *Hunter.*"

One of the most striking episodes from this section of Hunter's narrative, as the writer in the *Monthly Review* pointed out, was "a hunting
expedition of sixteen moons duration, commencing up the Arkansas; and
in the course of which he and his party crossed the Rocky Mountains, and
reached the Pacific Ocean on the south side of the Columbia river." On
their return, Hunter had recorded, the Osages, who "had looked upon us
as lost . . . greeted our arrival among them in the most joyful and
tumultuous manner. My Indian mother and sister wept aloud, and the
squaws, young and old, danced around us to the cadence of their festival
songs, and decorated our persons in the same manner as though we had
returned triumphant over the enemies of our country."

The incident that led Hunter to leave the Indians was also remarkable.
A trader named Colonel Watkins, who had an encampment on the
Arkansas, had given Hunter a number of small presents, treated him with
particular attention and kindness as a white, and repeatedly urged him
to accompany his party back to the settlements. Hunter refused, attached
as he was to Indian habits and their manner of life. But then occurred the
event which "produced a highly important revolution in my life; a revolution which, I am persuaded, few circumstances, and perhaps no other,
could have effected."

The circumstances were these: Six of a hunting expedition of thirty, of which Hunter was a member, visited Watkins on the Arkansas, bartered for whisky, stole six of his horses on leaving, killed and scalped a French trader who had his camp nearby, and returned to the main party of Osages with their booze, spoils, and bloody trophy. Embittered by the incursions of whites into their hunting lands and also maddened by the whisky, the rest of the hunters joined the six in plotting to murder Watkins and take all his goods. Though "these proceedings produced, in my bosom, the most acute, and indescribably painful sensations," Hunter kept his silence. He hid his feelings so effectively he was allowed to stand guard while his companions slept off the effects of the liquor. He thereupon "silently and cautiously removed all the flints from the guns, emptied the primings from the pans, took my own rifle and other equipments, and, mounting the best horse that had been stolen on the preceding day, made my escape, and gave the alarm to Watkins and his party."

Hunter arrived in Watkins' camp "badly lacerated, bleeding, and much exhausted" after riding all night through twenty-five or thirty miles of rough country. His warning naturally alarmed the trader. At first Watkins refused to listen to the urging of his men that they make an immediate retreat:

> He instantly ordered the preparations to be made to repel any attack that might be made on them, and I was requested to join in the defence, should one become necessary: but I refused, stating that it was sufficient for me to have betrayed my countrymen, without augmenting the crime, by fighting against, and possibly killing some of them. Colonel Watkins replied that they were not my countrymen; that I was a white man; and what I had done, and what he requested me to do, were no more than my duty to the white people required me to perform.

But Hunter refused with rising vehemence, his prejudice against whites generally as strong as ever: "I now hated the very looks of Colonel Watkins, who, before, had appeared so amiable and good; despised myself for the treachery of which I had been culpable, and almost regretted the part I had performed." Sensible of the obligations he was under to Hunter, Watkins gave up his plans for a stand and ordered preparations to break camp. The former captive accompanied the Watkins party down the Arkansas River and away from his red brethren.

And such, in greatly foreshortened form, was the outline of Hunter's captivity which reviewers put before their readers.

3

Unlike the usual run of captivity chronicles, already a stylized and stale popular genre, Hunter's *Memoirs* provided an entrancing tale of adventure, believable ethnological information, and more.[8] In a long and important article in the *Quarterly Review,* an anonymous critic commenced with an abstract of Hunter's life, for to his mind the narrative, which "does not form above one third of his volume . . . is by far the most interesting part of it; . . . besides the attractions inseparable from the relation of such a course of adventure, the information which it gives of the character and condition of the Indians, is thus conveyed in a much more easy and pleasing manner than it can be in formal and elaborate dissertations." [9]

The *Quarterly* critic also found it valuable for reaching a better understanding of the impending fate of the aborigines of North America. For some two hundred years they had been the victims of "the oppression and encroachment of whites." Despite their devotion, courage, and fortitude, the warlike tribes had resisted in vain "the extinction we confidently anticipate." Thus it was most important to have authentic memorials of their character, customs, and opinions before these "living ruins" disappeared forever, "for the remains of the Indian tribes are become to America what the shattered column, the broken arch, and the falling cloister are to Europe. The iron hand of time has not made deeper ravages on these, than the relentless cruelty of civilized men has inflicted upon the wretched remains of the aboriginal children of the lake and forest."

Hunter's book offered the *Quarterly Review* critic an opportunity for frankly discussing the relentless cruelty in detail. His view of "the transatlantic white population" was not sympathetic. He held that the Indian traders, with their "insidious supply of ardent spirits," were "usually the most ignorant, and depraved, and dishonest" individuals within that society. A close second in the process of corruption and destruction of the

8. For a useful survey of the chronicles, see Roy H. Pearce, "The Significances of the Captivity Narrative," *American Literature,* XIX (March 1947), 1–20.

9. This and subsequent quotations are from *Quarterly Review,* XXXI (December 1824), 76–111.

Indians were the settlers of the western states: "We affirm, without fear of contradiction or of error, that there is not to be found on the face of the globe a race of men so utterly abandoned to vice and crime—so devoid of all fear of God and regard towards man, as the outsettlers of Kentucky, Ohio, and the other back states." The writer, who wrote as a veteran of "the last war of the Canadas," had personally experienced their ferocity:

> If the mode of warfare of the Indians was ferocious, that of the enemy with whom we had to contend was equally so. Every man who has served in that country can attest the fact, that the Kentuckians invariably carry the tomahawk and scalping knife into action. . . . It would surely have been a despicable submission to the mawkish sensibility of our patriots, to have rejected the cooperation of the Indians in repelling an invading enemy, who at least equalled them in their most blood-thirsty qualities.

Against "the perpetually advancing deluge" of such settlers, the Indians stood little chance: "However it may be attempted to preserve appearances by fraudulent and compulsory purchases of Indian lands, and declarations of benevolent intentions towards their injured possessors, it has always been the boast of American policy, that 'the Indians shall be made to vanish before civilization, as the snow melts before the sunbeam.'" And not all the humane and praiseworthy efforts of the religious societies—"more commendable for zeal than judgment"—were likely to save a remnant of the tribes. Besides, the Indians had reason to be skeptical of the preaching of the missionaries from their Good Book. "When the Indians converse on these subjects, observes Hunter, they say, 'The white men tell Indian to be honest: Indian have no prison; Indian have no gaol for unfortunate debtors; Indian have no lock on his door.'"

The writer of the *Quarterly Review* essay used this powerful current of social criticism, which frequently bobbed to the surface of the narrative, to pursue the family squabble with his American cousins. He apparently remained unaware that Hunter's criticism flowed beyond such parochial concerns.

The *Memoirs* made perfectly clear that Hunter still had mixed feelings about the great change in his life. The incident involving Colonel Watkins was a case in point. Had the trader not brought whisky to the Brushy Fork of the Arkansas to drive the Indians out of their minds,

Hunter presumably would still have been contentedly roving across the prairies with his red brothers. Afterward he "almost regretted the part which I had performed" and, though he had "the consolation of the most entire conviction that I had acted rightly," he was still torn by his sense of having betrayed "those I sincerely loved and esteemed." [10]

Earlier he had recalled that, when passing from tribe to tribe as a boy, he had observed three or four other white children who appeared, "like myself, to have been at first forced to assume the Indian character and habits; but time and a conformity to custom had nationalized them, and they seemed as happy and contented as though they had descended directly from the Indians, and were in possession of their patrimony."

Since the day of Increase Mather transplanted Europeans had feared that men were as ready as ever "to run wild into the woods again"; generations of emigrants had been upset by the refusal of white captives, during the colonial wars, to part from their captors. Perhaps unwittingly, Hunter twisted the knife in this old wound with his placid observation of "a remarkable fact, that white people generally, when brought up among the Indians, become unalterably attached to their customs, and seldom afterwards abandon them." The real reach of Hunter's criticism, then, raised serious questions about both the American and the European consciousness. It was precisely as deep and as broad as the famous sentence in Crèvecoeur, that something in the Indian social bond was "singularly captivating, and far superior to anything to be boasted of among us; for thousands of Europeans are Indians, and we have no examples of even one of those Aborigines having from choice become Europeans!"

How could any child be "happy and contented" living with savages? Above all, how could *white* children? How could they possibly become, as Crèvecoeur and Hunter asserted, "invincibly attached" to Indian life? "Thus far," Hunter believed, "I am an exception, and it is highly probable I shall ever remain such." It was, however, a near thing and his old life, he confessed, still had seductive appeal:

> The struggle in my bosom was for a considerable time doubtful, and even now my mind often reverts to the innocent scenes of my childhood, with a mixture of pleasurable and painful emotions that is altogether indescribable. But my intercourse with refined society, acquaint-

10. Hunter, *Memoirs,* pp. 13–14. Except where otherwise stated, references will be to the third English edition (1824).

ance with books, and a glimpse at the wonderful structure into which the mind is capable of being moulded, have, I am convinced, unalterably attached me to a social intercourse with civilized man, composed as he is of crudities and contradictions.

"A glimpse at the wonderful structure into which the mind is capable of being moulded"—Hunter had surely written a striking and singular work. Beneath its adventurous surface, as in James Fenimore Cooper's Leatherstocking Tales, snags threatened the complacency of civilized man, with all his "crudities and contradictions."

Mingling with the City's Throng

2

In the course of our conversation, which ran upon pipes, upon Indians, and Indian countries, his royal highness [the Duke of Sussex] said he had reasons for asking me if I had known Hunter. . . . He said he had known Hunter familiarly while he was in London, and had entertained him in his palace, and thought a great deal of him.

GEORGE CATLIN,
Notes of Eight Years' Travels, 1848

Though he had left his "captivity" abruptly, Hunter did not immediately take up a new life in the white settlements. "If I had been ushered at once from one extreme to the other," he afterward maintained, "it is highly probable that a mutual dissatisfaction, and perhaps disgust, would have been the result." Several short steps, however, helped reconcile him to the great change.

Before the Watkins party reached the mouth of the Arkansas, Hunter struck off on his own, traveling north to the White River in search of some tribe which would take him in. His solitude was complete:

> The country around was delightful, and I roved over it almost incessantly, in ardent expectation of falling in with some party of Indians, with whom I might be permitted to associate myself. Apart from the hunting that was essential to my subsistence, I practised various arts to take fish, birds, and small game, frequently bathed in the river, and took great pleasure in regarding the dispositions and habits of such animals as were presented to my observations.[1]

Lying in the shade, he amused himself for hours watching ants store food, spiders move on their prey, mason-flies at work. One day a tremendous rushing noise warned him of the approach of a herd of buffalo, a thousand or more, running directly toward him. Finding shelter behind

---

1. For the quotations from Hunter in this section, see *Memoirs,* pp. 109–34.

the large tree under which he had been sitting, he watched them thunder by. At the rear of the herd was a panther, which he wounded and then succeeded in killing. He dressed and cured its skin over a fire and later found it "a source of some amusement: for I used frequently to array myself in it, as near as possible to the costume and form of the original, and surprise the herds of buffalo, elk, and deer, which, on my approach, uniformly fled with great precipitation and dread." In the mornings he sometimes awakened to find a rattlesnake coiled up next to him. Sharing the Indian respect for this reptile, he killed it only if he could find no other way to end their dangerous intimacy. He preferred to roll out of its reach, when this was possible, or to lie quiet "till the snake saw fit to retire."

Time was the full face of the moon, a gentle tide that carried him further into his friendly intercourse with the creatures of the prairie land and sky. But one day, after "several moons" according to his recollection, he was unpleasantly surprised by the appearance of five white hunters. His resentment of their intrusion ceased when one of the men spoke to him pleasantly in the Osage language. The sound of the familiar words changed his feelings "and I actually danced for joy."

The five were Frenchmen in search of trapping country. Hunter related that he was able to cut short their explorations by telling them what he knew of the area. They prevailed upon him to accompany them down-river to a place called Flees' Settlement. On his arrival he discovered that a number of the inhabitants suffered from fevers, and he was able to draw on his knowledge of Indian materia medica to prescribe remedies for their relief. And it was there that he learned his first words of the English language and was persuaded to put on white man's clothes—though, as he put it wryly, "it was a long time before I became reconciled to these peculiarly novel fetters."

The frontier circumstances of his new acquaintances made it possible for him to use skills he had already acquired among the Indians. According to his narrative, he trapped that fall and winter in the White River country he had explored so thoroughly. The next season he joined two young men named Tibbs and Warren in trapping along the west fork of the St. Francis. With his new partners he later signed on as a boatman and helped some Kentuckians float their produce down the Mississippi.

Nothing in Hunter's experience, not even the relatively settled St. Louis, had prepared him for New Orleans. The clash of empires and cultures was visible in the faces he saw in the public square, where

Pawnee
village ▲

NEBRASKA

La Platte (Platte) ▲ R.

Big Blue R.

Smoky Hill R.

Republican R.

KANSAS

Arkansas R.

I O W A

I O W A Y S

Missouri River

Des Moines R.

Grand R.

Mississippi River

Illinois R.

ILLINOIS

Old Kansas
village ▲

Kansas village ▲

Kansas R.

Fort
Osage ▢

Boone's
Lick ●

Boonville

Missouri River

St. Louis ●

Marais des Cygnes R.

Francis R.

Osage R.

Gasconade R.

Meramec R.
(Meramec)

Fort
Kaskaskia ▢

Great Osage village ▲

Little Osage village ▲

Grand R.

O S A G E

H I G H L A N D S

M I S S O U R I

Cape Girardeau ●

Crossing
Place the of
L. Osages ○

Verdigris R.

Grand (Neosho) R.

Settlement of
Delaware Indians ▲

New Madrid ●

Clermont's
Band of Osages ▲

Grand Saline R.
(Cimarron)

N. Fk. Canadian R.

Canadian R.

B O S T O N   M T S.

C H E R O K E E S

Arkansas R.

White R.

Flee's
Settlement

St. Francis R.

Mississippi River

TENN.

O Z A R K

OKLAHOMA

Fort
Smith ▢

Dwight

A R K A N S A S

O U A C H I T A

M T S.

Hot
Springs

French
Hunting Camps

Arkansas
Post ▢

Washita (Ouachita)

M I S S I S S I P P I

Pawnee
villages ▲▲▲

Little R.

Old Caddo village
Pecan Point
(Peccan)

Quapaw
village ▲

Choctaw
village ▲

Red R.

T E X A S

Caddo
village ▲

Yazoo R.

L O U I S I A N A

Natchitoches ●

Nacogdoches ●

Red River

OSAGE LOCALITIES
1823
*Names, points of interest, and the lo-
cations of villages are based on data
which first appeared on a chart drawn
by Zebulon M. Pike, issued in 1810,
and on a map of the Mississippi River
drainage area, drawn by Stephen H.
Long and published in 1823. Modern
state boundaries are shown for
reference only.*

0   100   200
scale of miles

Spaniards, Frenchmen, Yankees, Englishmen, Choctaw Indians, blacks, and individuals of every hue from black to white came together in the marketplace. Once he made his way into the city, perhaps carrying the goods of the Kentuckians up the wooden stairs to the top of the levee and to the stalls beyond, and had a chance to look around the market, he must have marveled at all the wares, the meat, fish, and oysters, white and sweet potatoes, pecans, wild ducks, tin kettles, dry goods. There was even a bookseller, whose stock of English and French volumes announced the presence of formal learning. The architect Benjamin Latrobe, who was in New Orleans at this time, recounted that as he looked across the square to the cathedral and the large buildings flanking it, the clanking of chains drew his attention to a work gang of slaves from the nearby jail, followed by overseers with long whips.[2]

Hunter's own account was cryptic but made clear that the experience was novel and moving:

> Here new scenes for both my admiration and disgust presented themselves to view. The arrangement, comparative elegance, and number of buildings; the magnitude, finish, and great collection of ships or vessels; the vast multitude of people, and the extent and bustle of business, excited the former; while the tumultuous revelry, intemperance, and debauchery of the boatmen and sailors, the abandoned demeanor of some unfortunate females, and the assemblage of a filthy multitude of blacks and whites, motley in all the intermediate shades, scarcely submitting to any moral restraints, and degraded in servitude and its concomitant vices, too low to be associated in the scale of rational human beings, were but too well calculated to produce the latter.

His admiration for the "bustle of business" suggested that his acculturation to white American ways had proceeded rapidly. This "eternal bustle," as Latrobe also referred to it, came from the ceaseless activity of Yankees who had recently streamed into the city to make money and who showed only contempt for the Spanish and French attachment to the graces of leisure.

Returning with his employers to Kentucky, he crossed the Choctaw and Cherokee nations on the way and then continued on back to the Missouri Territory. On a trading expedition the next fall he met Daniel

2. While in New Orleans to erect his waterworks, Latrobe kept a vividly written journal. See Samuel Wilson, Jr., ed., *Impressions Respecting New Orleans by Benjamin Boneval Latrobe: Diary & Sketches, 1818–1820* (New York: Columbia University Press, 1951).

Boone, then living at Boone's Lick on the Missouri, and struck up an affectionate relationship with the old man. On his return downriver he exchanged the furs he had collected in St. Louis for produce from Kentucky and then sold the.latter at a profit on the New Orleans market.

These experiences taught Hunter a good deal about white people. Whenever he had a chance, moreover, he went to school to learn to read and write. His first teacher was an old French woman who hoped to make a Roman Catholic of him. She made little progress toward this end, Hunter reported, but she did teach him the elements of English. His knowledge of the language increased during six weeks in a school in Cape Girardeau. While there he was called "by as many different names as there were pupils in the school," he explained, so he retained Hunter as his surname and, "as Mr. John Dunn, a gentleman of high respectability, of Cape Girardeau county, state of Missouri, had treated me in every respect more like a brother or son, than any other individual had since my association with the white people, I adopted his for that of my distinctive, and have since been known by the name of John Dunn Hunter."

At a seminary near Pearl River, Mississippi, he pursued his studies between trading seasons. The whole period of his formal schooling, he calculated, amounted "to about two years and a half, exclusive of about six weeks, which I passed, in the autumn of 1821, at Mr. Samuel Wilson's academy, near Walnut Hills, in Mercer county, Kentucky." At first he had real difficulty with the pronunciation and meaning of words, but once beyond this obstacle he found that he could move easily through all the common readers that came to hand. Between periods of formal schooling, he had access to "some respectable libraries" and carried books along on his trading ventures. As he put it, he "became literally infatuated with reading":

> My judgment was so much confused by the multiplicity of new ideas that crowded upon my undisciplined mind, that I hardly knew how to discriminate between truth and fable. This difficulty, however, wore off with the novelty, and I gradually recovered, with the explanatory assistance of my associates, the proper condition of mind to pursue my studies . . . with great interest and solicitude. They were confined to reading, writing, English grammar, and arithmetic.

But he soon moved beyond these elementary subjects to a point where he could think seriously of becoming acquainted "with some one of the learned professions."

Devout friends had meanwhile worked to bring him to a better understanding of Christianity and the Protestant virtues. He learned of the identification of the Great Spirit with the Creator and of the need to exercise "self-denial, charity, and truth, and to *square* my life by them, as acceptable offerings to the Great I AM." He was taught the value of "industry, perseverance and prudence." He also came to understand "the difference between the comparatively natural rights enjoyed by the Indians, and those essential to the harmonious preservation of civilized society."

Thus prepared and armed with letters of recommendation from his respectable friends, Hunter crossed the Allegheny Mountains in the autumn of 1821 to pursue his education and to publish a history of his life. After a year and a half in the East, primarily in New York and Philadelphia, he departed, probably in February or March 1823, for England. He carried with him high goals that were scarcely less remarkable than the narrative which he had just finished. He dared to think "of nothing less than the subjugation of the empires of science and literature, and when this had been accomplished, to have penetrated into unexplored regions in search of new truths."

2

Sometime after his arrival Hunter sought out Sir James Smith, the distinguished botanist. In a letter to a friend the scientist related that he had taken Hunter to visit the Norfolk estate of Thomas William Coke in October 1823:

> I introduced there Mr. Hunter, a native American, brought up among the Indians, and now going back with the noble design of improving them on the wisest and best principles. If you . . . have not read his Memoirs of his Captivity, pray do. The Duke of Sussex and Mr. Coke were delighted with him. He came to Europe with every possible recommendation from people whom I know.[3]

Unhappily, Smith did not go on to name names.

3. Smith to Mrs. Corrie, March 21, 1824, in *Memoir and Correspondence of the Late Sir James Edward Smith, M.D., Fellow of the Royal Society of London, etc.*, ed. Lady Smith (London: Longman, Rees, Orme, Brown, 1832), I, 513–15. Smith was the author of *English Botany,* the great work which was sometimes called *Sowerby's* after the name of its illustrator.

Quite possibly Jefferson and Madison were among Hunter's referees.[4] Almost certainly they included Richard Rush, the American Minister to the Court of St. James's.[5] From Jefferson, Rush, or someone, in any event, Hunter had learned of Coke's agricultural experiments at Holkham and had decided he must meet him. A. M. W. Stirling, Coke's biographer, asserted that the hope for such a meeting was the reason for Hunter's trip to England: "The fame of Coke as an agriculturist having reached him, he decided to journey to England in the hope of procuring an introduction to the man who, he learnt, could best aid him." [6]

The name "Coke of Norfolk" was deservedly famous throughout the country and even known to farmers abroad. According to the story, when he inherited the Holkham estate in 1776 the land was so barren there were two rabbits fighting for every blade of grass. Even if his reforms were afterward exaggerated, Thomas William Coke had made of his vast holdings—he left "just on 50,000 acres" to his son—"one of the wonders of East Anglia." [7] When he started, knowing little about agriculture, he had hit on the ingenious notion of inviting farmers from neighboring districts to Holkham once a year to visit and suggest improvements. These meetings became famous as the Holkham Sheepshearings, annual festivals which also attracted members of the aristocracy and reformers, and which included three days of sheep shearing, ploughing matches, and cattle exhibits. When Rush attended in 1819, about fifty guests stayed in the great house and another six hundred came each day to participate in the discussions and activities. By then, of course, Coke had made his name as a leading agricultural reformer. He had rich marl dug up and spread over the sandy soil, rotated crops, experimented with livestock, and planted woodlands which, among other more obvious uses, provided cover for thousands of partridges, pheasants, hares, and deer. Meanwhile, his income, according to Rush, had mounted to 60,000 pounds sterling a year.

4. Elias Norgate, *Mr. John Dunn Hunter Defended* (London: John Miller, 1826), pp. 33–35; John Neal, "Mr. John Dunn Hunter," *London Magazine*, V (May–August 1826), 319n, 340.

5. Rush, *Memoranda of a Residence at the Court of London . . . from 1819 to 1825* (Philadelphia: Lea & Blanchard, 1845), pp. 132–45, mentioned a visit to Holkham Hall in 1819, where he observed, among the hundreds of guests, Robert Owen of New Lanark. Rush had thus known Coke and something about Holkham for years. As will be shown, he befriended Hunter, presented him at court, and so on.

6. Stirling, *Coke of Norfolk and His Friends* (London: John Lane, 1908), II, 318.

7. W. A. Dutt, *The Norfolk and Suffolk Coast* (London: T. Fisher Unwin, 1909), pp. 259–76; *Gentleman's Magazine*, XVIII (1842), 316–17, 677.

Coke's home itself covered an acre of ground. Holkham Hall was one of the most imposing of the eighteenth-century "Great Houses." The large central block and four wings, connected by rectilinear corridors, rested on plans "according to Palladio." [8] Moving from the plain exterior and rather small doorway, a visitor entered a hall which rose to a dome fifty feet above, with decorations from a design of Inigo Jones, and which was surrounded on three sides by a gallery. The builder, Coke's great-uncle and a descendant of the famous Lord Chief Justice, filled the Hall with the treasures he had acquired during an extended grand tour of the Continent. Had Hunter been given the Green State Bedroom to stay in, for example, he would have slept on a bed upholstered in Genoa velvet and, upon awakening, looked up at walls hung with Brussels tapestry depicting the continents of Europe, America, Asia, and Africa. As he wandered through the halls and rooms, he may have marveled at this imperial accumulation of objects from distant ages and foreign lands. The statues included the famous headless Diana, which was supposed to have belonged to Cicero. The glory of the library was a collection of all the editions of Livy. And among the paintings by Titian, Veronese, and other old masters, Rubens' *Return from the Flight into Egypt* may have pricked Hunter's interest—though the subject came from Matthew in the New Testament, its flight motif drew the viewer back to Moses and one of the very earliest of our captivity stories.

Yet even relatively informed speculation is disappointing, and the importance of Hunter's stay at Holkham makes the absence of specific evidence on his personal reactions doubly frustrating. In broad outline, however, his days there had to be similar to those of Chester Harding, his friend and countryman. Harding went to Holkham in the first place at the request of Hunter, who had persuaded Coke, as a special favor, to sit for a portrait.[9] Luckily Harding's diary entries during this period have survived.[10]

The morning following his arrival in January 1824, Harding sat down to breakfast with "five and twenty ladies and gentlemen, the latter in their

8. James Laver, *Holkham Hall* (Holkham, Norfolk: Privately printed by the Earl of Leicester, 1960), p. 13.

9. Stirling, *Coke*, II, 320. Apart from secondhand accounts, such as Sir James Smith's, the only direct evidence on Hunter's response to Coke is a long letter, dated February 15, 1824, and reproduced in full in Stirling, II, 320–22. Aside from the original of this document, which is in Holkham Ms. 747, Vol. III, a search of the archives at Holkham Hall, for which I am indebted to Doctor W. O. Hassall of the Bodleian Library at Oxford, did not turn up a single relevant item.

10. Margaret E. White, ed., *A Sketch of Chester Harding, Artist* (Boston: Houghton, Mifflin, 1929), pp. 65–69.

shooting dresses." The guests were seated around a long table in the middle of the room and from time to time got up and helped themselves to the fish and game on the loaded side tables. After breakfast the party set off "in terrible array, with guns, dogs, and game-keepers," for a day in the field. On their return, they dressed for dinner. The splendor of the service, which had even impressed Ambassador Rush, elicited Harding's awe:

> Every dish was of silver, gold knives or forks for dessert, and everything else about the table of corresponding costliness. The ladies retired about eight; and the gentlemen, with a few exceptions, gathered around a smaller table, and sat until nine, and then joined the ladies and took coffee. After coffee, some of the company retire to their rooms; others to side-tables to write letters; and such as have nothing else to do play whist or chess, or some other games, until ten, when a supper is served up on a side-table, where the company stand, and eat or drink what they wish.

After this final gathering, the guests customarily asked for a bedroom candle and retired by eleven o'clock.

Participating in the routine of such days, Hunter came to know his unusual host. A Gainsborough portrait which hung in the Hall showed the Coke of Norfolk of four decades earlier, as a young man of twenty-eight, dressed in the broad-brimmed hat, shooting jacket, and long boots he wore when he petitioned George III for American independence. As others have observed, the painting seemed to say that Coke was not a courtier but a country gentleman; his clothes emphasized the point. He was one of the Whig landowners, a follower of Charles James Fox, and a supporter of protection for agriculture. As a matter of course he was elected a Member of Parliament and, by the time Hunter and Harding met him, he had already served nearly fifty years to become "Father of the House."

But Coke was more than a predictable expression of "the Whig interest." When he was young, he was reputed to be one of the boldest riders and best shots in England. He was also a friend of the American Revolution, an opponent of the war against revolutionary France, and a supporter of the Roman Catholic Relief Bill. He was a landlord whose response to his tenants must have impressed Hunter, as it did Harding: the latter noted with surprise that "Coke has very humanely provided for the servants who have grown gray in his service, by building them neat little cottages near the Hall, with a small piece of ground attached for the garden; and, in some instances, he has given a pension for life." Though he was himself primarily interested in the arts of cultivation, he respected men of talent, whatever their field, and made of Holkham Hall a gathering place for artists, writers, and scientists. "Live and let live!" was the libertarian toast he offered his guests when Rush was at Holkham.[11]

Coke's broadness and depth, and more specifically, his interest in American affairs, made him responsive to the needs of his guest. According to his biographer, Coke developed a deep interest in Hunter but found him difficult to talk to, for the latter had learned from the Indians that it was presumptuous in a young man to take the initiative in conversation. But once Coke had conquered this reserve, Hunter told him of his sensation on first beholding a city, his astonishment at the first sight of the Pacific Ocean, and of his surprise on entering London. "I can never be surprised again!" he told his host.

> In the agriculture at Holkham he evinced the keenest interest, and wished to obtain models of all the farming implements which he saw there. But when Coke pressed him to accept some of these as a gift, he refused, saying he would never take anything which he could not purchase. For the same reason, he told Coke, when he first went to New York, and the philanthropic people offered to educate him, he said: "No, if you educate me, you will expect me to think as you do. I have money, I like to think and judge for myself." [12]

Coke was understandably pleased by this independence and intrigued by Hunter's account of his life. With his friendship, Hunter could feel that he might more easily prepare himself to help the Indians. At the very least, Coke's support meant that his stay in England would be more productive and pleasant.

---

11. According to Harding, "Mr. Coke is most decidedly American in his feelings; he often says it is the only country where one spark of freedom is kept alive," White, *Harding*, pp. 68–69. Coke was also fond of saying that the Tory was "not a friend to liberty and to the revolution," *Gentleman's Magazine*, XVIII (1842), 316–17, 677.

12. Stirling, *Coke*, II, 319–20; see also *Memoirs of Sir William Knighton*, ed. Lady Dorothea Knighton (London: Richard Bentley, 1838), II, 56–63.

3

When he arrived in London, John Neal, the American writer, stopped near the statue of King Charles at Charing Cross to inquire the way to Fleet Street. In his *Wandering Recollections* Neal related a rather curious story of how he found his way:

> As I looked up, a stranger was passing, of whom I inquired the way to Fleet-Street. "I am going that way," said he, "and will show you." After a while, he stopped, and said, "This is Fleet-Street; I am going no further. What number do you want?"—"Number 481."—"This is 481. Whom are you looking for?"—"Mr. Charles Toppan, the engraver," said I. "That is my name," said he. Now, when I wrote . . . [an article about the incident], I honestly believed I was telling the simple truth, as a part of my own experience. Judge of my amazement, when I heard from my daughter in New York, that Mr. Toppan had mentioned the subject, and assured her that the strange coincidence happened not to me, but to Mr. John Dunn Hunter, the author of "Hunter's Captivity among the Indians!" How are we to explain this, supposing Mr. Toppan to be right and I wrong? [13]

How Neal chanced to appropriate the incident, immediately tempting as the question is, can wait for explanation in another chapter. It was a good anecdote, anyhow, and it related to Hunter: in a city of almost a million souls, he bumped into a stranger who turned out to be the very man he was looking for.

As it happened, both Hunter and Neal took lodgings in the neighborhood where the coincidence occurred. "Immediately on his arrival in London," Hunter's friend Elias Norgate testified, "chance directed him to the same house in which I lodged. He remained in England somewhat more than a year, making occasional excursions into the country, and visiting many families of the first consequence and respectability." [14] Hunter became a boarder of Mrs. Mary Halloway's at 7 Warwick Street, Charing Cross. After he had been there several months and had established a close friendship with Norgate, John Neal arrived and rented two rooms on the ground floor—the very rooms, Neal was fond of saying,

13. Neal, *Wandering Recollections of a Somewhat Busy Life* (Boston: Roberts Brothers, 1869), p. 271.
14. Norgate, *Hunter Defended*, p. 3.

which Washington Irving had occupied when he wrote *The Sketch Book of Geoffrey Crayon, Gent.*[15] Neal was directed to the Halloway house by Charles Leslie, Hunter's first portraitist. Leslie had known of the place since at least 1820, when he visited his friend Irving there; he apparently was in the habit of giving this address to Americans looking for rooms and had probably suggested it to Hunter in the first place.[16]

Norgate felt fortunate to have shared the same room and dined at the same table with Hunter for over a year: "With daily intercourse, with daily listening to his narrative, and daily watching the strong workings of his mind," he affirmed, "I became, to a certain degree, interested in the object of his pursuit; but I feel a much deeper interest in his fortunes, and a still deeper interest than all in the integrity and honour of his character, which are impeached in impeaching the veracity of his story." One such attempt to impeach his character was Isaac Candler's contention in *Summary View of America* that Hunter was merely the "professed" author of his narrative.[17] Norgate correctly responded that only after his arrival in England had Hunter made the additions to the American edition, including the entire section "Indian Anecdotes":

> As much of this was written in the room, whilst I was sitting by his side, I know positively that it was never revised, but passed directly from his hands to those of his publishers. I have many of his private letters in my possession, and a perusal of them would satisfy the most incredulous of his competency to have written the book, of which I firmly believe he was the *real* as well as the *professed* author.[18]

Norgate accompanied Hunter on some of his excursions into the countryside—probably including that to Holkham, which occurred some six months after they first met—and on three occasions took him for extended holidays to the home of his father outside Norwich.

An American traveler, who had met Hunter casually in New York in

15. Neal, *Wandering Recollections*, pp. 243, 313–14.

16. Irving T. Richards, "The Life and Works of John Neal" (unpubl. Ph.D. diss., Harvard, 1932), I, 469. Neal became a boarder at the house in February 1824. For Leslie's friendship with Irving, see Leslie, *Autobiographical Sketches*, ed. Tom Taylor (London: John Murray, 1860), pp. 63, 140.

17. In *Summary View of America* (London: T. Caldwell, 1824), p. 362, Candler had reported that Hunter's work was interesting but not skillfully compiled: "This book is so evidently the workmanship of some other person than the professed author, that it should have been mentioned in the preface, and the third person used instead of the first."

18. Norgate, *Hunter Defended*, pp. 4, 10.

1821, met him again in London in the company of Robert Owen. His account of Hunter's life at this time rings true:

> He, with the equally famous John Neale, and one other person, con-
> stituted all Mrs. H's boarders. In this obscure place, Hunter received
> the visits of many of the first gentlemen in London. His card rack was
> crowded with notes and cards, from persons of the highest distinction.
> I saw one of two very sentimental notes of condolence from the Duke
> of Sussex to Hunter while the latter was confined to his room, by a
> dislocated shoulder: which, by the way, was attended to, in behalf
> of the Duke, by his surgeon, Dr. Petingale.[19]

Ladies of the highest rank and fashion pressed around Hunter at the many social events he attended, showed themselves eager to converse, and were charmed by him, though, according to this witness, Hunter was small, ill-made, and ill-mannered:

> It is remarkable, that Hunter never seemed flattered with these atten-
> tions. His dress was plain; his manners, though coarse, were always
> grave; he seldom smiled, and even when surrounded with beautiful
> women, whose eyes yielded a tribute, that might have turned the head
> of a giddy fellow, he seemed to be unconscious of their notice and
> indifferent to it.

He also dined frequently with scientists and writers, with men like Sir James Smith and Joseph Sabine, both Fellows of the Royal Society, and strongly excited their interest. Their attention too he seemed to take in his stride: "He seldom spoke of the notice taken of him," the traveler remarked, "and never within my observation, unless in an incidental way."

Apparently Hunter maintained his grave composure even after Minister Rush presented him to George IV at Carlton Palace.[20] Yet, if all this attention did not turn Hunter's head, it did cause one of his fellow boarders to turn and squint his way. Later, in an unsigned piece on "Late

19. "Viator," Natchitoches *Courier*, March 20, 1827. The writer noted that his meeting with Hunter in London was in January 1824. There is a note in the Autograph File, Houghton Library, Harvard, dated January 1, 1824, written and signed by Hunter and very probably addressed to Dr. Petingale, which helps establish the authenticity of "Viator's" observations.

20. Norgate, *Hunter Defended*, p. 32.

American Books" in *Blackwood's Magazine,* John Neal described Hunter
as "the shrewd, light-haired North American savage, wearing white kid
gloves, at a patrician party here; and going to court, in breeches, with
hair powdered—a bag, a lace frill, and a small sword, of which he was
in greater peril, by far, than he ever had been, or ever will be, of a
tomahawk or a scalping-knife." [21] Possibly Neal's commitment to republican simplicity was all the stronger for his not having been invited to go
to court with Hunter in breeches and powdered hair. But he did have a
point: Carlton Palace was a far cry from the Brushy Fork of the
Arkansas.

4

The wilderness which Hunter had left to appear so improbably in England was to almost everyone he met something mysterious, known about
only through books, a distant and dreamlike West. No doubt he was
asked many questions which seemed rather silly: when he exhibited his
great collection of paintings and Indian artifacts in London two decades
later, George Catlin's audiences still wanted to know whether all Indians
were cannibals, went about entirely naked, ate raw meat, could reason,
had beards, were as amorous as whites, raised tea, ever ate the scalps.[22]
Though no record remains of what Hunter was asked by men on Fleet
Street or The Strand, there are accounts of conversations he had with
some of the Whig politicians and virtuosi who had virtually adopted him.
From these emerges some sense of Hunter standing before their drawing-
room fires gravely replying to their queries.

There was general agreement on his appearance: "In person he is
rather short, with a swarthy complexion," wrote one witness, "not handsome, but with eyes full of intelligence; and his countenance lights up
unusually in conversation, in which he takes great delight, though . . .
he is silent unless particularly addressed." [23] Cyrus Redding, the working
editor of the *New Monthly Magazine,* met Hunter at the home of a friend
in Mayfair and reported that he was "a strongly built, well-looking man,

21. Neal, *Blackwood's Magazine,* XVIII (September 1825), 319.
22. Catlin, *Notes of Eight Years' Travels and Residence in Europe, with His
North American Indian Collection* (New York: Privately printed by George Catlin,
1848), I, 48–49, 148.
23. Knighton, *Memoirs,* II, 57.

about the middle size, and of a grave carriage." [24] "Dr T——, of Liverpool," observed that "Hunter appeared modest, rather taciturn, seldom
mentioned his own adventures, but willingly answered questions, with
perspicuity." [25]

The directness of Hunter's response to a query about marriage among
the Indians was a case in point. For the Indians, Hunter pointed out,
marriage was a state by which "mutual happiness is to be highly increased" and, so long as it was, the partners remained together. When
it was not, they were at liberty to change. Affection was "the sole motive
of this connexion":

> Mr. Hunter spoke with great warmth of his horror of the usual motives
> for marrying in England. "Here," he said, "you marry for money, for
> rank, for beauty, for anything but love; therefore you must be bound
> to each other for life, to prevent greater confusion. But with the Indians
> it is otherwise; and I think the bond of marriage would take away all
> their love. The warriors love the squaws with their whole heart; but
> they would not be their slaves."

When Hunter was asked at this point whether the squaws were not considered inferior beings, he replied:

> "You mistake the term: squaw means woman. They are our mothers;
> they form us: we leave our young warriors to their care, and they
> [are] held in estimation just in proportion as our children are brave
> and virtuous, or the contrary, for we think education all-powerful in
> the formation of character." [26]

These replies were shrewd as well as perspicuous: they showed Hunter
to have an alertness to cultural differences and the capacity to make
balanced, perceptive judgments. Thus "Dr. T——" was impressed that
Hunter neither magnified the virtues of the Indians nor exaggerated their
vices: he held them to be merely a people of many good qualities who
were placed in the very unfortunate circumstance of facing extermination at the hands of white Americans.

24. Redding, *Personal Reminiscences of Eminent Men* (London: Saunders,
Otley, 1867), III, 43.
25. "Dr. T—," possibly Sir James Smith, quoted in the *Quarterly Review*, XXXI
(December 1824), 88–89.
26. Knighton, *Memoirs*, II, 60–61.

Cyrus Redding and an American friend who had some experience with Indians carefully probed for any sign that Hunter was an adventurer and a charlatan. They concluded that all the evidence was to the contrary:

> He was a very quiet man, apparently self-possessed. His manners were perfectly simple, and his temper said to be amiable; his garb plain, with not a shadow of ostentation, intelligent as to all that he noted. I do not credit a word of the slanders spoken against him, as they are against all who are envied. Injustice is the price of the coin paid for notoriety.

In a long life during which he met and wrote about many interesting individuals, Redding declared, "I have seen few that interest me more than this singular man." The idea of man living in the state of his earlier history had always captivated him, and "Hunter by his conversation increased this feeling." [27]

5

On February 15, 1824, Hunter wrote to Coke to thank him for sitting for Harding's portrait. His letter provided some information on his activities:

> His Royal Highness [the Duke of Sussex] is very highly pleased with your portrait. He was very well on yesterday. I dined with him at the Beef Steak Club. Lady Anson is much pleased with it, and I am very glad she is, for she must be a good judge of its correctness. I called with her to see Hayter's painting of Lady Ann and her fine little boy. Harding was well pleased with it. I think the infant exceedingly well done. I hope yet to have the happiness to see you again before I leave the country. I am now engaged in a series of lectures of Botany, Chemistry and Mechanical Philosophy. My whole time will be taken up by that; I did intend embarking by the 8th of March packet Ship. By increasing in useful knowledge, however, I may increase my power of acting on my return.[28]

27. Redding, *Reminiscences,* III, 46–47, 51, 53–54.
28. Stirling, *Coke,* II, 321.

He went on to note that he could not forget Coke's remark that he never found the day too long or time heavy on his hands, for it was in full accord with his own feeling: "I never find the days long enough; though I have found that by a proper arrangement of hours one may do a great deal."

How Hunter spent his days was especially impressive to one of his friends. Chester Harding recorded in his diary that he was "often vexed to hear the Americans abuse Mr. Hunter in the manner they do. I have spent much time in his company, and I think him one of the most remarkable men I ever knew." With his own want of schooling weighing heavily on his mind, Harding believed that one of Hunter's most admirable achievements was his success in self-education:

> He first went to school at the age of nineteen or twenty; and the proficiency that he had made in the various branches of scholastic education proves the absurdity of the common opinion, that a man of twenty is too old for studying the sciences, unless he has had the first principles beat into his head by the schoolmasters. Mr. Hunter is a good English and, I am told, a good Latin scholar. He is qualified to practice physic; he is a good mathematician; in short, there is scarcely a branch of science that he has not made some proficiency in. His society is courted by the great, partly, no doubt, because he is a wonder; but the very thing that makes him wonderful is that which reflects his greatest honor. I think him an honor to the country that claims him, and I am happy to find that he is devotedly attached to that country.

With such an example before him, Harding decided, he should not complain: "If knowledge is worth pursuing, I think that any man can obtain it." [29]

Harding was in his own right a remarkable man. Born in Massachusetts into a poor farm family, he had been a drummer during the War of 1812, a chair maker for two years, and a tavern keeper in a country village in western New York. Seeking a change, though he knew not what, he put his wife and child aboard a flatboat and floated with them down the Allegheny River to Pittsburgh. After working there as a sign painter, he tried to teach himself to paint portraits. He commenced in Paris, Kentucky, but soon found that he needed competently painted models to study. After returning East to study Thomas Sully's work in Philadelphia,

29. White, *Harding,* pp. 60–61.

he relocated in St. Louis. Among his sitters there, apart from well-to-do merchants and their families, were Governor Clark and an Osage chief who had come to see Clark as a member of a tribal delegation. In June 1820 he traveled a hundred miles up the Missouri to paint the portrait of the ancient Daniel Boone. Later he achieved a measure of success in Washington and Boston as "the self-taught backwoodsman." [30]

Harding met Hunter at one of Minister Rush's Sunday-evening gatherings in early December 1823. Though on this occasion Robert Owen held sway for hours with a moving discussion of the new system of education he had established at New Lanark, they met again shortly and quickly became good friends. It would have been surprising had they not, for they had much in common. Both had lived in the wilderness—though Hunter was for most of his life on the other side of the frontier—both enjoyed hunting and the outdoors, and both just a few years earlier had been in the backwoods of Missouri. They even shared the experience of a pilgrimage to see Boone. It was possible, indeed, that they had unknowingly passed each other on the streets of St. Louis in 1820.

Hunter introduced his new friend to the Duke of Sussex, and the latter generously offered to sit for Harding. The artist recorded on January 14, 1824, that he had begun the duke's portrait: "In this country, it is looked upon as a mark of great distinction to be allowed to paint one of the royal family. For this honor I am indebted to my friend Hunter." [31] There followed the portrait of Coke and one of Lord Archibald Hamilton, another in the circle of Hunter's supporters. While in London Harding also painted a portrait of Robert Owen, which was, according to John Neal, a work "of extraordinary plainness, power, and sobriety; and some others, which were shown at Somerset House, and Suffolk Street." Of them all, the "one of Mr. John D. Hunter . . . is decidedly the best." [32] Thanks to Hunter's introductions and his own

30. White, *Harding*, pp. x–xxi, 6–26; William Dunlap, *A History of the Rise and Progress of the Arts of Design in the United States* (Boston: C. E. Goodspeed, 1918; orig. publ. 1834), III, 65–72.

31. White, *Harding*, p. 62.

32. Neal, "North America Peculiarities. State of the Fine Arts. Painting," *Blackwood's Magazine*, XVI (August 1824), 135–36. In 1843 George Catlin saw Harding's portrait of Hunter in the library of the Duke of Sussex at Kensington Palace and thought it "an admirable likeness," *Notes of Eight Years' Travels*, pp. 79–85. The Duke of Sussex had magnificent collections of paintings and manuscripts, which were dispersed after his death in 1843; see L. Gleuck Rosenthal, *A Biographical Memoir of the Duke of Sussex* (Brighton: P. Gardner, 1846). An extended search for Hunter's portrait has failed to turn it up.

talents, Harding established for good his reputation as an accomplished portraitist.[33]

Hunter and Harding were great favorites of the Duke of Sussex. Born Prince Augustus Frederick, the sixth son of George III, he had as a young man shown himself a rebel by opposing his father's wishes in his first marriage. Early on he became "a decided Whig" and was known as a "man of liberal ideas": he opposed the slave trade, favored the repeal of the penal laws against Roman Catholics and of the civil disabilities of Jews, and even protested against the imprisonment of Napoleon. Like his friend Coke of Norfolk in so many ways, he welcomed to Kensington Palace "all those who cultivated the arts, sciences, and literature." [34] Minister Rush, who frequently dined at Kensington Palace, found the duke a "liberal minded and excellent Prince," one who spoke in favor of constitutional liberty "with his accustomed frankness and vigor." [35] The duke informed George Catlin years later that he still "highly valued" Harding's portrait of Hunter.

On a fine Sunday morning toward the end of April 1824, after six months of dampness, fog, mud, and smoke, Hunter and Harding rejoiced in the coming of spring. They called on the Duke of Sussex and found him, as usual, "very polite and kind." Their conversation perhaps turned upon one of their host's favorite themes, the imprisonment of Napoleon. Afterward the two young men took a long walk to see the green grass and the fruit trees in blossom. They thought and talked about their country, and compared it to England with results "favorable to the land of our birth," Harding recorded. "In the course of our rambling, we got into a boat, and floated with the tide from the Waterloo Bridge to the Iron Bridge." Upon viewing the former, they discussed the captivity of Napoleon and remarked how that had cast an indelible stain "upon the great conqueror of the age," for Wellington had had it within his power to show magnanimity to his once powerful but now fallen foe. It was truly a lovely day:

---

33. Before his death in 1866 Harding had painted, along with many others, Boone, Charles Carroll of Carrollton, John Marshall, Presidents Madison, Monroe, and John Quincy Adams, Senators Henry Clay, John C. Calhoun, Daniel Webster, and, as one of his last sitters, General William Tecumseh Sherman. See White, *Harding, passim;* Osmund Tiffany, "Chester Harding, the Self-made Artist," *Lippincott's Magazine of Popular Literature and Science,* XIII (January 1874), 65–74.

34. Rosenthal, *Memoir of the Duke of Sussex,* pp. 10–30; *Dictionary of National Biography.*

35. Rush, *Memoranda,* pp. 461, 478–79.

On the Thames we had a most beautiful view of the city. The sun was just setting, but still shone bright upon St. Paul's stupendous dome, and some other prominent points of the city, such as Somerset House, the Adelphi, etc.; and, as we floated along under the several bridges, which never look so strikingly grand as when seen from beneath, we concluded it would be many years before our country could boast such monuments of art.[36]

Moved by such thoughts of home, the two friends scarcely noticed they were floating farther and farther from their native wilds.

36. White, *Harding,* pp. 73–74.

Reflections on Civilization 3

> He told me he would not exchange an Indian life
> for the most luxurious in Europe; that such a life was
> far preferable, and was a scene of perfect enjoyment
> in the bosom of freedom and nature. There was but
> one drawback—it was a fearful one—and that was
> the insecurity from the attack of a hostile tribe.
>
> CYRUS REDDING,
> *Personal Reminiscences of Eminent Men,* 1867

The demands of new friendships and the whirl of social occasions did
not swerve Hunter from his aim of preparing himself to help the Indians.
Time and time again those who met him were struck by his preoccupation with what Sir James Smith called "the noble design of improving
them on the wisest and best principles." Another observer reported that
"his whole mind is engrossed with the plan he has formed to rescue
fifteen thousand Indians, who inhabit North America from the north-west
to the south-east, from the certain destruction that awaits them." [1] Somehow Hunter was able, amid all his other activities, to put his plan on
paper in the form of a new chapter, "Observations on Civilizing the
American Indians," and an essay entitled "Reflections on the Different
States and Conditions of Society." [2]

At the outset he revealed that his experiences with the great figures of
English society had not knocked him off his feet:

> The writer of the following lines has had an opportunity of seeing Man
> in almost every condition in which he exists in North America and Great
> Britain, from the free and high-minded tenant of the forest, to the
> highest ruler of civil society; and while he has enjoyed the blessings,
> and admired the improvements of civilisation, he cannot be blind to

1. Lady Dorothea Knighton, ed., *Memoirs of Sir William Knighton* (London:
Richard Bentley, 1838), II, 57.
2. "Observations on Civilizing the Indians," *Memoirs of a Captivity . . .*
(1824), pp. 360–73; "Reflections on the Different States and Conditions of
Society," pp. 453–62.

the evils, and the affecting miseries, which accompany its purest age, and which upon a superficial examination seem to be unavoidably connected therewith.

But a "thorough inspection" of this problem revealed that the evils and miseries were not inherent in civilization. And, "in its proper place," he added tantalizingly, he would trace them "to their real and true cause."

Meanwhile, he essayed a contrast between the primitive and civilized conditions of man, and before his sentence limped to a halt he placed heavy, perhaps insupportable demands on his reader:

> On contrasting the condition of that man or that society of men, who occupy a respectable station in a civil community, where the highest intellectual improvement and the deepest sense of moral obligation are united, yet free from the fetters of superstition, and above the tyrannic power of avarice; with that man or society, whose vices and virtues are mostly under the domination of passion, whose virtues are rather the momentary effusions of a generous sympathy than the sound maxims of morality necessary to the greatest happiness of life, and whose vices, which, though few, are sometimes flagrant, and frequently disproportioned to their cause;—we find a considerable balance in favour of the former; or that society whose intellectual improvement has proved the hand-maid to virtue, and has added purity of heart to the embellishments of the mind.

The "sound maxims" of the morality of Hunter's more pious teachers most likely found their way into this extraordinary sentence, as did his own mixed feelings about the blessings of civilization. Its obscurity and homiletic tone, in any event, suggested a poorly digested lesson. What he seemed to be trying to say was that in the contrast between civilized intellectuality and primitive passion, the balance of value swung toward the former. From this point of view, it was intrinsically desirable to "civilize" the Indians.

The necessity of doing something to save them was much more easily demonstrated. Here Hunter's sentences rang with felt conviction as he listed four major reasons the Indians were going to be destroyed unless something was done fast:

(1) The rapid encroachment of white settlers pushed them off their hunting grounds onto those of others. The impact of settlement thus thrust tribe back upon tribe and left that closest to the frontier to war with whites on one side and reds on the other.

(2) The destruction of game threatened their means of support. Hunter found the "wantonness of civilised man" dumfounding. Probably thinking of the boasts of the contemporary Davy Crocketts and certainly anticipating those of all the Buffalo Bills to come, he noted the peculiar desire of white hunters to have it said "that they have killed so many buffalo, deer, &c. Many have I seen shot down from mere wantonness, when the circumstances of the party did not permit them even to take off the skin."

(3) Being duped out of their land deprived the Indians of what Hunter called "national pride of character." This estrangement from themselves and their traditions, a condition characterized as "alienation" or "anomie" by later writers, drove the natives "into all manner of dissipation and vice; disease and poverty follow in their train, and wretchedness and ignominy close the melancholy scene."

(4) "The introduction of ardent spirits" among the Indians was the most hopeless problem of all. Though remedies for the other evils might be devised, he could see only a "sickly prospect" for stopping the sale of liquor to the Indians. What point was there in appealing to the humanity of whose who made "money their idol"?

Any attempt to save the Indians and better their condition manifestly had to start out from some understanding of their character, habits, and morals. With the possible exception of the work of the Society of Friends, Hunter noted, all the previous measures had lacked such understanding and were consequently feeble and "of a very doubtful, if not of a decidedly injurious nature." Would-be benefactors seemed incapable of understanding that it was "an insult to an Indian to suppose it necessary to tell him he must believe in a God." Young missionaries he knew had exhorted Indians "on morality, original sin, vicarious atonement, &c," without understanding that the quiet attentiveness with which they were received by no means implied understanding and acceptance. The Indians were merely being polite to guests and, besides, were quite capable of reflecting on moral issues.

At the base of all the erroneous views of the Indians was an inability or unwillingness to see them as *persons*.[3] Three-quarters of a century earlier Montesquieu had pointed to a similar difficulty when it came to slaves: "It is impossible for us to suppose these creatures to be men,

---

3. In his "Reflections" Hunter referred to "the OSAGE tribe, which consists of about five thousand seven or eight hundred *persons*," *Memoirs*, p. 455. By his italics Hunter no doubt wished to give emphasis to the fact that there were that many Osage *human beings*.

because, allowing them to be men, a suspicion would follow that we ourselves are not Christians." Though Hunter could not rise to the epigrammatic wisdom of the French essayist, he had cut down to the same tap root: "The title of the Indians to the distinctive character of human beings, from their moral and physical endowments, is as good, considering the circumstances in which they are found, as that of any other race of men on the face of the earth." He had only scorn for "the philosophers of the day [who] would rank them in their moral and physical endowments and capacities to improve, as intermediates to their own proudly cultivated race, and baboons or apes."

And if the Indians were men, then there was no way to justify their past destruction and, of those remaining, their impending annihilation. The present policy of the United States was cruel and unjust in too many instances. Hunter cited one

> which is mild in its features compared with others of more remote occurrence. I allude to the recent location of the Cherokees in the neighborhood of the Osage nation. These people, till the late treaty was effected between them, had been, it was well known, for a long time past implacable enemies; and the least knowledge of their character must have clearly pointed out the consequences that actually did result from the measure; namely, offensive operations, and the death of many warriors belonging to both nations. Now the powers that be, could have effectually prevented this, without endangering the interests of the American people in the slightest degree; they, therefore, as before asserted, have evidently been guilty of cruelty and injustice, to say the least of their conduct, towards both these tribes.

"The powers that be" in the United States could hardly have been expected to welcome this charge or appreciate Hunter's observation "that the American community in particular, which has become great and powerful as it were on the destruction of the Indians, owes the accomplishment of this measure [of saving and helping them], as far as is practicable, to its own character, to justice, and to moral right."

Since the bloody annals of Indian–white relationships offered precious little hope that American authorities would soon recognize and accept their moral responsibilities, Hunter went ahead with his plan to help the Indians help themselves. He started out sensibly by recognizing the extreme difficulty in promoting radical changes in the life of any group. The Indians were men and like mankind generally held stubbornly "to the prejudices and errors derived from custom and early education; and with how much greater force they cling to opinions that have received the adoption and concurrent testimony of immemorial usage, in support of their sanctity and truth." Though he did not use the word "culture," he was clearly addressing himself to the problem of how to redirect the cultural conditioning of character and life styles. For example, he was aware of the phenomenon that is now called "culture shock": "Those Indians who had been induced to leave their forests and vagrant pursuits for academic education," he pointed out, naturally made little progress and naturally preferred "their own country, and the society of kindred and friends." This was also naturally so, he added perceptively, in a country "where their colour alone is an insuperable barrier to all social and friendly intercourse."

An Indian characteristic was to seek "to indulge all their wants, so far as the means are attainable, and seldom restrain themselves except when old, though repeatedly admonished by experience and suffering." The Indian love of indolence and unrestrained freedom Hunter still found "peculiarly fascinating," but it meant that they would not willingly give up their personal freedom or yield obedience to anyone. Those who would bring them "to comprehend and adopt the doctrines and mysteries of revealed religion," therefore, could only do so through "constant, steady, and potent experiments." His tips to prospective teachers were shrewd: in words that have a familiar ring, he recommended that they "learn the language of the tribes in which they are respectively located." They should be consistent, fearless, and independent, but not stern and authoritarian. They should take advantage of the Indian love of praise and distinction. Assuredly they should not think of quick results, for "the opinions and prejudices of nearly all their grown people are so firmly fixed, that it will require much sound policy and good management to obtain permission, in the first place, to interfere with the education of those who are younger."

In his own scheme Hunter took all of these considerations into account. He was convinced that the basic cause of the Indian plight was want of proper education so that they could comprehend the advantages of civilized ways. Attempts to bring force to bear on them would simply increase their resistance and hence hasten their extermination. Their instruction would take place in their "native wilds." It would take advantage of their customs, their passion for glory, love of liberty, contempt for mean and unprincipled actions: "How pleasing the task to teach such minds the peaceful arts of civilised society; to reclaim such prolific soil to the choicest productions, to transform the fertile forest to a blooming garden!" The agrarian metaphor was no accident: Hunter identified civilization with agriculture and proposed, through personal example, to wean the Indians gradually away from their dependence on hunting and to persuade them to become copper-colored farmers, red yeomen who would turn Western America into a "blooming garden." [4]

More specifically, he planned to establish a settlement in Arkansas near the Quapaw Indians:

> I own a tract of land near them. I wish to let them see my improvement; my comfortable house; my rich meadows; my full barn; my fine stock: in short, every comfort which industry, seconded by art, can afford. Invite them frequently to see me; show them my independence; let them see that I have not to run after the game, and expose my health in the wet and cold; and my life and liberty to my enemies. This will be an appeal to his pride, and his honour, on which points they are extremely sensitive; emulation would be the consequence, for they hate to be outdone.

He did not think of inducing them to abandon wholly their habits. He would continue to shoot for amusement, for the Indians admired someone who could shoot well, and to pass the pipe as a sign of hospitality. But he would depend more on action than words to teach his red brothers the desirability and necessity of taking up the plow. His great object, he wrote with no evident irony, was "to convert the rambler over the forest to a domestic character." The times seemed propitious to Hunter, for after the fall of "the brave and gallant" Tecumseh, the wise and experienced Indians were coming to realize "they must either become tenants of the soil or be soon lost in the sea of forgetfulness."

Hunter argued for his plan in language that was sometimes obscure and marred by the unfortunate literary mannerisms of the day—an age when even a Hazlitt referred to a "tempest" instead of a storm. His leading assumptions were hardly original. His belief in the peculiar virtue of tilling the soil came, of course, from Jefferson—indeed, Hunter may have discussed this proposition directly with the aged ex-President at

4. For the dream of America as a garden, see Henry Nash Smith, *Virgin Land* (Cambridge: Harvard University Press, 1950); Leo Marx, *The Machine in the Garden* (New York: Oxford University Press, 1964); Roderick Nash, *Wilderness and the American Mind* (New Haven: Yale University Press, 1967).

Monticello before he left for Europe.[5] And, like Cooper in his Leatherstocking Tales, Hunter drew on eighteenth-century theories of the "march of civilization" and therewith fell into difficulties.[6] From Condorcet's *Equisse d'un tableau historique des progrès de l'esprit humain* (1795), or popularizations of the ideas therein, came the theory that all societies pass through fixed stages, from hunting to herding to farming to—to whatever, obviously, the present writer was advocating. For the Indians of North America, Hunter's argument had this kind of specific application: at stage "A" the Indians had "erroneous customs"; they should leave these behind for stage "B" and, moreover, had better do so in a hurry to avoid annihilation. But by what standards was it an advance in "civilization" to go from "A" to "B," when moving to the latter meant joining a society capable of killing an entire people?

Still, the surprising thing was not that many of his "Reflections" were cloudy; it was rather that some of them were clear and penetrating comments on man and society. Though the intellectual terrain was most difficult, he grasped the importance of understanding their whole way of life for any attempt to help the Indians. His use of the term "mode of life" approached the anthropologist's use of the term "culture" to refer to a complex of customs, habits, beliefs, traditions, myths, language.[7] He discussed the hold of "immemorial usage" in a way that anticipated Sir Henry Maine on "the cake of custom." In short, he adumbrated a theory of the cultural determination of character. And his analysis of the reasons for the threatened extermination of the Indians at the hands of American whites was dangerously close to the mark. He even showed real understanding of the colonial mentality in his remark about those whites who could not see Indians as *persons* but saw them suspended as "natives," halfway between baboons and themselves. Moreover, if in his judgment a colored skin in the United States acted as "an insuperable barrier to all social and friendly intercourse," then were not the Indians virtually forced to take up Tecumseh's old dream of a red confederacy? Finally, his thoughts on how best to reach the Indians were in the tradition of some of man's most remarkable teachers, of those who, from

5. Elias Norgate, *Mr. John Dunn Hunter Defended* (London: John Miller, 1826), p. 33.

6. For Cooper's similar conceptual scheme, see Henry Nash Smith's fine introduction to *The Prairie* (New York: Rinehart, 1950).

7. See Raymond Williams, *Culture and Society, 1780–1950* (London: Penguin Books, 1961), pp. 16–18 *et passim*, for an illuminating discussion of changes in thinking about and use of the word "culture."

Socrates to Sequoyah, have insisted on the importance of personal example, of joining thought to action, of sharing the fate of their students.

2

Hunter finished, signed, and dated his "Reflections" on June 27, 1823. Three days later J. Adams Smith wrote a letter of introduction for him to "R. Owen, Esq.":

> I beg leave to recommend to you my countryman Mr. Hunter. I called with him to present him to you last week but had not the good fortune to find you. He is going out of town tomorrow but will himself, before he goes, make another attempt at finding you at home. It will give me great pleasure to know that he has seen you as he is, as I am, much interested in the present prospect of improvement in the degraded condition of civilized man.[8]

Hunter delivered the letter and thus commenced his friendship with one of the founding fathers of English socialism and the cooperative movement.

Hunter was naturally interested in meeting the famous Robert Owen. His was one of the earliest and most spectacular success stories to come out of the Industrial Revolution. Without much formal schooling or what one of his sons called a "thorough culture in youth," Owen had nevertheless risen rapidly "to a giddy height. At ten years of age, he had entered London with ten dollars in his pocket; at forty-five, he was worth a quarter of a million. Then his Essays on the Formation of Character, backed by his success, had won him golden opinions."[9] In 1823 Owen was still manager and principal owner of the largest spinning mill in

8. Smith to Owen, June 30, 1823, Owen Papers, Holyoake House, Manchester. J. Adams Smith should not be confused with Sir James Smith or with the James Smith whom John F. C. Harrison refers to as a "Quaker visitor" to New Lanark in 1820, in Quest for a New Moral World: Robert Owen and the Owenites in Britain and America (New York: Charles Scribner's Sons, 1969), p. 155.

9. Robert Dale Owen, Threading My Way (New York: G. W. Carlton, 1874), p. 191. The younger Owen, incidentally, used the word "culture" in the already archaic sense of human cultivation or training.

Britain. He was also famous for his benevolence—on taking over the management of his mill, for instance, he had refused to employ pauper apprentices or any child under ten years of age.

Thousands flocked to New Lanark, Scotland, to inspect Owen's model factory village. Between 1815 and 1825, notes one authority, "the number of names recorded in the visitor's book was nearly twenty thousand, including the Grand Duke Nicholas of Russia." [10] They included as well an entry on August 29, 1823, for "John D. Hunter of Mississippi. American." [11] Hunter was no doubt impressed by the size of the establishment, which had a labor force of about 1500, the housing at moderate rent, the free medical services, the store which sold goods at cost, and, probably most of all, by the Institution for the Formation of Character, which "served a threefold purpose, as an infant school, a day school, and a centre for adult education and recreation." [12] As he walked through the village on the banks of the Clyde, perhaps accompanied by Owen, and observed the workers' garden plots, he no doubt looked for tips to apply to his own plans for a settlement in Arkansas.

But Owen was above all "a man of splendid visions," in the good phrase of the Hammonds,[13] and these more than his past achievements must have most attracted Hunter. As his correspondent J. Adams Smith and a whole generation knew, Owen was dedicated to doing something about misery and poverty, about "the degraded condition of civilized man." While others contented themselves with talking about "the state of the poor," he proposed to act now and thought he knew how to proceed. The previous year, for example, largely through his exertions, the British and Foreign Philanthropic Society was formed, with a long list of notables, including Coke of Norfolk, on its "acting committee," and with the following object: "to carry into effect measures for the permanent relief of the labouring classes, by Communities for mutual interest and co-operation, in which by means of education, example and employment, they will be gradually withdrawn from the evils induced by ignorance, bad habits, poverty and want of employment." This statement of purposes set forth in outline the entire Owen program. In 1823 he

10. Harrison, *Quest,* p. 152.
11. For which information I am much obliged to Mr. Andrew Inglis, former general manager of the New Lanark Mills (letter of February 14, 1970).
12. Harrison, *Quest,* pp. 154–60.
13. J. L. and Barbara Hammond, *The Town Labourer: 1760–1832* (London: Longmans, Green, 1917), p. 163.

completed some lectures in its behalf in Ireland and argued for his "villages of co-operation" before a select committee of the House of Commons.[14] It may well have been these activities, which were widely reported in the press, which first aroused Hunter's interest in Owen.

Owen told his Dublin audience that the fertile soil of their island was capable of supporting many more than the present seven million inhabitants. Yet he had found these same millions living in squalor, the landlords anxious about their rents, the peasants so poor that women were eager to get work for two pence a day, and men glad for a chance to work a fourteen-hour day for eight pence. The cause was not in the land or the people but in a misguided *system*. It was misguided because of "a secret, which, until now has been hidden from mankind." The hidden truth which he revealed was that "man's character is formed for him by circumstances, pre-natal and post-natal." Therefore his plans for cooperative commonwealths were designed to change circumstances and relieve man's misery.

Owen thus told all who would listen, including his critics among the political economists—David Ricardo was on the select parliamentary committee which inquired into his proposals—that the Industrial Revolution could be made human. There was no inevitability, he was contending, in the clouds of smoke and black-running streams, the prison-factories with their iron discipline, the servitude of men and the yoking of women and children to machines. To be sure, "machines were eating men" in the sense that they were replacing manual workers and accentuating the unemployment problem in the post-Waterloo years. Instead of destroying the machines or allowing them to continue starving millions, Owen proposed, enlightened men of good will should commence settling the poor in new "villages of co-operation," where they would work primarily in intensive agriculture. He presented drawings to the committee which showed a sample village, with a square or parallelogram made up of public buildings in the center—a communal kitchen, nursery school, library, and so on—surrounded by small houses on three sides and by dormitories for children on the fourth. He suggested there should be 800 to 1200 persons occupying the buildings on an estate of 600 to 1800 acres. Between the buildings in the square were trees and playgrounds, and beyond the square was land for a sort of green belt of gardens and

14. Frank Podmore, *Robert Owen* (New York: D. Appleton, 1907), I, 276–82.

trees, which would separate the village from any industries.[15] The communities would be largely self-supporting, and if more food was needed within the community or for other communities, more land could be cultivated until, in Owen's words, "the whole earth is a garden."

The details of Owen's proposals, which had just been put fully before the public, were bound to fascinate the newly arrived Hunter. Like Owen, Hunter saw in rural communal living a solution to his problems; he too wanted to turn the land into a "blooming garden." But it was Owen's leading idea—his only idea, said uncharitable critics—which probably helped Hunter most. The contention that "man is a creature of circumstance" was hardly a secret, and not even very new. It was a direct descendant of William Godwin's premise in *Political Justice* (1793) and a collateral descendant of other eighteenth-century theories, including those of the Scottish moral philosophers.[16] But Owenism went beyond its sources to focus on the crucial question of how character was formed by the social process. In brief, it put Hunter within reach of, however rudimentary the conceptual tools and moralistic the language, a critical social psychology and social anthropology.[17] It was along the same lines as his own attempt to deal with Indian manners and customs as an entire culture, and it gave him additional means for understanding the "machinery of society" and the ideological fuels—idea systems, myths, prejudices—which made it run. And Hunter too placed his ultimate reliance—until driven to more explicitly political action—on education to change men and bring about a new moral world.

In a speech welcoming Joseph Lancaster to Glasgow in 1812, Owen had gone so far as to say that education was "the primary source of all the good and evil, misery and happiness, which exist in the world." It accounted for the differences among men. "Man becomes a wild ferocious savage, a cannibal, or a highly civilised being," he had asserted, "according to the circumstances in which he may be placed from his

15. Margaret Cole, *Robert Owen of New Lanark* (New York: Oxford University Press, 1953), pp. 107–10. Mrs. Cole, from whose able exposition I have been drawing, points out that this is the earliest known suggestion of the green-belt idea and that Owen seemed to have in mind something like the garden-city developments carried out generations later by Sir Ebenezer Howard (pp. 110, 137).

16. George Woodcock, *William Godwin* (London: Porcupine Press, 1946), pp. 248–53; Podmore, *Owen*, I, 108, and II, 646–47; Harrison, *Quest*, pp. 83–85. Norgate observed that Hunter spent some time in the home of Dugald Stewart, the leading living member of the Scottish group (*Hunter Defended*, p. 32).

17. Harrison, *Quest*, pp. 78–87.

birth." [18] When Hunter arrived with his letter of introduction, it was as though a spectacular illustration of his point had appeared on Owen's doorstep.

Thereafter the two men spent a good deal of time together.[19] Their discussions must have been lively. Largely self-educated, "self-made" men, they had never learned the schoolmaster's lesson that nothing can be done about poverty and misery. And notwithstanding the vast differences in background, both men were addressing themselves to precisely the same problem, namely how to achieve or restore community. Owen's "villages of co-operation" were designed to bring community back to a society fragmented by the new industrialism. Hunter's agricultural settlement was to restore "pride of character" to, a people whose lives had been shattered by Western expansionism.

Like Coke, the Duke of Sussex, and other men of radical inclinations—in an age when the United States still had the goodwill of the British Left—Owen had long been in sympathy with the struggles of the republic across the Atlantic.[20] But he may have been induced by his new friend to take a more active interest in the possibilities for social experiment there. It was after he met Hunter, in any case, that he began to consider helping the Indians and to think of laying the foundation for his empire of peace and goodwill across the Atlantic. Later he remarked that America was already a sort of "half-way house" to the future.

Owen and Hunter probably visited their mutual friend John Smith in the House of Commons.[21] Owen may have introduced Hunter to Jeremy Bentham, his friend and partner, and to William Godwin, his friend and intellectual mentor, who was then an old man living in a house on The Strand.[22] He certainly introduced Hunter to a wider circle of London radicals: Owen's formidable friend and supporter, Anna D.

18. Podmore, *Owen*, I, 107.

19. For instance, Chester Harding met Hunter and Owen on December 8, 1823; on Christmas day following he breakfasted with Hunter and again encountered Owen, Margaret E. White, ed., *A Sketch of Chester Harding, Artist* (Boston: Houghton, Mifflin, 1929), pp. 59–60; the next month another American met Hunter with Owen, Natchitoches *Courier*, March 20, 1827; when John Neal thought back to his fellow boarder on Warwick Street, he thought of him as "associated with Mr. Owen, as a philanthropist for the restoration of our Indian tribes," *Wandering Recollections* (Boston: Roberts Brothers, 1869), pp. 313–14.

20. In *America and the British Left* (London: Adam and Charles Black, 1956), Henry M. Pelling discusses this fund of radical goodwill and how it was gradually dissipated by the United States.

21. White, *Harding*, p. 60; Norgate, *Hunter Defended*, p. 32.

22. Robert Dale Owen, *Threading My Way*, pp. 207–08, observed that his father was in the habit of visiting Godwin at this time.

Wheeler, the feminist known as the "Mary Wollstonecraft of her day," wrote John Neal that in her home "Mr. Hunter will always be welcome." [23] Mrs. Wheeler, who was also interested in the ideas of Fourier and Saint-Simon and was a friend of William Thompson, the Irish radical and atheist, declared in the same letter that it was impossible to make men just and fit for the New Moral World so long as they had women upon whom they could exercise their ancient rights of cruelty and oppression.[24]

Without more evidence, however, Owen's direct influence is hard to trace. Even before the two men met, Hunter had shown signs of having come in contact with Anna Wheeler's kind of radical feminism: in his "Reflections," he had rather surprisingly hoped for a day when the warrior would "elevate his burthened squaw to his equal in society, to a companion of his toils and a partner of his joys." Nevertheless, Owen very probably changed Hunter's thinking in one area in particular. Though Hunter had leveled some harsh words against missionaries in his remarks on civilizing the Indians, he had still welcomed an intelligent process which would finally educate them to understand the "mysteries of revealed religion." Owen, on the other hand, had been denouncing all organized religions for years. Through him Hunter came in contact with a secular humanism which enabled him to bypass religious rhetoric about original sin and man's innate evil. Owen's skepticism—he was a deist—advanced with all the magnetism and persuasiveness for which he was well known, must have had an impact on his young friend.

When Hunter came to write an afterword to his thoughts on civilization, an addition which he finished and dated August 2, a little over a month after he met Owen, he had no more to say about revealed religion. Instead, he showed that he had advanced his understanding of the source of the evils which beset contemporary society. And his analysis had a secular, radical tone:

> Those countries in which the arts and sciences have been most successfully cultivated, and where civilised man has received his highest polish, have all, so far as my acquaintance extends, been enjoyed at the ex-

23. Transcript of a letter from Mrs. Wheeler to John Neal, n.d. (1824), in Irving T. Richards, "The Life and Works of John Neal" (unpubl. Ph.D. diss., Harvard, 1932), IV.

24. In 1825 Mrs. Wheeler coauthored with Thompson a work engagingly entitled *An Appeal of One-Half of the Human Race, Women, against the Pretensions of the Other Half, Men, to retain them in Political and thence in Civic and Domestic Slavery.*

pense of some other nation. Those who took possession would naturally be haunted by fear of invasion; and the employment of a portion of those people, instead of adding to the general stock of wealth and improvement in their country, has not only proved a heavy tax, but an evil example to the community. The plan of settling any country by conquest is attended with many other evils too tedious to name. It causes a feudal system in the distribution of rewards; while some are made the wealthy lords of whole territories, others are left destitute.[25]

This indeed was a radical interpretation: that what was wrong was not the nature of man but the nature of imperialistic societies. And Hunter, probably thanks to Owen, was at the edge of the truth when he discerned that whenever learned men talked about "civilization," they really meant industrial capitalism, an order that left many men destitute and most men without community, an essential ingredient of any true civilization.

3

Hunter was not the first savage to invade and conquer Britain. In the age of Queen Anne there was the famous visit of the four Indian "kings" to London. Even more memorable was the visit of ten Creek Indians in 1734. Brought by James Oglethorpe from Georgia, they too were presented at court, given an audience with the Archbishop of Canterbury, and taken to Eton College, where they requested a half-holiday for the boys.[26] And, of course, from the time Pocahontas arrived with her baby and white husband, Indians were of great interest to the English public. One study shows that Hunter's reception was not out of the ordinary: Indian visitors often had their portraits painted by famous artists, were received at court as fellow kings and queens, were showered with gifts of money and clothing, and were the guests of honor at gala performances of plays and operas. Even white women were attracted to them, observes the student of Indians abroad with a distaste going beyond the conventional primness, with some disgracing themselves "by their pursuit of the Indians and several of the chiefs boasted on their return home of the number of white wives they had acquired abroad." [27]

25. "Addition," *Memoirs*, pp. 463–68.
26. Douglas Grant, *The Fortunate Slave: An Illustration of African Slavery in the Early Eighteenth Century* (London: Oxford University Press, 1968), p. 152.
27. Carolyn Thomas Foreman, *Indians Abroad, 1493–1938* (Norman: University of Oklahoma Press, 1943), pp. xvii–xix.

Manifestly no racial or sexual assumptions about the level of disgrace suffered by *white women* who chased after savages should keep us from observing here that Hunter undoubtedly received similar attentions and had similar opportunities. "Viator," the American visitor in London that winter who encountered him surrounded by beautiful women, "whose eyes yielded a tribute," still concluded that he "seemed to be unconscious of their notice and indifferent to it." But was he? Could he have been? Later on a traveling companion's diary will provide us with clues on how Hunter lived in his body, but here our way is blocked by lack of evidence: for the present the interior life of our subject must remain essentially unexplored and uncharted. All we have are some rather dark hints from John Neal about Hunter consorting with the women of the streets and the following engaging sketch of his merry-making with the ladies of high society:

> Did he eat his dinner in his shirt sleeves, or throw aside his knife and fork, or open his mouth very wide, look very savage at the women, flatter them to their faces, threaten to jump down their throats before a room full of company—O the delicious creature! every thing he did was so natural! Did he romp with them as they had never been romped with before, seize hold of their feet and propose to throw them out of the window . . . why even that, of which a real Hottentot would have been ashamed, was but a new proof to the advantage of our hero.[28]

In this instance it would be nice to think that Neal, for all his unfriendly intent and very serious limitations as a witness, takes us behind the external, public self which Hunter presented to new friends like Coke and Owen. Real Hottentots notwithstanding, I like to think of Hunter romping with the ladies and betraying not the slightest indifference to their yielding eyes.

Yet, after all the precedents have been duly registered, we may still conclude that the response to Hunter had unique features. No other savage visitor to Britain was white or, to my knowledge, had written a book. Moreover, Hunter had the good fortune to arrive at a moment when thoughtful men were raising fundamental questions about the condition of England and the nature of Western culture.

In a few short pages entitled "Signs of the Times," published in the *Edinburgh Review* of June 1829, Thomas Carlyle somehow caught the

28. Neal, "Mr. John Dunn Hunter," *London Magazine*, V (July 1826), 322–23.

mood of the decade and the direction of underlying currents: "There is a deep-lying struggle in the whole fabric of society; a boundless, grinding collision of the New with the Old. The French Revolution, as is now visible enough, was not the parent of this mighty movement, but its offspring." The parent was "Mechanism," the phenomenon to which he was later to give the name "Industrialism": "This age of ours," he pointed out, is "above all others, the Mechanical Age. It is the Age of Machinery, in every outward and inward sense of that word." Man's relationship to man was guided by the same calculation and contrivance, based on self-interest. The distance between the rich and the poor was increasing. Men had lost belief and had grown mechanical in head and heart. Not even the mountains or seas could escape their cold determination: "We war with rude nature," read a clairvoyant sentence, "and, by our resistless engines, come off always victorious, and loaded with spoils." He was also sadly prophetic about his own development, as well as the collective fate, in his assertion that "in all senses, we worship and follow after power."

"The time is sick and out of joint." Carlyle's conclusion was of course shared by Owen. William Blake would have agreed; he died in 1827, but his earlier and still more terrifying "visions in the air" were of the coming of an age in which the "dark horrors of war" were interrupted occasionally by intervals of uncertain peace.[29] The range of men who shared these first shocked apprehensions of the significance of industrialism was surprisingly broad; from their writings during this "first great critical period," Raymond Williams observes, comes "the greater part of our language and manner of approach." [30] Hunter could not have pursued his goal of penetrating into "unexplored regions in search of new truths" at a better time.

The time also shaped the intensity of the response to him. Over the years the reception of the different parties of Indian "kings" had depended to some extent on the idea that they represented the primitive freedom and simplicity of the West whence they came. As far back as 1670, in John Dryden's Conquest of Granada, the "noble savage" ran wild in the woods, "as free as Nature first made man,/ Ere the base laws of servitude began." In the 1730s Alexander Pope's An Essay on Man

29. See David V. Erdman, Blake: Prophet Against Empire: A Poet's Interpretation of the History of His Own Times (Princeton, N.J.: Princeton University Press, 1954), pp. viii, 308–9, 432.
30. Williams, Culture and Society, p. 287.

held out hope for "some safer world in depth of woods embrac'd," where "the poor Indian" would have refuge from the Christian "thirst for gold." [31] By the 1820s, however, the dream of a Lost Eden had a rather desperate tone. "Canto the Eighth" of Lord Byron's *Don Juan* paired off "Nature," symbolized by a Daniel Boone as fresh and free as "a torrent or a tree," with "Civilization":

> And the sweet consequences of large society,
>   War, pestilence, the despot's desolation,
> The kingly scourge, the lust of notoriety,
>   The millions slain by soldiers for their ration.[32]

The tone was mocking, but Byron's despair over "these sad centuries of sin and slaughter" was real enough. Two years later, in April 1824, he died in a squalid room at Missolonghi, sick to death of Western civilization.

At about the same moment, Hunter was preparing to return to the New World. That he was influenced by the idea of the "noble savage" will be clear to anyone who reads his narrative. Yet the response of his readers and those who met him had a poignancy which was more than a testimonial to him personally: it expressed the increasingly urgent and pervasive sense of the disjointedness of the times. For anyone who remembered the land, the smoke and grime and ugliness that settled on Manchester or Bradford or Glasgow were profoundly disturbing. And in this new industrial order, as the Hammonds put it so well, "the spirit of fellowship was dead." [33] Imagine, then, the appeal of the following lines:

> I asked what were his first impressions upon seeing civilized life? He replied, amazement. He could not have imagined seven years ago, which was the first time he saw New York [actually, New Orleans], that anything he now sees could exist. He also added: "I can never be surprised again: but what made me unhappy was to see the distress of the poorer inhabitants, for among the Indians none are suffered to want."

31. Still useful is Hoxie N. Fairchild, *The Noble Savage* (New York: Columbia University Press, 1928); see also Fred A. Crane, "The Noble Savage in America" (unpubl. Ph.D. diss., Yale University, 1952).
32. Byron, *Don Juan*, Intro. by Peter Quennell (London: John Lehmann, 1949), pp. 289–324.
33. *Town Labourer*, p. 329.

The warmth and fidelity of their friendships cannot be conceived by common minds: they will sacrifice even their life for their friends, and the chiefs defend and provide for their tribe in every way. Their hatred for their enemies is in the same proportion; every species of deceit is considered laudable, and is practised against them: but Mr. Hunter said that to each other they wére truth itself, and enjoyed a social happiness amongst themselves which he never witnessed in any other nation.[34]

Stirred by their own fading memories of community, Hunter's new friends learned of this social happiness with a yearning that "cannot be conceived by common minds."

Social happiness was an enviable state. Cyrus Redding, the magazine editor, wrote that he was captivated by Hunter as a "man living in the state of his earlier history." He really meant, the context makes clear, "living in the state of *man's* or of *society's* earlier history." Within this earlier history men as dissimilar as Carlyle and William Cobbett found a source of community in the Middle Ages.[35] The aboriginal societies of North America offered another possibility, as Redding's remark suggested. It was thus quite understandable that Sir Walter Scott, with his well-known affection for "lawless Highland chieftains," should express deep interest in Hunter's plan to help the Indians.[36]

All this is to say that Hunter was received most enthusiastically by those who were in some measure hostile to the Age of Machinery. The group of Tories gathered around the *Quarterly Review,* including the critic who reviewed his book and Sir Walter Scott, who was very nearly the periodical's creator, found Hunter useful not only to pursue their quarrel with republican America, but also as a means to express their own nostalgia for the organic unity of vanished societies.[37] Despite their very different political allegiances, both Coke and Owen were partly in this "squirearchical" tradition. Coke expressed the traditional concern for his servants and loyal tenants by building them cottages and otherwise providing for them in ways that elicited the admiration of Harding and, presumably, Hunter.

34. Knighton, *Memoirs,* II, 58–60.
35. Carlyle, *Past and Present* (London: Oxford University Press, 1957; orig. publ. 1843); Williams, *Culture and Society,* pp. 37–39.
36. "Viator," Natchitoches *Courier,* March 20, 1827.
37. See Walter Graham, *English Literary Periodicals* (New York: Thomas Nelson & Sons, 1930), pp. 241–44, for a discussion of the founding and publishing policy of the *Quarterly.*

Owen was a more difficult case. Part of his thought, as I have tried to indicate, was rooted in the libertarian tradition which came to him from Godwin and Shelley and which he would pass on to the early trade union and cooperative movements. Moreover, by the time he met Hunter, Owen had become thoroughly disenchanted with the possibility of doing something about child labor or anything else through the state. Very shortly he would list, right behind religion, the governments of the world as one of the major sources of evil. This distrust of centralized authority and conventional political action, which found responsive chords in Hunter's experience with "the powers that be," implied a radical rejection of the way the world was going. It meant that the real revolution had to be social, as men like William Morris and Oscar Wilde were later to argue. On the other hand, part of Owen's thought was grounded in conservatism, or, if you prefer, the traditional values of the eighteenth century. Though he was not lord of the manor, his model factory village was the counterpart of his friend Coke's cottages for tenants. His benevolence rested just as firmly on a concern for stable human relationships and a sense of responsibility for helping the poor and the infirm. Owen could immediately sympathize with Hunter's project for the Indians, for they were, in a sense, counterparts of Britain's "savages." Owen believed the "lower orders" too had to be taught "to become rational beings" and began with the question: What were the best arrangements by which they could be "lodged, fed, clothed, trained, educated, employed, and governed?" [38]

Domestic analogs aside, the North American Indians were, of course, of direct interest to Coke, Owen, the Duke of Sussex, Sir James Smith, and the other philanthropists and savants of the day. They turned to Hunter eagerly to find out all they could about his red brethren. But their eagerness stemmed in part from their own unease about the cost of empire. Ultimately the question raised by slavery had to be applied to other nonwhites: Were natives men? The waves raised by the antislavery controversy had not subsided by any means. In the spring of 1823 William Wilberforce, to whom Owen conceivably introduced Hunter, failed in an attempt to push through Parliament a bill to abolish

---

38. Quoted by E. P. Thompson, *The Making of the English Working Class* (New York: Random House, 1964), p. 781. Thompson's discussion of Owen's paternalism is first-rate, though to my mind he neglects Owen's libertarian, radical side—perhaps in part because he finds it so difficult to sympathize with the "kindly Papa of Socialism: Mr. Owen, the Philanthropist."

slavery in the West Indies.[39] And as if to quiet concern about the British record there and in Africa and Asia, the critic in the *Quarterly Review* used Hunter's book as an occasion to dwell on the atrocities of the United States. But this would not do for those who were friends of America, as most of Hunter's supporters were, and would not do for those who were genuinely worried about the question of natives elsewhere in the British sphere—in Canada, for example.

The timeliness of Hunter's concerns was affirmed with the publication of John Halkett's *Historical Notes Respecting the Indians of North America: With Remarks on the Attempts to Convert and Civilize Them.* A lawyer and colonial administrator, Halkett was a veteran of Lord Selkirk's battles with the Northwest Fur Company in the Red River Valley of Canada. He had first-hand observations of the Indians to draw on from his travels in North America and an intimate knowledge of the difficulties of attempts to "civilize" them. His book revealed that he drew on Hunter as well for information and assistance, spent a good deal of time in his company, and profited from their conversations and his reading of Hunter's *Memoirs.* Hunter thus demonstrably spoke to the mounting interest in the topic and made his own indirect contribution to one of the first and best histories of Indian–white relations. That an author who wrote with such remarkable sensitivity and intelligence should have sought guidance from Hunter was in itself no small tribute.[40]

Before Halkett's book was published, however, Hunter returned to the United States, in the late spring of 1824, carrying with him the best wishes of all his English friends. "Mr. Hunter is gone again to the woods of the Missouri," wrote one reviewer, "with the advantage of much knowledge acquired both in England and America, to attempt some amelioration of . . . [the Indians'] condition, and we trust our colonial Government will profit by the example thus set before it." [41] Another expressed confidence that he would accomplish his noble purpose: "And we can vouch from our own observation, that uniting the intrepid and persevering character of the Indian with the intelligence of the educated

39. R. Coupland, *Wilberforce* (Oxford: Clarendon Press, 1923), pp. 475–81. Worth noting here is the fact that the copy of Hunter's *Manners and Customs . . .* in the Ayer Collection at the Newberry Library, Chicago, was once owned by William Wilberforce.

40. For Halkett's reliance on Hunter, see *Historical Notes* (Edinburgh: Archibald Constable, 1825), pp. 197–200, 204–5, 229–30, 324n, 343, 347–48, 355, 387, 389, and esp. 398–408.

41. "Indian Anecdotes," *New Monthly Magazine,* VIII (July–December 1824), 278.

European, he is eminently fitted to achieve this grand design, and change the face of an important race of mankind." [42]

Not everybody was so sanguine. According to John Neal, one person "of great worth" declared that Hunter had much to fear from Americans and their government: the "American people are his worst enemies." [43]

42. *Literary Gazette*, April 19, 1823, p. 242.
43. Neal, "Hunter," *London Magazine*, V, 325.

PART TWO

IMPUDENT IMPOSTOR?

BALLAD
[to the tune of "Liberty Tree"]

Americans, rise at the voice of distress,
   'Tis virtue to succour the brave.
The force of your arms distant realms shall confess,
   Join'd with those whom your valour may save.

Savage nations shall learn by your conduct to rise
   Above the untractable state,
Drop their customs of malice, and learn from the wise,
   To be civiliz'd, gentle and great.

But those who presume against reason and right,
   To spread terror, destruction and fire,
Shall perceive the advantage of art in the fight,
   Shall be taught real worth to admire.

The wilderness then shall bloom forth as the rose,
   Tall forests give place to rich grain,
While unity, peace and contentment disclose
   Their beauties to crown the domain.

The native delighted—secured in his claim,
   And instructed to stick to his word,
Shall abandon the tomahawk, arrow and flame,
   And the hoe shall take the place of the sword.

Our eagle shall then his wild pinions extend,
   To the ocean that rolls in the west,
Dissension and discord be brought to an end,
   And the world be permitted to rest.

From *The Remarkable Adventures of Jackson Johonnet
of Massachusetts; Who Served as a Soldier in the Western
Army in the Massachusetts Line, in the Expedition under
General Harmar and the Unfortunate General St. Clair.
Containing an Account of His Captivity, Sufferings, and
Escape from the Kickapoo Indians.* Written by Himself,
and Published at the Earnest Importunity of His Friends
for the Benefit of American Youth (Boston: Samuel Hall,
1793).

Father of the West:
General Lewis Cass

4

> Mr. John Dunn Hunter is one of the boldest impostors, that has appeared in the literary world, since the days of Psalmanazar.
>
> *North American Review,*
> January 1826

Two parties of canoeists kept their rendezvous at Michilimackinac (now Mackinac) on June 25, 1825. One, led by General Lewis Cass, Governor of the Michigan Territory and ex-officio Superintendent of Indian Affairs, had come up from Detroit along the coast of Lake Huron. The other, headed by Henry Rowe Schoolcraft, Indian Agent at Sault Ste. Marie, had descended the straits from Lake Superior the day before. With Cass in command, the entire force left Michilimackinac on July 1, fought headwinds down Lake Michigan to Green Bay, ascended the Fox River with its numerous portages, crossed over to the Wisconsin, descended to its mouth, and paddled a league up the Mississippi to reach Prairie du Chien on July 21. General William Clark, who was coming upriver from St. Louis, was expected shortly. Clark and Cass had been appointed commissioners by the Secretary of War to negotiate a treaty which would settle the disputes among the tribes of the upper Mississippi and fix the boundaries of their territories.

The scene at the old French settlement of Prairie du Chien presented an unforgettable tableau. As Schoolcraft observed in awe, "no such gathering of the tribes had ever before occurred." On the banks of the river, for miles above and below town, on the island opposite, and in the meadow behind, the ground was covered with tepees. To Schoolcraft's way of thinking, "the Dakotahs, with their high pointed buffalo skin tents, above the town, and their decorations and implements of flags, feathers, skins and personal 'braveries,' presented the scene of a Bedouin encampment."

Of all the tribes assembled, of the Dakotas, Winnebagos, Chippewas, Menomonees, Potawatomis, and Ottawas, the most striking were the Iowas and the Sac and Foxes: They came to the treaty ground as a war party, armed with spears, clubs, guns, and knives. They came nearly nude, painted, bearing flags of feathers, beating drums, whooping, and appearing "the very spirit of defiance," Schoolcraft recorded. "Their leader stood as a prince, majestic and frowning. The wild, native pride of man, in the savage state, flushed by success in war, and confident in the strength of his arm, was never so fully depicted to my eyes." This majestic chief, Keokuk, stood with his war lance, high crest of feathers, and daring eyes "like another Coriolanus." But Coriolanus' kind of defiant rebellion against the authorities was completely out of place at Prairie du Chien.

Day after day Clark and Cass, "the explorer of the Columbia in 1806, and the writer of the proclamation of the army that invaded Canada in 1812," joined in a task that boded "so much good to the tribes." Inside Fort Crawford the commissioners conferred with the delegations and pored over bark maps and drawings which helped them establish just boundary lines. "The thing pleased the Indians. They clearly saw that it was a benevolent effort for their good." The Treaty of Prairie du Chien was signed on August 19 and laid "the foundation of a lasting peace."

One incident at the close of the council slightly marred this picturesque scene. Some of the tribes had argued during the negotiations that the real reason the United States government spoke against the use of "ardent spirits" was the expense and not the principle. To show that the government was not cheap, the commissioners ordered their men to place tin camp kettles, each holding several gallons, in a long row on the grass in the council area. Teetotaler Cass then spoke sternly to the Indians "on the sin and folly of drunkenness." At the close of his remarks, "each kettle was spilled out in their presence. The thing was evidently ill relished by the Indians. They loved whiskey better than the joke." [1] Joke?

1. Schoolcraft, *Personal Memoirs of a Residence of Thirty Years with the Indian Tribes on the American Frontiers* (Philadelphia: Lippincott, Grambo, 1851), pp. 213–17. See also Andrew C. McLaughlin, *Lewis Cass* (Boston: Houghton, Mifflin, 1891), p. 128. Clark wrote to Secretary of War James Barbour on September 14, 1825, about the council: see Office of the Secretary of War, Letters Received, Indian Affairs, St. Louis Superintendency, National Archives, Record Group 75. Hereafter references will be to microfilms. For the Treaty of Prairie du Chien, for instance, the reference is M(icro Copy) 668, R(oll) 5, N(ational) A(rchives), or M668, R5, NA.

Actually, the picture Schoolcraft tried to depict for his readers was deeply marred from top to bottom by a lack of sensitivity and verisimilitude. Keokuk, that Sac Coriolanus, was in fact a venal soul who soon ceded tribal lands wholesale, to the dismay and anger of Black Hawk, his great rival. The treaty was negotiated for white Americans by representatives of the United States War Department. Both commissioners came to the council highly accomplished in the art of relieving Indians of their land. Clark arrived late, in fact, because he had stayed in St. Louis to wind up the details of a treaty by which the Osages ceded the great bulk of their remaining land to the United States.[2] Though the purpose of the deliberations at Prairie du Chien was not land cession, the commissioners' benevolent work for the good of the Indians was not without their own in mind. Stabilization of the relationships of tribes pushed back on one another helped the fur trade. And, preoccupations with the picturesque aside, Schoolcraft had on an earlier trip noticed the lead mines "on the west bank of the river twenty-five leagues below" Prairie du Chien.[3] Others had been no less observant. The Indians were soon to be called back to the fort to sign another treaty, which took away their lead regions in southwestern Wisconsin and northwestern Illinois.[4] And, of course, the agreements reached at Prairie du Chien in 1825 did not produce "a lasting peace."

But it was this paper-thin frontier pageant that provided the essential backdrop for Schoolcraft's presentation of a subplot entitled "Impostor":

> Among the books which I purchased for General Cass, at New York, was the narrative of one John Dunn Hunter. I remember being introduced to the man, at one of my visits to New York, by Mr. Carter. He appeared to be one of those anomalous persons, of easy good nature, without much energy or will, and little or no moral sense, who might be made a tool of. It seems no one at New York was taken in by him, but having wandered over to London, the booksellers found him a good subject for a book, and some hack there, with considerable cleverness, made him a pack-horse for carrying a load of stuff about America's treatment of the Indians.

2. Clark to Office of Indian Affairs, June 8, 1825, M18, NA.
3. Mentor R. Williams, ed., *Henry Rowe Schoolcraft: Narrative Journal of Travels* (East Lansing: Michigan State College Press, 1953), p. 221.
4. Francis Paul Prucha, *Broadax and Bayonet: The Role of the United States Army in the Development of the Northwest, 1815–1860* (Madison: State Historical Society of Wisconsin, 1953), p. 8.

Only the wary reader, suitably forewarned, could slip through this thicket of misstatements—to stop and argue with so fanciful a guide about whether it was some hack *here* rather than *there* would not help, and to insist that some persons in New York were in fact taken in by Hunter might even hurt.

Nevertheless, probably Schoolcraft had picked up Hunter's narrative in New York and packed it along on the trip to Michilimackinac. He probably gave it to Cass and

> C. reviewed the book, on our route and at the Prairie, for the *North American*, in an article which created quite a sensation and will be remembered for its force and eloquence. He first read to me some of these glowing sentences, while on the portages of the Fox. It was continued, during the leisure hours of the conferences, and finally the critique was finished, after his visiting the place and person, in Missouri, to which Hunter had alluded as his sponsor in baptism. The man denied all knowledge of him. Hunter was utterly demolished, and his book shown to be as great a tissue of misrepresentation as that of Psalmanazar himself.[5]

Real Indians were appropriately whooping and beating their war drums in the background as Cass composed his famous exposure. But the why and the how of it were again a little more complicated than Schoolcraft's account would suggest.

General Cass made clear in a letter to Colonel Thomas L. McKenney, head of the Office of Indian Affairs in the War Department, that he was after larger game:

> The article in the Quarterly Review, which was the subject of your very just and forcible animadversions, contains such a tissue of misrepresentations, and is so calculated to injure the character of our country abroad, that I have determined to prepare an article for the next North American Review, to contain a refutation of those calumnies. The essay must of course be miscellaneous in its general features, and a variety of topics must be introduced. But the object will be steadily kept in view.[6]

Hunter was thus incidental, merely one of a variety of topics to be introduced while Cass steadily pursued his real objective.

5. Schoolcraft, *Memoirs*, p. 217.
6. Cass to McKenney, July 30, 1825, M234, R419, NA.

McKenney's earlier "animadversions" had appeared, the letter revealed, in an unidentified "national journal." This made it likely that he was the author of an anonymous "Communication" in the *National Intelligencer* of April 26, 1825. The writer there angrily rejected the "stale and stupid slanders" of the article in the *Quarterly Review;* he was particularly incensed by the "gross slander" against the Kentuckians who served in the late war. They were not ferocious, he stated flatly: "Ferocity is not, and never has been, a distinguishing trait in the American character; on the contrary, it is remarkable for humanity, and in the midst of the most appalling scenes of bloodshed, the American never loses that sensibility and sympathy, which the scenes of horror around him might be supposed to destroy or deaden." As for the Indians, if they "have been treated with cruelty, it has not been by the order or the connivance of the government, or with the approbation of the mass of the American people." Besides, the reviewer had misconceived the character of the savage, for "the Indian is ferocious, cruel, and blood thirsty by nature." He was certainly not a proper subject, the writer pointed out, to be embodied "into the creations of the poet or the fictions of the novelist." And here, in sum, were the major lines of attack that Cass was to pursue, even including an assault on the novels of Cooper.

On the same day that he wrote to McKenney from Prairie du Chien, Cass also wrote to Jared Sparks, editor of the *North American Review,* offering to contribute an article for the January issue, when Congress would be in session, to combat the "peculiar malignity" of the *Quarterly Review.* He took to the field with some misgivings, he said, for "it is a task for the proper execution of which I certainly feel my general incompetency, and I regret for the sake of our common country that it is not in other and abler hands." [7] Cass accompanied General Clark on his return down the Mississippi. On September 1 the two commissioners wrote from St. Louis to Secretary of War James Barbour that the treaty had been signed and that, since it involved "the whole of our Indian relations upon the upper Mississippi and upper Lakes," Cass would bring the treaty to Washington in time for the commencement of the next session of Congress.[8] Two days later Cass wrote triumphantly to McKenney that his "article for the N. American, like other infants, grows apace." He was worried only about space, since "I have brought

7. Cass to Sparks, July 30, 1825, Sparks Manuscripts, Houghton Library, Harvard.
8. Clark and Cass to Barbour, September 1, 1825, M234, R419, NA.

together a vast multitude of facts." [9] On September 12 Sparks replied
that he would welcome "a full and impartial account of the comparative
policy and conduct of the American & British governments towards the
Indians" and added that "a temperate but firm refutation of the false
statements of the Quarterly Review will be desirable in this connexion."
In late October Cass sent the article to Boston in time for the January
issue of the *North American*.[10]

Even the chronology of its preparation testified to the political nature
of Cass's document. The sensation it created was carefully calculated for
maximum political impact. Cass was on hand for the opening of Congress to see that "it takes well." [11] Another Cass subordinate, also in the
employ of the War Department, sent a copy in pamphlet form to Schoolcraft with the comment that Sparks, "who had unlimited authority,
availed himself of it to lop off many excellent branches, among others
the severest cuts at the *Quarterly*. I should send more than one copy,
but the others were all transmitted to the Gov[ernor] at Washington,
there to be distributed no doubt to the general advantage of the
Department." [12]

At first glance the quarrel over Hunter's *Memoirs* that followed seemed
to be between the transatlantic reviews, the *Quarterly* and the *North
American*. The former had earned a reputation for vituperation and un-
fairness in its defense of the crown and the established church, established standards, established everything.[13] Its American counterpart had
ponderously tried to create a counterestablishment through native literature and native scholarship. And the reviews had locked horns over
Hunter and the Indian policy of the United States. But to those charged
with carrying out that policy the *Quarterly*'s attack seemed against an
entire institutional structure; their response was from the beginning
official or quasi-official. The long article in the *National Intelligencer* was

9. Cass to McKenney, September 3, 1825, M234, R419, NA.
10. Sparks to Cass, September 12, 1825; Cass to Sparks, October 23, 1825,
Sparks Mss., Houghton.
11. Cass to Schoolcraft, February 6, 1826, in Clarence Edwin Carter, ed., *The
Territorial Papers of the United States*, XI, *The Territory of Michigan* (Washington: Government Printing Office [hereafter, GPO], 1943), 945.
12. Charles C. Trowbridge to Schoolcraft, January 23, 1826, *ibid.*, XI, 935–37.
13. Walter Graham, *English Literary Periodicals* (New York: Thomas Nelson
& Sons, 1930), pp. 241–48. For a discussion of what Frank Luther Mott has
called "the Paper War, which lasted for more than a hundred years after the
Revolution, and which still breaks out occasionally," see his *History of American
Magazines* (New York: D. Appleton, 1930, 1938), I, 188–89; on the editors and
policies of the *North American*, see II, 219–61.

really a kind of White Paper in defense of the national character and of United States Indian policy. Cass entered the lists "for our common country." Men on War Department missions undertook to defend their bureaucracy from allegations of cruelty, injustice, callousness, murder. For these men the stakes were no less than the national interest.

In this context, Sparks, the hard-headed former Unitarian minister, was improbably ingenuous to have expected from Cass a full and impartial account of anything. To be sure, Cass later undertook to instruct the editor on the proper role of his journal. The reputation of the *North American,* he wrote, "is the property of the nation. In all questions affecting the literature, the history, or the policy of the United States, it must stand between our country and her traducers." [14] But of course, no one had to threaten to commandeer the *North American,* for Sparks seemingly saw nothing wrong in opening his pages to a high official in the War Department for an anonymous defense of the War Department.[15]

2

So did General Cass come to expose Hunter as one of the boldest impostors since Psalmanazar:

> His book, however, is without the ingenuity and learning, which, like redeeming qualities, rendered the History of Formosa an object of rational curiosity. It is a worthless fabrication, and, in this respect, beneath the dignity of criticism; compiled, no doubt, by some professional book maker, partly from preceding accounts, and partly from the inventions of Hunter. *Our only motive for introducing the work into this article is, that, by exposing so gross an imposition, the public may be put upon its guard for the future, and not give credit to tales supported neither by intrinsic nor extrinsic evidence* [italics added].[16]

14. Cass to Sparks, April 22, 1826, Sparks Mss., Houghton.
15. Some editors have not changed all that much. A modern counterpart was the editor of *Foreign Affairs,* who a few years ago (April 1965 and April 1966) accepted two articles on the "faceless" Vietcong from George A. Carver, Jr., without notifying his readers that Carver was a government employee, in this instance, a CIA agent.
16. "Indians of North America," *North American Review,* XXII (January 1826), 53–119. Cass and Schoolcraft knew a good phrase and obviously found a name like Psalmanazar irresistible. The reference was to George Psalmanazar, the author of *An Historical and Geographical Description of Formosa* . . . (London: Dan Brown, 1704). Psalmanazar claimed to be "a native of said Island," but later admitted, in the next installment of his *Memoirs* . . . (London: R. Davis, 1764), that he was merely "a reputed native."

This was an expression of lofty motive but not a very reassuring statement of purpose, for it was not strictly true.[17] Still, misrepresentation of
intent did not necessarily invalidate Cass's demonstration of the worth-
lessness of Hunter's book. Let us examine one by one the major counts
of his indictment.

No evidence whatsoever identified the "professional book maker" or
even established the fact of his existence. No evidence pinned down the
narrative's dependence on "preceding accounts." That left Hunter's
"inventions."

Cass commenced his exposure of these with an analysis of Hunter's
fraudulent use of Tecumseh:

> Hunter has inserted what he calls a speech, delivered by Tecumthé to
> the Osages. And it is but a poor comment on the *tact* and judgment of
> the reading community, that this speech, and the reflections in which
> Hunter says he indulged on his arrival at the Pacific Ocean, have been
> already quoted into three respectable works, as valuable specimens of
> aboriginal taste and feeling.[18]

Of the moving "extemporaneous utterance" which he tried to reproduce
in his narrative from memory, Hunter had noted apologetically that "the
richest colours shaded with a master's pencil, would fall infinitely short
of the glowing finish of the original." [19] Cass faulted readers for swallow-
ing Hunter's invention by showing that "no Shawnee had, in 1812, ever
visited the Osages as a friend, nor was Tecumthé ever within many hundred miles of a party of that nation," and that the speech could not have
been his anyway, for his spontaneous remarks were not eloquent.

With sure strokes Cass proceeded to destroy any possibility that
Hunter had ever seen Tecumseh among the Osages. "*We happen to
know,*" he asserted, "that on the 27th of September 1811 he arrived at
Vincennes, and sought an interview with General Harrison." Since he
also knew that Tecumseh had returned from his recruiting trip among

17. On October 10, 1825, Cass wrote Sparks that "his primary object . . . was
to repel the calumnies which have been heaped upon us by some of the English
journals," Sparks Mss., Houghton.

18. Cass did not specify the "three respectable works." If he included the
Quarterly article as one, the other two were John Halkett's *Historical Notes Respecting the Indians of North America* (Edinburgh: Archibald Constable, 1825),
pp. 347–48; and James Buchanan's *Sketches of the History, Manners, and Customs
of the North American Indians* (London: Black, Young, & Young, 1824), pp. 5–6.

19. For Tecumseh's speech, see Hunter's *Memoirs*, pp. 43–48.

the southern tribes in December 1811 and knew that thereafter he "never was again further west than the Tippecanoe," the possibility of his visit among the Osages was decisively ruled out. But Tecumseh had first arrived at Vincennes on July 27, 1811, General Harrison's correspondence establishes, and returned from the South about March 1812.[20]

Upon demand of their credentials, the general's other "facts" lost their assurance with equal rapidity: Cass said Tecumseh was "a half Creek, his father being of that tribe." But the Indian leader was almost certainly "wholly a Shawanoe," as Benjamin Drake asserted on good evidence. The notion he was half-Creek came from Harrison, who informed the War Department that Tecumseh's *mother* was a Creek. And it was risky to be very certain about Tecumseh's movements and whether he ventured west of Tippecanoe in early 1812. As General Harrison had informed his superiors the preceding summer, his great adversary was elusive: "For four years he has been in constant motion. You see him to-day on the Wabash, and in a short time hear of him on the shores of lake Erie or Michigan, or on the banks of the Mississippi; and wherever he goes he makes an impression favorable to his purposes." [21]

Now was there any positive evidence that Tecumseh "was ever within many hundred miles of a party of that [Osage] nation"? In the late 1780s, according to an Indian biographer, Tecumseh and his brother Tenskwatawa, the Prophet, left the Ohio country for three years, crossed the Mississippi, and joined the Osages and other tribes in buffalo hunts.[22] In 1808 and 1809 Tecumseh visited the Shawnees of Missouri, which assuredly put him within many hundred miles of the Osages. Actually, he seems to have visited the Osages on this trip too.[23] In 1810 and 1811 there was word of the activities of Tecumseh and his brother in the area. John Bradbury's *Travels in the Interior of America in the Years 1809, 1810 and 1811* passed on the report that the Prophet had sent the distant Otoes a wampum belt with an invitation to join the confederacy.[24] In the fall of 1810 General Clark forwarded to General Harrison informa-

20. Benjamin Drake, *Life of Tecumseh and of His Brother the Prophet* (Cincinnati: E. Morgan, 1841), pp. 139–42; Glenn Tucker, *Tecumseh: Vision of Glory* (Indianapolis: Bobbs-Merrill, 1956), p. 353n.

21. Quoted in Drake, *Tecumseh*, p. 142.

22. John M. Oskison, *Tecumseh and His Times: The Story of a Great Indian* (New York: G. P. Putnam's Sons, 1938), p. 48.

23. Louis Houck, *A History of Missouri* (Chicago: R. R. Donnelley & Sons, 1908), I, 220; Tucker, *Tecumseh*, pp. 214–17.

24. Bradbury, *Travels*, Vol. V of *Early Western Travels, 1748–1846*, ed. Reuben Gold Thwaites (Cleveland: Arthur H. Clark, 1904), 227.

tion that the Prophet had sent belts of wampum to the tribes west of the Mississippi.[25] George Champlain Sibley, the Osage Indian agent, wrote a long letter to the War Department complaining about the way the tribe had been neglected and mistreated, and noted that there was danger from British agents; [26] the Jesuit *Annals of the Osage Mission* suggests the identity of one of the "agents" in 1811: "Tecumseh, the famous Shawnee Chief, visited the Osages in Missouri and on the Neosho and Verdigris rivers in an effort to get the Indians to join him in a confederacy to fight against the U.S." [27]

Though he could only reproduce "the shadow of the substance," Hunter noted apologetically, his recollection made clear why Tecumseh's speech had made an impression on his mind, "which, I think, will last as long as I live":

> *Brothers*—When the white men first set foot on our grounds, they were hungry; they had no place on which to spread their blankets, or to kindle their fires. They were feeble, they could do nothing for themselves. Our fathers commiserated their distress, and shared freely with them whatever the Great Spirit had given his red children. They gave them food when hungry, medicine when sick, spread skins for them to sleep on, and gave them grounds, that they might hunt and raise corn. . . .
>
> The white people came among us feeble; and now we have made them strong, they wish to kill us, or drive us back, as they would wolves and panthers.

As Hunter set it down, the speech was a torrent of anger against whites, a splendid appeal—shaped by Tecumseh's vision of an independent Indian country—for the unity of the oppressed, and had as well an eschatological conclusion which anticipated the Ghost Dance religion decades later:

25. Drake, *Tecumseh*, p. 132. Clark probably got his information from Manuel Lisa, the fur trader. See Lisa's letter of 1817 reminding Clark of this, reproduced in Hiram H. Chittenden, *The American Fur Trade* (New York: Press of the Pioneers, 1935), II, 883–86.

26. Sibley's letter was reproduced in Edwin James, *Account of an Expedition from Pittsburgh to the Rocky Mountains Performed in the Years 1819 and '20* (Philadelphia: H. C. Carey & I. Lea, 1823), II, 244–49.

27. William White Graves, *Annals of the Osage Mission* (St. Paul, Kan.: Published privately by the author, 1935). William Edward Park, "Tecumseh: The Climax of the Indian Tragedy," *Canadian Magazine of Politics, Science, Art and Literature*, XLII (Toronto, 1914), 219, notes that Tecumseh "penetrated the Texas country."

Brothers—The Great Spirit is angry with our enemies—he speaks in thunder, and the earth swallows up villages, and drinks up the Mississippi. The great waters will cover their low-lands, their corn cannot grow, and the Great Spirit will sweep those who escape to the hills, from the earth with his terrible breath.

Brothers—We must be united; we must smoke the same pipe; we must fight each other's battles; and more than all, we must love the Great Spirit; he is for us; he will destroy our enemies, and make all his red children happy.[28]

This was the "invention" that Cass thought the "reading community" should have seen through straight away.

Exactly why he thought so was not made clear in his article. Since Cass was fighting several enemies at once—Tecumseh, Hunter, the critic of the *Quarterly Review,* and the British as a people—his attack sprayed out like pellets from a shotgun. Insofar as it was directed against Tecumseh, Cass granted that he was a brave warrior and a skillful leader, but still held he was a tool of the British—he had been "tampered with by British agents"—and a man filled with desire for self-aggrandizement. In a sentence, Tecumseh was not a Good Native; he had none of the makings of a "pet Indian," as Cass called those who were properly obedient.[29] Unforgivably, he had "seceded from the *'legitimate'* authority of his tribe," most of whom had "adhered with unshaken fidelity to the cause of the United States." Readers should have known, Cass seemed to be saying, that the speech reported by Hunter could not have been delivered by the disaffected, self-interested Tecumseh. More explicitly, Cass discredited the speech on the grounds that Tecumseh had ghost writers or prompters. Three Wyandot chiefs, he maintained, had actually prepared the major speeches for which Tecumseh had received credit: "Tecumthé was not an able composer of speeches. We understand he was particularly deficient in those powers of the imagination, to which we have been

28. Tecumseh's reference to the Great Spirit speaking "in thunder, and the earth swallows up villages" was to an earthquake which occurred in 1811 and which swallowed up part of New Madrid on the Mississippi; see Drake, *Tecumseh,* p. 145. For the role of Tecumseh and the Prophet in the tradition leading up to Wovoka and Sitting Bull, see James Mooney, "The Ghost-Dance Religion and the Sioux Outbreak of 1890," *Fourteenth Annual Report of the Bureau of American Ethnology* (Washington: GPO, 1896), II, 665–78; for a still larger context, see Vittorio Lanternari, *The Religions of the Oppressed: A Study of Modern Messianic Cults,* trans. Lisa Sergio (New York: Alfred A. Knopf, 1963), pp. 123–24 *et passim.*

29. Frank B. Woodford, *Lewis Cass: The Last Jeffersonian* (New Brunswick, N.J.: Rutgers University Press, 1950), p. 93.

indebted for the boldest flights of Indian eloquence. He was sometimes confused, and generally tedious and circumlocutory."

The evaluation of General Harrison was appreciably more generous: "The implicit obedience and respect which the followers of Tecumseh pay to him, is really astonishing," he wrote of his enemy, "and more than any other circumstance bespeaks him one of those uncommon geniuses which spring up occasionally to produce revolutions and overturn the established order of things." Many eyewitnesses testified that Tecumseh was a superb orator. "The Great Spirit above has appointed this place for us, on which to light our fires, and here we will remain," he said in 1807. "As to boundaries, the Great Spirit above knows no boundaries, nor will his red people acknowledge any." This speech, with its obvious parallels to the one reported by Hunter, struck Anthony Shane, who worked for the Indian agent at Fort Wayne, as "a masterpiece of Indian oratory." Indeed, another eyewitness account held Tecumseh capable of "developing a power and a labor of reason, which commanded the admiration of the civilized, as justly as the confidence and pride of the savage." On his chosen theme he was most impressive: "His fine countenance lighted up, his firm and erect frame swelled with deep emotion, which his own stern dignity could scarcely repress; every feature and gesture had its meaning, and language flowed tumultuously and swiftly from the fountains of his soul." This handsome tribute to the Indian orator came to biographer Drake in a letter from none other than the then Minister to France, Lewis Cass.[30]

"A Lie will travel from Maine to Georgia, while Truth is pulling on his boots," went a saying popular in the 1820s, a saying Cass seemed to be trying to provide illustrations for in his writings. If a biographer turns to you as an Indian expert, write a letter telling him that his subject's oratory spoke for his genius. If an earlier writer you wish to destroy says that Tecumseh was an unforgettable speaker, dismiss this abruptly on the basis of your inside information that the Shawnee had three Wyandot ghost writers named Walk-in-the-water, Grey-eyed-man, and Isidore(!). A century later Truth tardily galloped up to point out that no Wyandot chief was available to Tecumseh during his first speeches in Ohio, nor did one accompany him on his southern tour, when "he made his greatest speeches. His spontaneous remarks were often eloquent, showing that, contrary to Cass' opinion, he possessed great powers

30. Drake, Tecumseh, pp. 228–29; for the response of Harrison and others to Tecumseh as a person and a speaker, see pp. 85, 92–93, 97, 142.

of imagination and fluent speech." [31] In truth, Melville's *Confidence Man* might have found Cass's approach to historiography a perfect fit. Its beauty lay in its relative invulnerability to critical analysis. But once the reader discovers, as in the general's use of the evidence on Tecumseh, that a kind of shell-game alertness is demanded of him, then the hand may not always be quicker than the eye.

Consider a few of the illustrations which abound in Cass's sensational *North American* article: he declared the circumstances of Hunter's supposed capture to be as fraudulent as his account of Tecumseh's visit. "His description of the scene shows, that it was an act of the most determined hostility. There were the war whoop[s] and the yells, 'the massacre of [my] parents and connexions, the pillage of their property, and the incendious destruction of their dwellings.'" But the sentence which he cited was quoted out of context; in the Philadelphia edition of the narrative, which Cass was using, the sentence began with the phrase "in these deluded spells" and continued with the images and sounds which came to him then, all of which made absolutely clear that Hunter wanted the reader to regard these seemingly "perfect remembrances" as delusory. Next, with his foundation resting on what Hunter did not say, the general declared the incident could not have occurred, for the period was one of profound peace in the Old Northwest. But in 1801 General Harrison, whom Cass cited as his authority, wrote Secretary of War Dearborn deploring murders and other horrors in his immediate neighborhood at Vincennes.[32]

Joined to Hunter's misrepresentation of the history of the region, according to Cass, were his falsehoods regarding the true ethnographic facts. The general pointed out that, contrary to the narrative, the Osages had no tomahawks, no canoes, and no rifles. If they had guns, which was rare, they were not the rifles mentioned by Hunter but the so-called northwest fusils. Perhaps Cass was technically correct about the rifles, though the archeological evidence presents a problem. Tracing the culture sequence of the Osages, Carl Chapman found that between 1780 and 1830 weapons for hunting and warfare were no longer manufactured

31. Tucker, *Tecumseh*, p. 348n. By way of anticlimax note also that in 1816 Cass had emphasized that Tecumseh established a formidable coalition "by his talents and ambition, and *above all, by his disinterestedness*" (italics added). Francis Paul Prucha and Donald F. Carmony, eds., "A Memorandum of Lewis Cass: Concerning a System for the Regulation of Indian Affairs," *Wisconsin Magazine of History*, LII (Autumn 1968), 38.

32. Quoted in Henry Adams, *History of the United States of America* (New York: Charles Scribner's Sons, 1889–90), VI, 71.

at home on a large scale and that field workers uncovered more gun flints than arrowheads. After 1800 the influx of trade materials was steady, with "flintlock rifles, iron axes, iron knives" among the most important objects. But the issue is not of great consequence. The Osages named the first fusil they ever saw, in about 1700, a *wa-ho-to'n-the* (it-causes-things-to-cry-out) and that remained their name for a rifle.[33] And Cass was simply wrong about the tomahawks. The archeological evidence and travelers' accounts confirm Hunter's statement that the ancient battle-ax made from flinty rocks had been "pretty generally superseded by the . . . steel tomahawk and scalping knife, procured from the traders." [34] As for canoes, *voyageurs* had visited the Osages for decades in the canoes they had purchased to the north from the Winnebagos; from the early 1700s the Sac and Foxes came down in canoes to fight them; explorers such as Pike and Bradbury had reported canoes on the rivers and streams of the Osage country. The "skin canoe" Bradbury reported seeing at the mouth of La Platte was no doubt made of buffalo skins in the Osage manner Hunter described in detail.[35]

"But one of his grossest errors," said Cass, "relates to the Ottawas. He speaks, in many places of his work, of the Ottawas, as a tribe of southwestern Indians." Cass cited pages 41, 95, 198, and 200 of the Philadelphia edition where Hunter did speak of Ottowas. His context made clear that he was referring to the Oto tribe of the Platte River country. Pike called them Ottoes, Long called them Otoetata, and Colonel McKenney, Cass's associate, was currently calling them Ottoas. In his list of the seventy-eight known variations in the spelling of the name, Frederick Webb Hodge quite willingly included Hunter's reference to them as Ottowas.[36] But a quick eye will do the trick here: note what Cass achieved by the simple substitution of vowels. It did seem that Hunter had blundered badly in mislocating the Great Lakes Ott*a*was.

---

33. Carl H. Chapman, "Culture Sequence in the Lower Missouri Valley," in *Archeology of Eastern United States,* ed. James B. Griffin (University of Chicago Press, 1952), pp. 145–47; John Joseph Mathews, *The Osages* (Norman: University of Oklahoma Press, 1961), pp. 132–34.

34. Hunter, *Memoirs,* p. 322; Bradbury, *Early Western Travels,* V, 65, 217; Francis La Flesche, "War Ceremony and Peace Ceremony of the Osage Indians," *Bulletin 101 of the Bureau of American Ethnology* (Washington: GPO, 1939), p. 14.

35. Hunter, *Memoirs,* p. 292; Mathews, *Osages,* pp. 170–71; Zebulon Montgomery Pike, *Exploratory Travels through the Western Territories* (London: Longman, 1811), pp. 128, 154; Bradbury, *Early Western Travels,* V, 71.

36. Hodge, "Handbook of the American Indians North of Mexico," *Bulletin 30 of the Bureau of American Ethnology* (Washington: GPO, 1912), Part II, 164–66.

The general also seemed to demolish Hunter's claims to knowledge of the geography and botany of the Osage prairies and hilly woodlands. He dismissed as "trash" Hunter's section on Indian materia medica. But contemporary whites in Missouri granted that the Osages "were most skilful in medicine." [37] Some of the remedies Hunter discussed have since found their way into the *U.S. Pharmacopeia;* the medicinal practices he listed have direct parallels with those of other tribes.[38] Another falsehood became apparent, Cass said, when Hunter spoke "of wild rice, as an article of food, which in fact is found in no part of the country, where he pretends to have lived." As the general made this claim, an item appeared in the *New York Religious Chronicle* of August 1825 which noted correctly that wild rice grew in greater or less quantity from Louisiana to the Arctic Circle. In fact, in 1819 Thomas Nuttall, the botanist, found *Zizania miliacea,* a species of wild rice, on the north fork of the Canadian River, which ran through Osage country, and so reported in his *Journal of Travels into the Arkansas Territory.*[39]

So did Hunter show his impudence to be exceeded only by his ignorance, according to Cass, and nothing revealed the depths of his ignorance more than the account of his party feeling religious awe when they first beheld the Pacific. "The Osages occupy a country of boundless plains," the general wrote. "They know nothing of the ocean, nor do they believe, that the land of departed spirits is beyond it. The Heaven of the Indians is as sensual as the Mahometan paradise." But in 1803 a delegation of Osages had visited Jefferson in Washington and probably then learned something about the Atlantic; in 1794 six Osages had accompanied Auguste Chouteau to New Orleans and probably then learned something about the Caribbean; and in 1725 an Osage had visited France, returned

37. Quoted from *Brown's Western Gazetteer* in Houck, *Missouri,* I, 180.
38. There is a section on Hunter in Vergil Vogel, "American Indian Medicine and Its Influence on White Medicine and Pharmacology" (Ph.D. diss., University of Chicago, 1966, now published by the University of Oklahoma Press). For uses similar to those discussed by Hunter of pipisseway, elm bark, oak bark, sassafras bark, balsam, sumac, and others, see, notwithstanding differences of tribe and region, Gladys Tantaquidgeon, "Mohegan Medicinal Practices, Weather-Lore, and Superstition," *Forty-third Annual Report of the Bureau of American Ethnology* (Washington: GPO, 1928), pp. 264–70.
39. Nuttall, *Travels,* Vol. XIII of *Early Western Travels,* 269. Albert Ernest Jenks, "The Wild Rice Gatherers of the Upper Lakes," *Nineteenth Annual Report of the Bureau of American Ethnology* (Washington: GPO, 1900), pp. 1022, 1032, approvingly quoted Hunter and found his account in accordance with his own findings that in the first quarter of the nineteenth century wild rice grew extensively in the expanse of country between the Mississippi and the Rockies.

to give the tribe his impressions of the French, and, beyond question, told them something about his ocean voyage.[40]

In truth, the Osages knew of the ocean from long ago, from before the white man came, before there were centuries, even before the living creatures had names. In the beginning the Little Ones, as they called themselves, came down from the sky to find the entire earth covered with water. They appealed to the Great Elk. The Great Elk helped by throwing himself on the earth and by "disturbing the water in all its vastness." According to the rites of the Puma gens (clan) the Great Elk threw himself on the vast waters four times until the ground was exposed and ready to receive men and animals. As he rolled about and arose, the hairs of his body clung to the soil and became the grasses of the earth. The inward curve of his neck made the ridges of the earth, the tip of his nose the end of the ridges.[41]

The assumption that savages were childish sensualists would forever bar Cass from guessing the richness of Osage cosmology.[42] In their intricate system, the mystic unity of the universe was given symbolic expression in the dual organization of the tribe. It was divided into Sky and Earth moieties, and the latter was in turn subdivided into Dry Land People and Water People. Sky, Earth, Dry Land, and Water corresponded with the cardinal points North, South, East, and West, respectively. For

---

40. Mathews, *Osages*, p. 357; Edward Francis Rowse, "August and Pierre Chouteau" (unpubl. Ph.D. diss., Washington University, 1936), p. 166; Carolyn Thomas Foreman, *Indians Abroad, 1493–1938* (Norman: University of Oklahoma Press, 1943), p. 132.

41. I am drawing on Francis La Flesche's account of the Great Elk myth in "The Osage Tribe: Rite of the Chiefs; Sayings of the Ancient Men," *Thirty-sixth Annual Report of the Bureau of American Ethnology, 1914–1915* (Washington: GPO, 1921), pp. 165–69, and "The Osage Tribe: Two Versions of the Child-Naming Rite," *Forty-third Annual Report of the Bureau of American Ethnology* (Washington: GPO, 1928), p. 49. According to one version, the Little Ones came up from the subterranean world: see J. O. Dorsey, "Osage Traditions," *Sixth Annual Report of the Bureau of American Ethnology* (Washington: GPO, 1888). In the other version they descended from the sky: La Flesche, "The Osage Tribe: The Rite of Vigil," *Thirty-ninth Annual Report of the Bureau of American Ethnology* (Washington: GPO, 1925), pp. 302, 338, 360–61; for the Great Elk Songs, see p. 338ff.

42. The huge body of materials collected by La Flesche, who was himself the son of an Omaha chief, provides Claude Lévi-Strauss with some of his most important evidence on *The Savage Mind* (University of Chicago Press, 1966). For an indispensable discussion of the complexity and richness of Osage thought, see esp. pp. 142–49, 170. On the "sensual" nature of Osage thinking, consider the following remark which Lévi-Strauss quotes: " 'We do not believe,' as an Osage explained, 'that our ancestors were really animals, birds, etc., as told in traditions. These things are only *wa-wi-ku-ska'-ye* (symbols) of something higher.' "

the Osage, then, the West "meant" Water, and was associated as well with the setting sun, night, mystery, death, Spiritland. The western side of the Rocky Mountains and Water therefore came to the same thing: if the Pacific had not existed, Osage thought might have required the invention of another ocean.

So these illustrations from Cass's extensive catalog of charges have, once analyzed, left the "impudent impostor" actually strengthened in his claims to authenticity. One matter, however, remains: What of the "vast multitude of facts" Cass reported to McKenney from St. Louis?

3

Cass followed up his list of charges with four letters "in confirmation of our statement, respecting the imposture of Hunter." The first was from General William Clark and merits full quotation:

In answer to your inquiries respecting the man, who calls himself Hunter, I have no hesitation in stating, that he is an impostor. Many of the most important circumstances mentioned by him are, to my certain knowledge, barefaced falsehoods. I have been acquainted in this country since 1803, and have resided in it since 1807, and for eighteen years have been connected with the Indian Department. It is not possible he could have lived with the tribes he mentions, and gone through with the scenes he describes, without some knowledge of him, and of his history, having reached me.

The second letter was from Baronet Vásquez, subagent for the Kansas, who declared that in all his nineteen years with the tribe there had been "no white man a prisoner, of any age or description among them." The third was from Pierre Chouteau, trader and former Osage agent, who declared that he had been associated with the Osages in one capacity or another for the preceding fifty years and during that period "there never was any white boy living or brought up by them." But the decisive stroke came from Mr. John Dunn, "a member of the Missouri Legislature," the gentleman "whom Hunter states to have been his great patron and friend, and for whom he was named":

I have the honor to state, in answer to your inquiries on the subject, that I have never known such a person as John Dunn Hunter, the reputed author of Memoirs of a captivity among the Osage Indians, between the years 1804 and 1820. I have been a resident in the vicinity of this place for the last twenty years, during which time I have never heard of a person, bearing the same name with myself, in this country. I am, therefore, confident, that the author alluded to is an impostor, and that the work issued under his name is a fiction, most probably the labor of an individual who has never seen the various tribes of Indians of whom he speaks.

I can further state, that I have known no man of the name of Wyatt in this county, who seems to have been mentioned as one of the friends of Hunter.

John Dunn's letter was dated September 4, 1825; the other three were dated at St. Louis on the preceding day.

The *Niles Weekly Register* immediately pronounced Cass's article decisive. Hunter had been "conclusively proved . . . an arrant impostor. . . . The North American Review is final on this subject." The *National Gazette* preferred to withhold judgment, but noted that the article was "likely to attract more general notice than any thing of the kind which has been published of late years, in this country." [43]

A long, angry response appeared in the May and June 1826 issues of the *New York Review*. Written by a literary Indian named Kass-Ti-Ga-Tor, the article took Cass to task for his ignorance of philology and more particularly for his gratuitous attack on the Reverend John Heckewelder's understanding of the Delawares and their dialect. Most infuriating to him were Cass's contentions that the venerable missionary was guilty of fabrications—not deliberate misrepresentations, that is, but examples made up "to meet the case," instances furnished by "the spirit of accommodation." [44] As for Cass's statement that Hunter "whines about the purchase of land, and the introduction of whiskey," he retorted, "what honest man does not, who knows the abominable frauds, the murders, and other nameless atrocities, which have so often been connected with those purchases?" Besides, he noted, Peter Stephen Duponceau, "our learned

43. *Niles Weekly Register*, January 21, 1826; *National Gazette*, January 25, 1826.
44. William Rawle counterattacked with *A Vindication of Rev. Mr. Hecke-welder's History of the Indian Nations* (Memoirs of the Historical Society of Pennsylvania, I [1826]), which Cass in turn reviewed in the *North American Review*, XXVI (April 1828), 357–403.

and distinguished fellow-citizen," had already shown that Hunter's book lacked authenticity.

Jared Sparks, editor of the *North American,* had every reason to be pleased. As he wrote to Alexander Hill Everett, the United States Minister to Spain:

> No article which has appeared in the Review has excited more attention, than the one on Indians by Governor Cass. It is a bold, spirited, and able performance. The notice which Hunter attracted in England was the reason why much excitement prevailed there when it was proved that he was an impostor. Pamphlets and reviews have been written there on the subject.[45]

One of the pamphlets Sparks had in mind was Norgate's *Mr. John Dunn Hunter Defended.*[46]

Hunter's fate, Norgate held, had been a little whimsical. First he was charged with not having written the book that passed under his name, and it was now being asserted "not only that he wrote the book, but that he invented the narrative!" To his mind the animus of the "reviewer" in the *North American* was to be seen in every line:

> The main spring to all his hatred, and the exciting cause of his disposition, to throw the black veil of falsehood over everything that Hunter asserts is to be found in his principle, that the Indians are not to be trusted, and that the Americans have used them but justly in depriving them of their lands, and in doing their utmost to exterminate them.

Though Norgate could say that he professed "to be a personal and intimate friend" of Hunter, he had no knowledge whatever that would enable him to deal with whether a grain of wild rice was to be found in the Osage country. A careful reading of Cass enabled him to make several perceptive observations, but he was obviously stunned by the letter from John Dunn: Why had the man waited three years to denounce

45. Sparks to Everett, September 12, 1826, Sparks Mss., Houghton. Everett succeeded Sparks as editor and owner of the *North American.*
46. The full title was *Mr. John Dunn Hunter Defended: or, Some Remarks on an Article in the North American Review in Which That Gentleman Is Branded an Impostor* (London: John Miller, 1826).

as forgery a book bearing his name? Surely it was most odd that Hunter had eulogized Dunn's kindness? Would not Hunter have been a very fool to have made such a detailed reference, if his story were all fabrication? "There is a mystery about this, which I profess not to understand. One day or other I doubt not that Hunter will clear it up, but time must be allowed him." Yet questions, important as they were, were not answers.

The *National Gazette* published Norgate's pamphlet in July 1826.[47] The editor, Robert Walsh, who was one of Hunter's American patrons, explained to his readers the repugnance he felt in thinking "such a man as Hunter appeared to be . . . an errant cheat. His deportment in this city was modest and amiable. He sought money only in seeking subscriptions for his book. Those with whom he associated were compensated for the time which they bestowed upon him, by the pleasure which they derived from his conversation, manner, and real or pretended history." According to one report which had reached Walsh, Hunter was "very remotely situated on [the] White River"; another suggested "that Hunter had engaged in a journey to the interior of Mexico." Until the accused could hear of the charges and make himself heard, judgment should be suspended. But Walsh was troubled: "We discovered nothing in the criticisms or testimony of the Reviewer, except the statement of Mr. John Dunn, of Cape Girardeau, which was necessarily to be esteemed very cogent. That statement is, doubtless, fitted to disturb the confidence of any of Hunter's acquaintance; and his English champion rather eludes than repels its force; but even that . . . [Hunter] may be able to explain."

The publication of Norgate's pamphlet in the *National Gazette* certainly disturbed the confidence of Hunter's enemies. Sparks wrote Cass that he did not doubt that "Hunter will come out in his own defence, and it may be necessary for the Review to take up the matter again. For this purpose all the facts should be collected, which can be come at. Gen. Clark and others I hope will be more full and explicit." [48] His next letter had a still more urgent tone. The excitement in England "could hardly have been produced by any other topic. In this country also, it has had its advocates and opponents, who have been warm in their praise and their censure. I know several persons who still believe in the truth of Hunter's narrative, and that he will yet come out in self defence. I think, therefore, that all proper means should be used to accumulate

47. *National Gazette*, July 13 and 14, 1826.
48. Sparks to Cass, July 26, 1826, Sparks Mss., Houghton.

other facts, and be prepared to meet a reply." He urged Cass to induce Clark to read the book and "to give you his comments on it freely," Cass should not "allude to John Dunn Hunter's case in any manner at the present, but I would collect facts as fast as possible. Should you think Gen. Clark does not possess a copy of Hunter's Narrative, you had better write to some friend in Philadelphia to forward one by mail, which may be done by taking off the covers." Speed, secrecy, the accumulation of facts by "all proper means"—merely a manner of speaking?—to all this Sparks added an interesting postscript: "On looking at General Clark's letter [which appeared in Cass's article], it seems quite certain that he has read Hunter's narrative, and perhaps has a copy of the work." [49]

Ten days later, which was about the length of time required for Sparks's letter to reach Detroit, Cass wrote to Colonel McKenney: "Will you do me the favour to purchase Hunter's narrative for me, and send it under cover of the frank of the Dept. to Gen. Clarke? I am anxious to have it done immediately." On the following day, Hunter now having become official War Department business, Cass wrote to McKenney: "I snatch a moment to say to you, that I will not trouble you to send a copy of Hunter's work to Gen. Clarke. I have found an opportunity of sending [one] from here." [50]

Cass replied immediately to Sparks as well, noting with some anger that the writer of the pamphlet had the "spice of impudence" and adding the peculiar and unprovable point that he had discovered the place where Hunter was supposed to have hit the Mississippi on his return from the Pacific "& I know he was never there." He later reassured Sparks that he had "written fully to Gen. Clark respecting Hunter and forwarded a copy of his work. Facts enough to put him down will be ready, should he turn to make battle." Anyway, the London pamphlet was "not worth notice." [51]

On the contrary, Norgate's pamphlet had helped clear up part of the mystery. Up to this point a greenhorn could follow Cass's trail: to his way of thinking, an article had been published by one of America's traducers. While on an official mission at Prairie du Chien, he entered the lists against this enemy of "our common country." Since Hunter had

49. Sparks to Cass, September 11, 1826, Sparks Mss., Houghton.
50. Cass to McKenney, September 21 and 22, 1826, M234, R419, NA.
51. Cass to Sparks, September 21 and December 16, 1826, Sparks Mss., Houghton.

been the principal instrument of the attack, Cass sought to parry the thrust of the narrative or, if possible, turn it against its wielder by exposing it as a fraud. To this end he accompanied Clark, his brother-in-arms and fellow Indian superintendent, to St. Louis, where he forthwith unearthed a "vast multitude of facts." Unfortunately these facts would not withstand careful scrutiny. And the publication of Norgate's defense of his friend spurred Cass into a correspondence with Sparks and McKenney which revealed that at least one of his four St. Louis witnesses had very probably not read Hunter's narrative. Now, since they themselves testified they had never met Hunter, they could have known about him only through his *Memoirs* or through hearsay. Any testimony based on what Cass told them about the book, given his demonstrated capacity to abuse and misuse evidence, lacked probative value.

4

From here on the trail runs over rocky ground and finally disappears across the Mississippi. There are great gaps in the evidence. Searches of the Clark collections in St. Louis and Topeka failed to turn up a single reference to Hunter. Most of Cass's papers were destroyed, apparently deliberately, by an heir.[52]

So let us reconnoiter: Looking back at Clark's letter, you can see that Sparks was right: Though Clark did not have a copy of Hunter's narrative or easy access to one, and hence had probably not read it, he wrote as though he had, confidently stating that "many of the most important circumstances mentioned by him are, to my certain knowledge, barefaced falsehoods."

Baronet Vásquez, writer of the second letter repudiating Hunter, had been the interpreter on the Pike expedition. Just as they got under way, Vásquez was arrested for a debt of some three hundred dollars owed to Manuel Lisa, the fur trader. On their return to St. Louis, Vásquez and his escort met James Wilkinson, Governor of the Louisiana Territory, and the latter personally became his security: Wilkinson wrote to his man Pike that "Manual is a Black Spaniard . . . I will teach them how to interrupt national movements with their despicable intrigues."[53] Of in-

52. Information supplied by Alice C. Dalligan of the Detroit Public Library, February 1, 1969, for which she has my thanks.
53. Quoted in Richard Edward Oglesby, *Manuel Lisa* (Norman: University of Oklahoma Press, 1963), pp. 36–37.

trigues there were no end, apparently, for Pike's letters to the conspiratorial Wilkinson were full of hints of Spanish plots and trading plots; at one point he remarked of his interpreter that he was thought to be "a perfect creature of ——— ———." [54] Even if Vásquez were not so perfect a creature of someone, obviously his testimony must be approached carefully.

The anonymous reference probably was to Pierre Chouteau, the third correspondent named in Cass's article. From 1794 past the turn of the century he and his half-brother Auguste, the wealthiest merchant in St. Louis, had held a trading monopoly with the Osages. When the monopoly was given to Lisa in 1802, Chouteau induced about half the tribe—some estimate as many as 3000 souls—to move to the Three Forks of the Arkansas, where he had trading privileges. He had accomplished this through recognizing as chiefs influential and ambitious men who were not, as the ethnologist La Flesche remarked, "in the established order of chieftainship. In this way a breach was made in the tribal organization—an organization that was interwoven with the religious rites of the people." [55] Chouteau farmed the Osages for furs—trade with the tribe he himself fixed at $40,000 per annum—and was jealous of intruders. When Chouteau requested that his monopoly of the trade be restored, Albert Gallatin wrote President Jefferson that Chouteau "seems well disposed but what he wants is power and money." In 1804 he was nevertheless appointed agent to the Osages. In 1808 he joined with his rival Lisa, William Clark, and others in the formation of the St. Louis Missouri Fur Company. When Cass requested his help in 1825, Pierre Chouteau was living in semiretirement in a castle on the edge of St. Louis, surrounded by stone walls which enclosed his house, barns, stables, and extensive slave quarters, all provided courtesy of the indolent savages of the Osage tribe. Had he read Hunter's strictures against traders, Chouteau would naturally have disapproved. But his letter provided no indication that he had read the narrative, and his statement that there never was a white boy living among the Osages was not quite what it seemed.

As always, so much rode with the word "white." From the beginning of the eighteenth century, *coureur de bois, voyageurs, Bohemes,* and other Europeans fathered children among the Osages. At the beginning of the nineteenth century there were children with light eyes, wavy hair,

54. Pike, *Travels,* p. 398.
55. La Flesche, "The Osage Tribe: Rite of the Chiefs . . . ," pp. 43–44.

lighter than bronze skin. Short and dark, Hunter, who lived with the tribe as an Osage and not as a "white" boy, would have had no trouble "passing." In the following decades trappers, explorers, adventurers, traders, and officials continued to mate with Osage women. But Chouteau knew all this. His son Auguste Pierre Chouteau, who was running the Osage trading post on the Verdigris, near its junction with the Arkansas, had an Osage wife by whom he had several children.[56]

In 1825 Chouteau joined Clark, before the latter went to Prairie du Chien, in getting the Osages to sign a treaty by which they were obliged to cede their vast holdings to the United States, give up their home along the Little Osage River, and move onto a reservation in Kansas. Hunter's accusation that the Indians were being duped out of their land and his particular concern for the Osages came up at a bad time for both Chouteau and Clark. There is no evidence Chouteau ever regretted his role in negotiating this treaty, but Clark later informed General Ethan Allen Hitchcock that this had been "the hardest treaty on the Indians he [Clark] ever made and that if he was to be damned hereafter it would be for making that treaty. It really seemed to weigh upon his conscience." [57]

None of Cass's four letter writers ever again took an active part in the denunciation of Hunter. Though Sparks had written requesting his aid in detecting the impostor's most "prominent blunders," Clark never went through Hunter's narrative in order to be "more full and explicit" for the record.[58] Instead, the second round of denunciations came from individuals at a lower echelon of the Office of Indian Affairs or the Army, or from less prominent traders. Clark apparently limited his assistance to Cass in the fast-as-possible collection of facts to delegating the responsibility to a subordinate, Major Thomas Biddle, the Army paymaster at St. Louis.

Born a member of the well-known Biddle family of Pennsylvania, Thomas Biddle served in the War of 1812 with distinction and at its conclusion stayed in the Army as a captain of artillery. In 1819 he accompanied the Long expedition as far as Council Bluffs, then returned

56. Mathews, *Osages*, pp. 168–69, 307–8. In 1910, of the 2100 enrolled by the Bureau of Indian Affairs as Osages, only 825 were "full bloods": La Flesche, "Rite of the Chiefs," p. 44. The younger Chouteau also sired children by three other Indian women (*Dictionary of American Biography*).

57. Clark to Office of Indian Affairs, June 8, 1825, M18, NA; Grant Foreman, ed., *A Traveler in Indian Territory: The Journal of Ethan Allen Hitchcock* (Cedar Rapids, Iowa: Torch Press, 1930), p. 56.

58. Sparks had written to Clark directly the same day he urged Cass to ask Clark for help, September 11, 1826, Sparks Mss., Houghton.

in the spring of 1820, to take up his duties as Army paymaster at St. Louis. Shortly thereafter he married a local girl, and by the time of his violent death a decade later was known as "an enterprising citizen. By his industry and prudence he had amassed a large fortune, which he is said to have left to his amiable widow." [59] As chief disbursing officer for the Army in St. Louis, Biddle was closely associated with the Chouteaus; he had married into a closely knit community with aristocratic pretensions; and in 1826 he was in the process of amassing a fortune, something that was hardly possible on the pay of a major in the United States Army.

Since Biddle could not have known Hunter, given his late arrival in St. Louis, and since he had no special competence in Indian affairs, it was difficult to understand why Clark and/or Cass had chosen him for the assignment. Aside from the fact, that is, that he had assisted Commissioners Clark and Cass at Prairie du Chien, where the campaign to expose Hunter started in the first place.[60]

Biddle first sent the documents he had accumulated to Sparks with the request that, if the editor could not get them in the next issue or thought they should be published elsewhere, he should send them on to the *National Gazette* in Philadelphia.[61] But the *Gazette's* editor, Robert Walsh, was sympathetic to Hunter, which apparently swayed Sparks to send the Biddle materials to the *National Intelligencer*, where they were prominently published on November 8, 1826.

Biddle's covering letter added nothing to the controversy. As he correctly pointed out, John Dunn's testimony alone should have been enough to prove Hunter an impostor, but he had no further communication from this obscure gentleman. He did find it easy to understand why Dunn had waited three years for his denunciation, for "I will venture to say, that the first time Mr. Dunn ever heard of Mr. Hunter's book was when he was called upon to refute its authenticity."

Biddle's second document came in the form of "Interogatories [*sic*] and Answers having reference to Mr. Jno. D. Hunter, put to a Delegation of Osages who were assembled at St. Louis to make peace with the Delawares, and other Tribes, Sept. 22d, 1826." One answer came from "Noel Maigrain (a white man) [who] has lived with the Osages twenty-

---

59. "Biographical Sketch of Major Thomas Biddle," *Illinois Monthly Magazine*, I (September 1831), 549–61. In 1831 Biddle was killed in a duel with Spencer Pettis, a U.S. Representative for Missouri (St. Louis *Beacon*, September 1, 1831).
60. *National Intelligencer*, October 5, 1825.
61. Biddle to Sparks, September 23, 1826, Sparks Mss., Houghton.

five years and never heard of such a man." This respondent was doubtless Noel Maugrain, who in fact was of Osage–French parentage, who had married the daughter of White Hair, the Osage "chief" said to be "a creation of the Chouteaus," and whose honesty was doubted by Meriwether Lewis when Maugrain and Pierre Chouteau pressed a claim for Osage lands.[62] The level of the interrogation was revealed in the fourth question and answer: "Did Tecumseh ever visit your nation? [Answer:] Mad Buffaloe, Sans Nerf, The Old Corn, La Montre, Noel Maigrain, all say, never. We have heard of Tecumseh, as we have heard of the Devil, but he was never at our nation."

Three letters wound up Biddle's presentation. The first came from John C. Sullivan of St. Louis, who said he had met Hunter in April 1825 when he was engaged in surveying the western boundary of the Arkansas Territory. Hunter was presumably on his way to the Red River "to locate himself on a farm." Sullivan testified, "I never heard of his intention of going among the Indians, nor had he the manners of a man raised among them, or those of man raised to the hunting life." Hunter did not or would not speak Osage and once asked him "if I had ever seen a book written by him, to which I replied in the negative. He spoke of knowing many persons at St. Louis, and mentioned Gov. Clark and the Chouteau family." From Hunter's mysterious conduct and miraculous tales of his captivity, Sullivan concluded he was an impostor and communicated this opinion to his associate, Joseph G. Brown, who "will no doubt recollect it." Sullivan's testimony was important mainly in his recollection that the impostor claimed acquaintance with Clark and Chouteau, something Hunter did not claim in his book and was never reported as claiming anywhere else.

Unlike Sullivan, who was not otherwise identified, Colonel Pierre Menard was introduced by Biddle as "one of the most wealthy and respectable citizens of Illinois, and was Lieutenant Governor of that State. In an intimate knowledge of Indians and traders, he is not surpassed by any one in this country." Menard was also a former partner of Chouteau and Clark in the St. Louis Missouri Fur Company and a long-time associate of the late Manuel Lisa. He claimed to have been well acquainted with Tecumseh and to have seen him in Missouri twenty-five years earlier on Apple Creek, but was certain he "never was at the Osage village." Moreover, he had "never heard of a trader of the name of Colonel Wat-

62. Mathews, *Osages*, pp. 386–87.

kins among the Osages, or of John D. Hunter." All in all, Menard simply took up where Chouteau left off and added little to the accumulation of facts.

The last letter, from Major William Davenport of the Sixth Infantry, U.S. Army, was the most interesting of the lot. Davenport reported that Hunter had visited Cantonment Gibson in the Arkansas Territory in April 1825 when he commanded there. Davenport, unlike any of the others, claimed to have read the narrative before Hunter's visit, but this was made somewhat doubtful by his observation that Hunter explained his lack of knowledge of the Osage language on the grounds that "he had been but a short time with them; and the little he had learn[ed] he had forgotten." Had Hunter wished to maintain an imposture, he would hardly have offered this explanation to someone who had read his narrative. Unlike Sullivan, Davenport reported that Hunter's manners "are rough and unpolished, and judging from them, he might have been brought up in a wigwam; yet they are by no means unpleasant." He also replied that "to my recollection, I have never been informed by Hunter that he knew, or had any acquaintance with Governor Clark, or either of the Choteaus." That the Osages might not care to admit to Davenport the circumstances of Hunter's escaping from them and warning Colonel Watkins was not too surprising. But this passage was: "Again he was informed while at the garrison, that his narrative was discredited and advised to call upon such of the Osages as he knew to come forward and corroborate his statement, that we might give him certificates to establish the truth of his story. He did not take this friendly hint." This occurred, according to Major Davenport, in April 1825. Yet Cass took full credit for discrediting the narrative in his article, which was published the following January. Of course, there is a chance, a slim one, that when Davenport reported that he had informed Hunter again "that his narrative was discredited," he was referring to his own conclusion to that effect, which had never before seen print. But, since he drew on Cass's charges and otherwise wrote as if, in April 1825, there were wide public understanding of the fraudulent nature of Hunter's narrative, the chances are that his chronological blunder stemmed from his efforts to be helpful.

This salvo was followed by one last round from the Army position. It appeared in the *National Gazette* of January 10, 1827, prefaced by Walsh's sad admission of defeat: "Major Hamtramck, whose letter concerning John Dunn Hunter we have placed in our first page, holds the office of Indian Agent for the Osage nation—We fear that the individual

Hunter is 'no better than he should be.'" John Francis Hamtramck was a career soldier, having been a sergeant in the First Infantry in 1813 and 1814, a cadet at West Point following the war, and a commissioned officer from 1819 to 1822, when he resigned to enter the Indian service. As Indian agent he reported directly to Clark.[63] Hamtramck too was certain Tecumseh had "never visited the Osages." After efforts to discredit Hunter's knowledge of Indian languages, Hamtramck flipped over his ace in the hole:

> The smattering knowledge which Hunter appears to have of the Osage and Kansas languages has been picked up while he was stationed at Fort Osage on the Missouri River, from whence he deserted in 1808, while belonging to Capt. E. B. Clemson's company, as will be made apparent before the lapse of many months, when we may hope to have the gentleman's services again in our army, to complete the term of his enlistment.[64]

We may only regret that the Army did not somehow get this gentleman back to complete his term of enlistment. For a deserter to write so convincingly of his first reactions to New Orleans and London, of wilderness delights, of the crudities and contradictions of civilized man—this AWOL would have been a greater wonder than Hunter appeared to his English friends. And for him to desert from the infantry in 1808, when he was eleven or twelve years old at most, would have made him still more wonderful.

5

In this underbrush sharp-eyed trailers might be hard put to find bent twigs. At the very heart of the mystery was Mr. John Dunn, member of the Missouri legislature and patron of Hunter. Biddle was certainly right: Dunn's testimony alone should have been enough. Why then, instead of

---

63. F. B. Heitman, *Historical Register and Dictionary of the United States Army* (Washington: GPO, 1903), I, 496. For instance, Clark forwarded to the Office of Indian Affairs on October 14, 1826, Hamtramck's abstract of expenditures for the preceding year—M18, NA.

64. Hunter had thus allegedly deserted from Hamtramck's old outfit, the First Infantry. For Eli B. Clemson, see Heitman, *Historical Register*, I, 309.

asking him to read the narrative and specify his refutations of Hunter's inventions, did Biddle round up a new panel of witnesses? If it was a good question why Dunn was not heard from before Cass called on him, it was perhaps a better one why he was never heard from again.

Look back at Dunn's letter again (pp. 77-78). His reference to Hunter as "the reputed author of Memoirs of a captivity among the Osage Indians, between the years 1804 and 1820" is intriguing. The title is wrong and the years are wrong and the phrase "reputed author" sounds like Cass's reference to the narrative as "a work, purporting to be written by an American." At a minimum, the sentence shows that Biddle was right in venturing to say that Dunn had never heard of Hunter's book until "he was called upon to refute its authenticity." Did Cass's account of Hunter's touching tribute to John Dunn, for treating "me in every respect more like a brother or a son than any other individual had," simply make John Dunn more indignant over the way his name had been abused? If so, the indignation was not expressed in the letter, certainly not by his stiff confidence "that the author alluded to is an impostor, and that the work issued under his name is a fiction, most probably the labor of an individual who has never seen the various tribes of Indians of whom he speaks." How could he possibly know that? How could he possibly know that the unknown writer had most probably never seen the various tribes unless he simply accepted Cass's word? But even Major Hamtramck granted Hunter a smattering knowledge of Indian languages and had an ingenious hypothesis to account for his presence among those selfsame tribes. Above all, how could this unknown individual have known of his own existence: that is, of the fact that there was a man named John Dunn living in Cape Girardeau County, State of Missouri?

Dunn's final paragraph was an anticlimax. Had he read Hunter's *Memoirs,* he would have known that a man named Wyatt *was* mentioned, and not "seems to have been mentioned," by Hunter. And had he read the narrative, he would have known that Hunter placed Wyatt at a settlement just above the mouth of the White River in the Arkansas Territory, and *not* at Cape Girardeau County, Missouri. Cass had misled the obliging John Dunn.

One of the caprices of history has made many more verifiable facts available about John Dunn Hunter, "the reputed author," than about John Dunn, "a member of the Missouri Legislature." In fact, in 1825–26 there was no such person as the latter. There was a John Dunn from Cape Girardeau County who had been in the third Territorial Assembly in 1816.[65] Perhaps Cass meant *former* member. The 1830 *Census of Missouri* (p. 456) listed a John Dunn at Cape Girardeau as head of a family which included four males and two females. And in 1806 one John G. Dunn had been listed on a petition without his home district identified.[66] But these were probably two different John Dunns, and there was probably yet a third. The naturalization papers of the third, for which he applied on August 13, 1838, announced that his name was John Dunn, that he intended to reside in St. Louis, that he had been born in Northumberland, England, forty-six years earlier, and that he was renouncing and abjuring forever his allegiance to Queen Victoria. A receipted bill of this John Dunn turned up in the Pierre Chouteau Maffitt Papers.[67] *Memento mori!*

To Hunter's detractors Colonel Watkins and the commanding presence of Tecumseh among the Osages were myths conjured up by an equally mythical author. Yet no one, not Cass, Clark, Chouteau, or Biddle, seemed to want to challenge Hunter's account of his relationship with Manuel Lisa, the undeniably real dreamer of fur-trade empires. Hunter had related in his *Memoirs* how, after his return from the Pacific (in about 1815), he had met Manuel Lisa, "a Spaniard or half Indian, who was now bound on a trading expedition up the Missouri, in company with a Mr. M'Lane, another trader, and several Spanish, French, and American boatmen. . . . This Manuel Lisa was an artful, cunning man: he had several private interviews with me, and used every argument in his power to persuade me to accompany him in his intended voyage."

Of all Hunter's accusers only Timothy Flint, the frontier chronicler, took up Hunter's account of Lisa's expedition. In a private letter to Jared Sparks, Flint wrote that the narrative was an ill-digested compilation from the journals of Pike, Brackenridge, and one of the members of the Lewis and Clark expedition, but he did note that the reference to Lisa was to a man he knew. He knew of no M'Lane, however, and suggested to Sparks that this might represent a mistake by the compiler, for there was a trader named Mclellan.[68] Flint presumed too much from his

65. Houck, *Missouri*, III, 7.
66. Carter, *Territorial Papers*, XIII, 479. I am much obliged to Mrs. Henrietta Krause of the State Historical Society of Missouri, Columbia, for her courteous assistance in trying to track down the real John Dunn.
67. This John Dunn's naturalization papers are at the Missouri Historical Society, St. Louis.
68. Flint to Sparks, September 12, 1826, Sparks Mss., Houghton. Flint later made public his feelings in a sarcastic reference to "the *thrice*-famous *John Dunn Hunter*" in *Western Monthly Review*, I, 69–71.

knowledge of local affairs: had he read Nuttall's *Journal,* he would have learned that the botanist had found a M'Lane running a house of entertainment on the Mississippi River at a placed called "M'Lane's Landing." [69] As if to demonstrate the difficulty of tracing such obscure references, Reuben Gold Thwaites added an editor's note to Nuttall's account, confessing "we find nothing positive to this individual, but it is interesting to note that Arkansas County was represented in the upper house of the territorial legislature in 1821 by Neil McLane, who may have been the same man." It is more interesting to note that Thwaites might have found something positive about M'Lane in Hunter's narrative.

In his *Memoirs* Hunter had related that he was one of a group of about twenty Osage and Kansas Indians who helped Lisa ascend the Missouri River. At its junction with the Kansas River, all the Kansas Indians in the party deserted to return to their tribe. Hunter decided not to join them because his ties were established with the Osages and because of "the artful persuasions and promises of Manuel Lisa." It was on this trip that he witnessed, "for the first time in my life, the wide and wanton destruction of game, merely to procure skins; and so much disgusted was I, on seeing the buffalo carcasses strewed over the ground in a half putrefied state, that my reluctance to fulfil my engagements was so much increased, as to occasion me to reflect seriously on absconding from the party." The Indians remaining with Lisa manned the towline for the boats and suffered from constant exposure during heavy rain or high waters. When they arrived among the Mandans, Hunter related, Lisa's attitude toward him changed. Instead of "well-dissembled kindness and indulgence," he undertook to make Hunter sensible of his power over him and of the fact that the presence of the Sioux to the south made absconding dangerous. Hunter refused to submit to his will, and they had harsh words. Only after Lisa asked his pardon did Hunter and his companions agree to go on. After they arrived at the Great Falls of the Missouri, however,

> on account of a general dissatisfaction at the conduct of Lisa, all the Osages, who were ten in number, and myself, after having explained our motives to the traders, and their party, abandoned them, and took our course down the river, in the most direct manner. Lisa did all in his power to prevent our departure, on account of the important services he well knew we were capable of rendering him, in procuring furs,

69. Nuttall, *Early Western Travels,* XIII, 96.

&c., and on which he had calculated with certainty and great expectations; but finding our determinations not to be changed, he parted from us apparently reconciled.

Hunter later learned, after a return trip of extraordinary hardship, that Lisa had complained of their conduct as having defeated his object of using them to negotiate with tribes along the Missouri. Even after Hunter had left the Osages, Lisa was hostile when they met again "and resorted to clandestine measures to prejudice the Indians against me, and defeat the object of my [own trading] voyage."

Hunter's account was remarkable in at least two respects. It provided the only known evidence for Lisa's activities in the winter and spring of 1816.[70] Furthermore, it agreed in all particulars with Lisa's operating techniques and his known capacity for quarrelsomeness, holding a grudge, authoritarianism, treachery. All the trustworthy accounts are in agreement with William H. Goetzmann's recent characterization: "A swarthy and sinister man, he was a combination of the conquistador and the frontier opportunist. . . . Meriwether Lewis detested him. Governor James Wilkinson feared him, and once ordered him stopped at all costs. His French rivals, particularly the Chouteaus, hated him, and spread rumors about his domestic affairs. On his trips upriver Lisa seldom found it safe to turn his back on his own engagés." [71] In his defense an earlier historian had written that "it is difficult to prove that his methods were more cruel or more treacherous than those of his rivals." [72] Hunter's was the second-best and most revealing account written by someone who claimed to have worked for Lisa.

The best account of one of Lisa's expeditions was Thomas James's *Three Years among the Indians and Mexicans.* Said to be "a pioneer type," James was six feet tall, muscular, and twenty-seven years old when he enlisted in 1809 for a voyage with Lisa. A Welshman and a man with broad sympathies, he liked the Indians he met and thought of them as "Chiefs with the dignity of Real Princes." He was outspoken in his dislikes as well, and wrote that he and the other Americans soon "thoroughly detested and despised Lisa." The trip up was marked by desertions, hard words, threatened violence. At their destination, James contended, the

70. Oglesby, *Lisa,* pp. 160–61.
71. Goetzmann, *Exploration and Empire* (New York: Alfred A. Knopf, 1966), p. 17.
72. Thwaites's biographical note in Bradbury, *Early Western Travels,* V, 97.

partners of the St. Louis Missouri Fur Company—Lisa, Colonel Menard, and Chouteau—went back on their word to supply guns and traps: "We found ourselves taken in, cheated, chizzled, gulled and swindled in a style that has not, perhaps, been excelled by Yankees or French." Threats were made to take away the arms and ammunition in their possession: "They seemed determined to turn us out on the prairie and among Indians, without arms, provisions, or ammunition." James bought supplies from the trapper John Colter and set off for furs on his own. On his return in August 1810 he found himself in debt to the company for over two hundred dollars. William Clark sued him in September for that amount, and James in turn sued the partners for breach of contract. When it was all over, James noted ruefully, he had lost three hundred dollars in a season of trapping on the headwaters of the Missouri.

James's account matched Hunter's in every significant circumstance. What happened to James may also have a close bearing on what had already happened to Hunter. Before his death in 1847, James received help from Colonel Nathaniel Niles in writing his *Three Years,* which was published by the War Eagle Press in Waterloo, Illinois, in 1846. The book was so vehemently attacked when it came out that Colonel Niles, according to one account, immediately suppressed it. Most copies were destroyed. It became a rarity indeed: in 1910 there were only two known copies. In his 1916 introduction to the Missouri Historical Society's republication of the work, Judge Walter B. Douglas dared to hope that the years had deprived James's "ill-natured accusations of all power to offend." Douglas' attempts to justify republication said all that needed to be said. The members of the St. Louis Missouri Fur Company, men like the Chouteaus, Lisa, Clark, and others, "were men of high character, ranking among the best citizens of St. Louis." Even if James's statements were true, the judge ruled, they were "ill advised." Statements against such men "were entitled to and could obtain no credence whatever." In St. Louis there were many persons quick to resent James's statements about kinsmen, he explained; it was therefore not surprising the book was promptly withdrawn. So spoke civic pride, in the guise of an editor, seventy years after James had been silenced.[73]

If Judge Douglas was right about James in the 1840s, how much more forcefully do his remarks apply to Hunter in the 1820s? The memory of the St. Louis Missouri Fur Company was still green in 1823. William

73. I have been drawing on Judge Douglas' introduction to James's *Three Years* (St. Louis: Missouri Historical Society, 1916), pp. 6–9.

Clark and Pierre Chouteau were in attendance just a few years earlier, in 1818, when their old partner Lisa married the widowed daughter of Stephen Hempstead.[74] In 1825, when Cass and Clark arrived in St. Louis, Lisa's widow was still very much alive, known as "Aunt Manuel," and revered as a saintly and lovable woman by all who knew her.[75] An attack on her late husband would be resented for her sake alone, were there no other reason. Indeed, in 1825 Clark spoke with sympathy of the "embarrassment" caused by the tangled affairs of "Manuel's estate," though he, Auguste Chouteau, and others were shortly to sue that estate for "incompleted services." [76] The suit showed that Clark and one of the Chouteaus were currently tied financially to a man attacked in Hunter's narrative.

Take protective feeling for kinsmen, add the fortunes to be made from former Osage lands, add the great wealth in the fur trade acquired and to be acquired in the forthcoming Saga of the Mountain Men, add a lingering fear of Indian combinations—take all this and you can imagine how sympathetically Cass was received on his fact-finding mission in the late summer of 1825. He hardly had to mention that Hunter was playing into the hands of the enemies of white America. Even if what Hunter said were true—to echo Judge Douglas' pronouncement on James—he had been ill-advised to say it.

Yet, just how this first phase of the attack on Hunter fitted into the larger context of Cass's role as "Father of the West" awaits more evidence and calls for analysis in the Epilogue. Meanwhile, others joined in the hue and cry.

74. Oglesby, *Lisa*, pp. 71, 167.
75. Chittenden, *Fur Trade*, I, 131–32.
76. Oglesby, *Lisa*, pp. 193–94.

Yankee: John Neal

5

Neal—John. A New Englander—a real brother Jonathan or Yankee; one of those audacious, whimsical, obstinate, *self-educated* men.

JOHN NEAL,
"American Writers," *Blackwood's Magazine,* 1825

The term Yankee is universally applied to all rogues in the western states, without any regard to their place of nativity.

JOHN DUNN HUNTER,
Memoirs of a Captivity, 1824

A reply to Norgate's pamphlet appeared in the *London Magazine,* Jared Sparks reported to General Cass, "in which the writer accords to your positions, and brings forward a good deal of additional testimony founded on the conduct of Hunter in England. The truth is, he was made so much a wonder in that country and was so much noticed by people of the first rank, that much mortification is felt in finding that they have been egregiously duped." Clearly Sparks had gladly accepted the writer's thesis that the English were so upset because they had been made fools of. The article was written by John Neal, who had boarded with Hunter and Norgate on Warwick Street in Charing Cross.[1]

Except for "whimsical," which was not quite the right word, John Neal was everything he said he was in the self-characterization of the epigraph above. He was obstinate and audacious, played the literary games of the day with gusto, had the necessary flair for invective, and was withal surprisingly frank about what he was doing. In a series entitled "American Writers" in *Blackwood's Magazine,* Neal presented a critical estimate of over a hundred authors from the assumed viewpoint of an Englishman familiar with the United States and anxious to promote better transatlantic understanding. His opinions were not hesitant, as

1. Sparks to Cass, September 11, 1826, Sparks Mss., Houghton; Neal, "Mr. John Dunn Hunter," *London Magazine,* V (July 1826), 317–43.

when he dismissed Thomas Paine, "whose memory is held in utter abomi-
nation throughout America. The mischief that he did was intentional: the
good—accidental." He generously devoted ten pages to Washington
Irving, eight to himself, six to Charles Brockden Brown, and a half page
to James Fenimore Cooper. In the section on himself, Neal observed that
he had written more than perhaps any other four of his countrymen,
yet he was only thirty-two years old and had been writing for only
seven years. He had already published several novels which deserved
high marks for their literary excellence. Of his *Randolph*, for instance,
he wrote that it was "about as courageous a book as ever was, or ever
will be, written; full of truth—alarming truth—to the great men of North
America. It struck them with consternation."

His self-portrait in the same eight pages was equally engaging. When
he was eleven or twelve he worked in his family's retail shop in Portland,
Maine, where he "learnt, without his poor mother's knowledge, how to
sell tape—lie—cheat—swear—and pass counterfeit money—if occasion
required—as it would, sometimes in a country, where that, which was
counterfeit, and that, which was not, were exceedingly alike, not only
in appearance, but in value." [2] In his *Wandering Recollections,* published
decades later, by which time he had become a wealthy man through
shrewd investments in Maine granite, Neal proudly returned to his pre-
cocity as a sharper: one reason for his success in passing counterfeit bills,
he related, was that he was the youngest person in the store "and by far
the most innocent-looking, with my blue eyes, golden-hair, and Quaker
bob-coat." It was his "pride and boast that I never failed in putting off a
bad bill, once committed to my charge." [3] But in his article in *Blackwood's* he recorded that he had grown tired of cheating "in a small way
and, after many years of adventure . . . undertook to study law; and, as
if that were not enough to employ his faculties—to support himself
meaningfully by his pen (a thing unheard of in America)." Neal compiled the *History of the American Revolution,* which was credited to
Paul Allen, and published *Keep Cool, Logan, Errata,* and *Seventy-Six*
between 1817 and 1823, when he abruptly left Baltimore to go abroad.
According to his account of what "sent me to England," he had been
angered and sorrowed by someone asking the Sidney Smith question:

2. Neal, "American Writers No. V," *Blackwood's Magazine,* XVII (February
1825), 190.
3. Neal, *Wandering Recollections of a Somewhat Busy Life: An Autobiography*
(Boston: Roberts Brothers, 1869), p. 125.

"Who reads an American book?" He determined then and there to "take passage in the first vessel I could find . . . and see what might be done, with a fair field, and no favor, by an American writer." [4] In reality, he seems to have been weary of law practice and desirous of trying to keep pace with the foreign reputations of Cooper and Irving. Neal's most faithful biographer notes reluctantly that "he appears to have been something of an opportunist in his use of the American theme." [5]

As Neal recalled why he had gone abroad, however, he had simply the patriotic motive of carrying on his personal war with the British. He wanted to get into the pages of *Blackwood's*, "the cleverest, the sauciest, the most unprincipled of all our calumniators": "If I could [only] manage to get possession of that blazing rocket-battery, and turn its fire upon the swarming whippersnappers, who were always lying about our institutions, and habits, and prospects." [6] Neal won access to *Blackwood's* in the spring of 1824, about the time Hunter returned to the United States, and used it as the vehicle for numerous articles in the next eighteen months.

In the fall of 1824 Neal advised the English not "to puff" American writers: "Nothing can be worse, for the stomach . . . than to dish up anything American—game or not game; wild meat,* or not—with a superabundance of sweet sauce, or Cayenne pepper." Neal's asterisk referred the reader to a note which read: "As in the case of Mr. John D. Hunter—for example; of whom a word by and by." [7] His next word came during the course of his discussion of Isaac Candler's *Summary View*, when he insisted that the American government had made and was making "stupendous exertions" for the safety and improvement of the red man: "As for [whatever] Mr. John D. Hunter (who knows nothing at all of the Indian History—or the designs of the American government) may say about 'his countrymen being the worst enemies of his *plan*,' it is all trumpery and stuff":

> We know him well, and we undertake to say positively, that, up to the day of his departure from London, he had no plan of his own, and

4. *Wandering Recollections*, p. 239. Sidney Smith, one of the founders of the *Edinburgh Review*, had asked, "In the four quarters of the globe, who reads an American book?"

5. Irving T. Richards, "The Life and Works of John Neal" (unpubl. Ph.D. diss., Harvard, 1932), I, 476.

6. *Wandering Recollections*, p. 245.

7. "American Writers No. II," *Blackwood's*, XVI (October 1824), 416.

was ready to adopt the suggestion of anybody; nay, more—we undertake to say, also, that the American government, will go heart in hand,
with him, or anybody else, who will produce anything like a digested,
rational plan for the protection of the Indians.[8]

Neal nevertheless took issue with Candler's contention that Hunter himself had not written his narrative by claiming to "have heard him talk
better than that book is written; and have seen him write better. The
manuscript was corrected—not written—by a New Yorker." In the next
to last of his "American Writers" series, Neal turned to Hunter as "a very
honest fellow, at bottom—spoiled by absurd attention here; with a world
of cunning; who forgot his part, as a North American savage, entirely,
before he left us.—He could now get up a better book, without assistance." Finally, in September 1825 he ridiculed Hunter for having appeared at court in breeches and with powdered hair.[9]

Cass's essay came as a windfall. Neal quickly concluded that the writer
of the *North American* article had to be someone who knew a great deal
about "the southern tribes of America," or "the writers, I should say, for
the article appears to be the work of two or three different people." Neal
was understandably impressed by someone who could write of Tecumseh, as Cass claimed he had, with "the Prophet and his son . . . sitting
with us." [10] When Norgate published his defense of his friend, Neal gleefully rushed into the fray. With the decisive authority of Cass's article
to go on, Neal assumed that he was finally free to raise his campaign of
ridicule and innuendo to the level of an outright attack.

2

Neal began by quoting Norgate: " 'I profess to be a personal and intimate friend of Mr. John D. Hunter' (so says the author of the pamphlet). 'Immediately on his arrival in London, chance directed *me* to the
same house in which *he* lodged.' " In the second sentence of his pam-

8. "A Summary View of America," *Blackwood's,* XVI (December 1824), 639.
9. "American Writers No. IV," *Blackwood's,* XVII (January 1825), 56. The
article read "he could *not* get up a better book," but in the next issue (February
1825), p. 186, Neal made clear that this was an error and that he meant *now.*
"Late American Books," *Blackwood's,* XVIII (September 1825), 319.
10. "Hunter," *London Magazine,* V, 330, 334. Cass made this most dubious
claim in "Indians of North America," *North American Review,* XXII (January
1826), 98.

phlet Norgate had in fact written: "Immediately on his arrival in London, chance directed him to the same house in which I lodged." Neal italicized the very pronouns he was juggling, as if to dare the reader to detect his sleight of hand. The reason for the deception remained obscure for several pages, however, until he returned to the sentence and argued that he could say with greater propriety than Norgate that "*chance* directed *me* to the house in which Mr. J. D. Hunter lodged." The false parallelism he was constructing had required the earlier misquotation, all of which presumably left the reader suitably bedazzled.

Neal contended that he knew as much and probably more about Hunter than Norgate, for "I am older by six or eight years; I have had a much better opportunity for the study of human character, than he has had; and I have slept under the same roof 'with Mr. Hunter, and dined at the same table'—perhaps for a longer time than Mr. Norgate himself did." Acceptance of this claim depended on the reader's ignorance, which Neal could safely assume, of two facts: that Norgate was already boarding with Mrs. Halloway when Hunter arrived in early 1823 and that Neal did not join them until about a year later, sometime in February 1824.[11]

With a parade of italics and a show of precision in stating the particulars of the matter, Neal suggested that Norgate was withholding important information:

> Now, another might say of Mr. Norgate here, that, in defending his hero he is defending himself, they having been so *very intimate* for such a length of time; another might say also, that few men have courage to own that they have been very grossly deceived by anybody under any circumstances . . . so too another might say, that Mr. Norgate having mentioned the Duke of Sussex, and Mr. Coke of Norfolk, as two of the many who thought so highly of his hero, should have mentioned that the *Duke of Sussex encountered Mr. Hunter at Mr. Coke's, where Mr. Hunter had been produced by Mr. Norgate himself.*

Though the reader could not be expected to know this, Norgate could scarcely be blamed for withholding information about something that did not happen. Hunter was introduced to Coke and Sussex at Holkham Hall, you will recall, by Sir James Smith, the botanist.

Norgate had written his pamphlet under the grievous handicap of not

11. Richards, "Neal," I, 469n.

knowing where his friend was: "When I last heard of him (Sept. 1825), he was at Pulaski, State of Missouri, but I know that he left the most polished society of England to teach the Native Indian of Western America the peaceful arts of civilized life." Neal asked the reader to "observe here that our hero has not been heard of even by Mr. Norgate for more than eight months (a long period for a *dear* friend to be left in suspense, a long period for such a friend to be left in the lurch)." As for Hunter's extended silence, why did he not respond to the charges in the *North American?* "Why does he not furnish the facts for Mr. Norgate? *He* has had full time enough, though he should be fifteen hundred miles off." Neal believed it most likely that "our hero" will never be heard of again and did not believe he had intended to return to the Indian tribes when he left England. To Norgate's contention that Hunter had returned to teach the Indians "at the peril of his life," Neal retorted: "Absurd!—What peril is there to Mr. John D. Hunter, more than to any other white, in going to live, or to *trade*, among the savages?" He recklessly undertook to insure Hunter's life, "throughout America, for a mere trifle." But his most explosive point was the following: "Mr. Norgate is not aware, perhaps, that there is no such place in the world as 'Pulaski, state of Missouri,' the place at which Mr. J. D. H.'s last letter was dated." Few readers, probably not even Norgate, would think to check into this confident declaration that Hunter had written from a place "which does not belong to our earth." In reality, Pulaski County, located in south-central Missouri, bordered on Osage County to the west and contained the site of an old Osage village. It was familiar ground to Hunter, for it was traversed by aboriginal trails and warpaths.[12]

With an air of injured innocence, Neal outlined his own dilemma. He had concluded that Hunter "was probably the child of some Yankee trader, perhaps by a red woman." But when he put this in one of his earlier *Blackwood's* articles, he had been charged with envy or jealousy. The tone of his present article, the envy and self-pity which seeped from his sentences, came out in the following passage:

> If I gave little facts to justify the opinion I expressed, and little facts were all that I could give, I should have been charged with tattle and gossip. If I only gave the opinion, the result—I was to be charged with prejudice, or it may be with misrepresentation, or with inability

12. Louis Houck, *History of Missouri* (Chicago: R. R. Donnelley & Sons, 1908), I, 226.

to produce the facts. I have not forgotten the uproar that followed what I did say—though I said barely enough to put people upon enquiry. I was attacked on every side—charged with assailing the defenceless; a pretty charge by the way, for assailing a man, who, though he had gone away, had left a multitude of friends—friends too of the highest rank, and of the highest talent here, to fight his battles: a pretty charge to make, while I was unknown here—literally unknown, without a friend, perhaps, in the whole country, to whom I could have appealed in a case of hardship. Mr. Norgate himself was one of that very multitude.

Though Neal slipped into several personal attacks, most of the time he preferred to regard Norgate as a warm-hearted, credulous fellow who, like so many of his countrymen, had been deceived by a "thorough-bred impostor." He even pretended to find this understandable: "He was overrated here, prodigiously overrated—but where is the wonder? The people of this country had never seen, what we see every day in America, savages bursting from the solitude—savages when they first appear—but, like their own rivers, growing beautiful as they approach the light." The young Englishman had to be excused for reason of his never having experienced this wondrous sight.

Norgate was not quite as young and impressionable as Neal would have him. He was not in fact six or eight years younger than Neal, but five. Named after his grandfather Elias Norgate, he was born in 1798, the eldest of the twelve children of Thomas Starling Norgate of Hethersett Hall.[13] Aside from his pamphlet on Hunter, Elias Norgate's only other published work was *A Brief Sketch of the Origin and Progress of the Norfolk & Norwich Horticultural Society* (1833), in which, despite his rather prosaic subject, he managed to show a warm concern for "poor cottagers" and a desire that they might learn to grow fruits, flowers, and vegetables on their little plots of land. After he left London, he assisted his father in publishing the weekly *East Anglian* between 1830 and 1833, when he died suddenly.[14]

Notwithstanding his friendship for Hunter, Elias Norgate was one of the few disinterested individuals in the whole controversy. Though he had not heard from his friend for months, as Neal taunted, he had the courage to go ahead with his pamphlet and to publish it at his own ex-

13. Walter Rye, *Norfolk Families* (Norwich: Goose & Son, 1913), p. 608.
14. I am indebted to Mr. Thomas Norgate of Deighton Hills, Taverham, Norwich, for these details. His grandfather was Elias Norgate's brother.

pense. He took the obligations of friendship seriously. And the testimony he offered deserved to be taken with equal seriousness:

> If Hunter is an impostor, never can I venture to place confidence in man again; Nature has stamped sincerity and truth upon his very countenance; his thoughts, words, actions—all correspond with this palpable and external impress. He bears the genuine mint-mark about him, and it is visible in everything he says, and in everything he does. With my feelings towards him, it would be affectation to make any apology for attempting his defence.

That Hunter had lived for over a year in close proximity to an alert, honest man without betraying his alleged imposture, has to be given considerable weight in any examination of the charges against him.

3

When he came to write his memoirs years later, John Neal remembered that his exposure of "the wicked and foolish imposture of Mr. John Dunn Hunter" in the *London Magazine* "was followed by a similar exposure, in a more serious vein, by the late Dr. Sparks, in the 'North American Review,' on the authority of no less a personage than General Cass." [15] It was entirely in character for Neal to claim priority for his own effort. Recall his similar claim (p. 26) to the noteworthy coincidence of bumping into Charles Toppan, the very man he was looking for among the hundreds of thousands of souls, on his arrival in London. Now we are in a position to answer his question as to how this could have happened: if some incident took his fancy, a remarkable coincidence or an exposé of an impostor, he simply appropriated it.

In the heat of battle, Neal was not above making up his evidence as he went along. He announced, for example, that "the beautiful though absurd poetry" about Hunter in the *Quarterly Review* was in "a paper written by a poet, who knows about as much of our North American savages, peradventure, as other men who deal in prose, know of the anthropophagi." Neal may well have been thinking of Robert Southey, one of the founders of the *Quarterly*, and guessed he had written the article. According to John Murray's "Register," however, it was written

15. *Wandering Recollections*, pp. 313–14.

by George Procter, a professional army officer and historian who wrote, under the pseudonym George Perceval, a well-known *History of Italy* (1825); the second edition, published in London in 1844, announced that it was "By Colonel Procter, late of Sandhurst College." [16]

Neal contended that Hunter's book had "excited no interest" in the United States "till it was so absurdly over-estimated here." But even the *North American* did not completely pass the narrative by "as a thing of no worth before," as Neal asserted, for in the course of a review of James Buchanan's study of the Indians in the October 1824 issue, the writer took Buchanan to task for referring to the narrative "with more respect than we imagine it deserves, as a well authenticated performance." [17] In fact, Hunter's narrative had excited sufficient interest in the United States to produce one of the most perceptive reviews to appear anywhere. Early in 1824 a writer in the *Cincinnati Literary Gazette* held that Indians appeared little better than brutes because they had generally been "represented to us by their enemies" and that, though Hunter's narrative was still not an account of the Indians by one of themselves, it came closer than anything "we had reason to expect during the lives of the present generation." As the work "bears unquestionable marks of candour and impartiality, as well as of sound understanding, it is entitled to more consideration than any work we have hitherto seen upon the subject." [18] The narrative was not praised more unreservedly in England or, as Neal would have it, more absurdly.

Neal turned to a real problem when he took up the question of the letter from Hunter which was prefixed to the second and third London editions of the narrative. The writer of a favorable account in the *Eclectic Review* had still wanted to know how the narrative got to the publishers and who the Edward Clark was Hunter had named in his "Preface" as his friend and assistant, and what he had to do with it.[19] Hunter sent the following letter, dated at London on August 2, 1823, to his publishers:

> The Editor of the Eclectic Review, in examining my Memoirs, has made a very natural enquiry, who is the gentleman alluded to in the Preface as my assistant? I am very happy to answer the question by

16. For the Murray entry, see Walter E. Houghton, ed., *The Wellesley Index to Victorian Periodicals* (University of Toronto Press, 1966), pp. 703, 1054.
17. *North American Review*, XIX (October 1824), 464.
18. *Cincinnati Literary Gazette,* January 1 and 10, 1824; the review was edited by John P. Foote.
19. *Eclectic Review*, XX (July–December 1823), 174, 180.

referring to Col. Aspinwall, consul-general for the United States to Great Britain, and Mr. Toppan, 69. Fleet-street, London. I might refer to many of the most respectable persons in all parts of the United States, but perhaps a few will suffice: Robert Walsh, Esq., Editor of the National Gazette, Philadelphia; Col. William Duarre, Editor of the Aurora, Philadelphia; Dr. Waterhouse, Boston; Dr. Mitchell, Dr. Hosack, and Mr. Silliman, of New York; Professors Patterson and Patter of Baltimore.

Norgate reprinted the letter and observed that Hunter would have had great effrontery to list all these personal references, if he were an impostor. In reply Neal wondered what Norgate would say, "If I were to tell him that his hero has not answered the question at all—nay, that he has referred to a number of people, a large part of whom were never heard of, in America!" The basis for this second charge was that Hunter had misspelled the name of Colonel William Duane, the Jeffersonian editor of the *Aurora,* that of Professor Pattison of Baltimore, and of others, or had associated their names "in some way, with mistake. For example, Robert Walsh is not the Editor of the National Gazette, Philadelphia; but Rob. Walsh, *Junior,* is." Neal was on strange ground here, in his role as a stickler for accuracy. Anyone who referred to Alexander Hamilton as "Secretary of State under the administration of Washington," as Neal did in his "American Writers" series for *Blackwood's,* was in no position to cavil at minor errors.[20]

But Neal's main point was almost lost amid all this quibbling. Hunter had not answered the question of who Edward Clark was. The question was, Who was Hunter's assistant? and he had replied, as paraphrased by Neal, "I am happy to refer you to A. B. and C. D. E. F. G. . . ." From Neal's point of view, failure to answer the question meant that Hunter was hiding something. From another point of view, the failure may merely have been a measure of Hunter's lack of familiarity with the language, especially language used polemically to marshal evidence, and his lack of familiarity with publishing, with how books are put together, with the roles of editor and author. From whatever perspective, the question was unanswered.

Such questions were terribly difficult to answer in a country where, as Neal had reason to know, that "which was counterfeit, and that, which

20. Neal, "American Writers No. IV," *Blackwood's,* XVII (January 1825), 56.

was not, were exceedingly alike, not only in appearance, but in value."
Who was the genuine John Smith? The true Pocahontas? In their archetypal American captivity story, what were the true circumstances of the
relationships of the intrepid captain and the dusky Indian princess? Who
was the real Daniel Boone? White Indian or pathfinder of civilization?
What were the true circumstances of the captivity stories associated
with his name? The truth is that Europeans brought their ancient myth
of the West with them; when they stepped off the ship, they commenced
to live it.

Travel books and captivity narratives made magnificent repositories
for the experiences which followed. The first narratives of miraculous
deliverances from captivity were put before readers as evidence of God's
illustrious providence. By the time of Cotton Mather's *Magnalia* (1702),
however, a certain "stylization" had become apparent.[21] The narrative
was with increasing frequency written up by an "editor" for its journal-
istic value as propaganda. Hatred could be channeled against Indians,
whose atrocities, depending on the particular point in history, were depicted as French-inspired or English-inspired. Soon it came not to matter
very much, for the narrative became a tale of woe carried along by the
terrifying activities of wilderness beasts who needed no outside
inspiration.

Inevitably, the "editor" sometimes worked singlehandedly: there was
no ex-captive whose experiences had to be wrought into the proper literary form. In investigating the *Affecting History of the Dreadful Dis-
tresses of Frederic Mannheim's Family* (1793?), Stanley Pargellis could
find no evidence in deed records or elsewhere that indicated Mannheim
was real enough to have twin sixteen-year-old daughters who might have
been tortured to death. Jackson Johonnet, from whose *Remarkable Adventures* comes the ballad on page 59, seems never to have lived in
Falmouth, Maine, or anywhere else.[22] Even when the captive had a
real existence he frequently related unreal experiences. The Charles
Rusoe who left a particular account of his sufferings during his eleven
years with the "Scanyawtauragahroote" Indians apparently was a captive,
though he reported seeing a monkey as he traveled with his captors to

21. The term used by Roy Harvey Pearce in "The Significances of the Captivity Narrative," *American Literature,* XIX (March 1947), 3.
22. Pargellis, "The Problem of American Indian History," *Ethnohistory,* IV,
(Spring 1957), 118.

the Spanish settlements in the Southwest.[23] A "second writer" or editor may have been responsible for the monkey, but sometimes it was the other way around. Mountain man Joseph L. Meek, for example, had undeniably real adventures which he related to Mrs. Frances F. Victor, who wrote them up in *The River of the West* (1870). The mischievous Meek told his admirer of his captivity with the Snake Indians, of being rescued by a friendly chief and taken into the woods, and of meeting there a beautiful maid named "UMENTUCKEN TUKUTSEY UNDEWATSEY, otherwise Mountain Lamb," so they could go galloping off together, on Mrs. Victor's sober prose, to Pierre's Hole.[24]

In the long career of the captivity story in American literature, Hunter's book was something of an anomaly. In her study of eighty-four such chronicles, Dorothy Behen found that their single most characteristic feature "was their emphasis on the gory details of violent physical abuse wilfully inflicted by their captors." Of the entire number only Hunter's narrative and two others showed Indians sometimes acting more humanely than whites would have in comparable circumstances.[25] That Hunter had no relish for gore and refused to cast the Indians in their conventional roles as villains made his narrative a relatively fresh approach to an old topic, if it was not, in itself, proof of his authenticity. But no matter how exceptional, his *Memoirs* automatically became part of a popular literary genre which had its own imperatives. Publishers and hack writers the country over knew that, in order to be salable, a narrative had to include at least some terrifying incidents and exciting escapes and deliverances.

Consider the following: While he was still with the Kansas, Hunter related, they had ascended the Platte several hundred miles to the entrance of the Dripping Fork, where they fixed their camp and explored a nearby cavern.

> Lighted up by our birch-bark flambeaux, the cave exhibited an astonishing and wonderful appearance; while the loud and distant rumbling or roar of waters through their subterranean channels, filled our minds

23. *Memoirs of Charles Dennis Rusoe d'Eres* . . . (Exeter, N.H.: Henry Ranlet, 1800), p. 46; Dorothy M. F. Behen, "The Captivity Story in American Literature, 1577–1826" (unpubl. Ph.D. diss., University of Chicago, 1951), p. 93.

24. Meek's "highly spiced fiction" is discussed in Leroy H. Hafen and W. J. Ghent, *Broken Hand: The Life Story of Thomas Fitzpatrick, Chief of the Mountain Men* (Denver: Old West Publishing, 1931), pp. 92, 296.

25. Behen, "Captivity Story," pp. 41, 190. She found the "roguery of the captors almost always emphasized" (p. 133).

with apprehension and awe. We discovered two human bodies partly denuded, probably by the casual movements of the animals which frequent this abode of darkness; we inhumed and placed large stones over them, and then made good our retreat, half inclined to believe the tradition which prevails among some of the tribes, and which represents this cavern as the aperture through which the first Indian ascended from the bowels of the earth, and settled on its surface.[26]

The tradition made sense, for, as we have seen, one of the versions of the genesis myth of the Osages had the first men ascending from the depths of the earth. But a close examination of the passage shows that Hunter must have read Charles Brockden Brown's *Edgar Huntly* (1799) before he entered "this abode of darkness": as if heeding Brown's famous preface, the Indians have a proper literary response to a Gothic setting which was the American counterpart of ruined castles and chimeras.[27] It comes as no surprise, therefore, to learn that the existence of the cave has been questioned.[28]

Hunter concluded the preface of the Philadelphia edition with a request to the reader "to keep the fact in view, that these details have been written from a recollective comparison between the information I have acquired since my assumption of literary habits, and the cursory and accidental observations of youth and immature manhood, when not the slightest suspicion existed of their ulterior recurrence, application or importance." [29] Did Hunter's "infatuation with reading" after he left the Osages and his subsequent "assumption of literary habits" lead him to add such colorful incidents to his narrative to assure it public appeal? Or did his Philadelphia publisher, James Maxwell, insist that such incidents be added? [30] More importantly still, did Hunter's "assistant," Edward Clark, insist on such additions as a literary touch, cooperate in adding them, or what? Neal's point thus touched on some very crucial issues indeed for any systematic assessment of the authenticity of all or parts of the narrative.

Neal may have unwittingly cut a path into these tangled matters. In

26. *Memoirs*, p. 29.
27. Brown, *Edgar Huntly or Memoirs of a Sleepwalker* (Philadelphia: David McKay, 1887), p. 4. Hunter's cave is like Huntly's underground pit in Ch. XVI.
28. "Dripping Fork of the Platte," *Nebraska History*, IV (March 1921), 22–23.
29. In the London editions the reference to his "assumption of literary habits" disappeared.
30. Maxwell printed the 1812 counterfeit publication of the expedition of Lewis and Clark but was also reputable enough to be the printer of the first Biddle edition of their travels.

his *Blackwood's* series he had written that Hunter "could *now* get up a better book, without assistance; although, we dare say, that, after all the pruning; alteration, correction, etc. etc. which the *'Narrative'* has undergone, there is not a paragraph left as it was written by him." [31] The "now" which was misprinted in Neal's article and which I have italicized above, may have been the critical word. In his attack on Hunter in the *London Magazine*, Neal granted that, "though he can talk well, and write well (for a savage), he is not to be depended upon—that is, when he does it well, it is by a happy accident." By way of illustration, Neal quoted some of Hunter's notes from the margins of a book:

> "He who would do great actions must learn to *empoly*, his powers to the least possible loss. The *possession* of brilliant and extraordinary talents, is not always the most valuable to *its possessor*. Moderate talent properly directed will enable one to do a great deal; and the most distinguished gifts of nature may be thrown away by an unskillful application of them. 15, May 1824." Here I have copied the passage (orthography, punctuation, perplexity, and all) just as it appears. It is enough, by itself, to show the character of the man—great good sense, a little quackery, no very clear ideas beyond a fixed level, as where he speaks of the *possessor* of a *possession*—yet altogether above what could be expected here (though not in our part of the world) of a white savage, who had got his growth before he was caught.

Whatever Neal had come to expect from white savages, he performed a real service in reproducing Hunter's earnest sentiments. The latter's difficulty in getting them down in proper form showed him still learning as he went along. His misspelling here and in his letter to his London publishers indicated he still had a fair distance to go. If an impostor, the success of his imposture did not depend upon his mastery of American-English. His failure to answer directly the question about his assistant was a further indication: otherwise, since he had never tried to keep Edward Clark's name a secret, his response was inexplicable. Besides, Hunter was quite clear about all this at the very beginning: in his Preface he had admitted a "total ignorance of the art of book-making."

It was, after all, in character for him to feel a stranger in the world of letters. His lack of preparation for dealing with publishers and editors was painfully obvious. His pathetic trust in their good offices, for example, was suggested by this publisher's note which was added to the

31. "American Writers No. IV," *Blackwood's,* XVII, 56.

pamphlet form of his *Reflections on the Different States and Conditions of Society:* "Mr. Hunter requested any necessary corrections might be made; but it was thought better to retain his own expressions, than to suggest any alterations beyond a few verbal corrections, and his manuscript is now printed for the *sole use* of the New England Company. *August,* 1823."

No circumspect, seasoned author would ever willingly request a publisher to make "any necessary corrections." If Hunter handed over his chapters or sections or whatever to James Maxwell—or to Edward Clark, which was more likely—with a similar request, then the Dripping Fork cavern incident in the narrative becomes more understandable. The reviewer in the *Literary Gazette,* which was associated with Hunter's English publishers, perhaps drew on inside information in his contention that the narrative "was wretchedly got up and published in America, so interlarded and *mended* by some editor who could not appreciate its value as it came untouched from the lips of its author." And the following passage from a letter of Hunter to James Madison becomes more understandable as well: "My publisher in this country treated me with much injury. I directed a number of names of persons to whom copies of my book were to be sent. I was gone to Europe and did not attend to it myself. I find the mortification that not many copies were sent, to those which I ordered free of expense. I fear you are among those neglected." [32]

If Hunter was totally lacking in knowledge of how to cope with bookmen, the role of Edward Clark was pivotal. The biographical data are scanty but suggestive. *Westcott's History of Philadelphia* has several entries: in February 1813 Clark "proposed to light the city with tallow and old fat, instead of with oil"; in 1814 he entered into an argument with William Rush, the carver, about the best way to bring water into the city and the same year "obtained a patent for lamps"; and in 1816 he was listed as "Corresponding Secretary of the Cabinet of Sciences." He was elected to membership in the Academy of Natural Sciences of Philadelphia on January 28, 1817. [33] The same year Hunter's narrative came out Clark published his *Description of a Plan for Navigating the Rapids in Rivers . . . ,* which had for an epigraph: "The comfort and hap-

32. Hunter to Madison, October 15, 1824, Madison Papers, Library of Congress.
33. David McNeely Stauffer, *Westcott's History of Philadelphia* (Philadelphia: Historical Society of Pennsylvania, 1913), XIV, 1004, 1033, 2296, and XVIII, 1305. I am obliged to Ruth E. Brown, Librarian of the Academy of Natural Sciences, for her letter of January 3, 1969, on Clark's membership in that organization.

piness of man, depend on human improvements." The following year he published *Proceedings of Two Meetings of the Citizens of Philadelphia Respecting Col. Clark's Plan for Ascending Rapids in Rivers and Thereby Improving the Navigation of the River Delaware, Beyond Trenton.*[34] Clark's plan involved the invention of a boat-pulling barge outfitted with paddle wheels and windlasses, which would be anchored by a cable or chain at the head of rapids in the Delaware, and which from there would pull craft over the falls. His outline of the plan indicated that his experiments on the Susquehanna near Columbia showed to his satisfaction that it would work on the Delaware.

Unquestionably this was the Edward Clark mentioned in Hunter's preface. That the two men remained in correspondence after the latter went to England was made clear in Hunter's letter to Coke in which he referred to a friend in Philadelphia who

> has lately sent me a plan for navigating rapids, by a very simple apparatus by which a boat will ascend the rapids with speed in proportion to the velocity of the current. . . . Several patents have lately been granted of machines highly important, my correspondent informs me, and says: "Never was the march of Human intellect more rapid than in America at the present time." [35]

After Hunter's return to Philadelphia, friends repeatedly met "Col. Clarke, an eminent civil engineer," at his home or in his company.[36] Decades later George Ord, an old Philadelphian, wrote a friend that he did not know whether Clark was still living, but that he had been personally acquainted with him as the compiler of the narrative: "He told me that when Hunter solicited his assistance, he perceived that he was deficient in learning, but that he placed reliance on his integrity and sincerity; but that had I [Clark] known he [Hunter] was as great a rascal as I afterwards found him to be, I would have had nothing to do

34. Clark, *Description of a Plan* . . . (Philadelphia: William Brown, 1823); *Proceedings* . . . (Philadelphia: Joseph R. A. Skerrett, 1824).

35. Hunter to Coke, February 15, 1824, in A. M. W. Stirling, *Coke of Norfolk and His Friends* (London: John Lane, 1908), II, 322.

36. Joel W. Hiatt, ed., "The Diary of William Owen from November 10, 1824, to April 20, 1825," *Indiana Historical Society Publications,* IV (1906), 29, 32–33; Caroline Dale Snedeker, "The Diaries of Donald Macdonald, 1824–1826," *Indiana Historical Society Publications,* XIV (1942), 208.

with him. Here our conversation terminated." [37] And here our evidence on Edward Clark ends.

This much we do know: Clark was a civil engineer, probably an honorific colonel, the inventer of ingenious contraptions for navigating falls of rivers, a booster firmly committed to the march of American progress, and, as long as Hunter was around, on friendly terms with him. If Clark discovered that the author of the narrative he had helped compile was a rascal, he did so only after Hunter left Philadelphia in late 1824 and did not broadcast his finding. Why he never spoke out publicly during the course of the controversy remains a mystery. About one thing, however, there is reasonable certainty: Clark was not, as Neal contended, "a New Yorker."

4

Neal touched on another puzzling question. In his narrative Hunter had included a letter from Colonel Watkins, dated at Cape Girardeau, March 15, 1821. The letter was both a tribute and an offer of assistance:

> I have just received information from Mr. Combs and Colonel L. Bean, that you are lying very low with the fever, at Shawneetown; yet am much gratified to hear from the same respectable source, that you are on the recovery.
>
> I am in haste, and am sorry I have but a few moments to devote to this tribute of gratitude and respect, for one to whose goodness and enterprise I am indebted, under Providence, for my life; and that too, at the sacrifice of every thing valuable to you. . . .
>
> I am willing to certify upon oath, at any time, if required, my delivery from inevitable destruction, by your timely and hazardous undertaking.
>
> I know your clerical friends were very solicitous for you to go

37. George Ord to Waterton, October 20, 1861, American Philosophical Society, Philadelphia. After Hunter's narrative came out, Clark had been demonstratively proud or at least unashamed of his role in seeing it through the publisher's. Two of the copies he gave to friends have survived. The first is inscribed "Lod Sharpe/ presented by his friend/ Col. Edwd. Clarke" and is in the Pennsylvania State Library, Harrisburg. The other is inscribed "Dr. Wm Swift/ from his friend/ Col. Ed^d. Clark/ Dec. 18th 1828 [?]" and is in the Orlando, Florida, Public Library. The relatively illegible last digit may make the date 1823; it is more likely 1828, which, if correct, would say a good deal about Clark's real response to the charges of imposture.

through Boston, and obtain a theological education. I cannot say what course to advise you, as to that:—I do not know the moral tendency of your mind, and cannot advise. Let me hear from you often: I shall be generally at Natches or Baton Rouge.

The writer signed off as George P. Watkins, "your most affectionate and sincere friend and well-wisher." [38] Watkins' reference to Colonel L. Bean in his first paragraph, incidentally, was noteworthy in light of Colonel Ellis P. Bean's presence then in the Osage country and of the leading role he later played in the events leading to Hunter's death.[39]

Norgate reprinted the Watkins letter, with the observation that "in common fairness" it should not have been suppressed by the writer of the article in the *North American Review*. Why Cass made no mention of it whatever was indeed intriguing. And why did Mr. John Dunn, who went out of his way to deny the existence of a man named Wyatt, fail to add that he had never heard of Colonel Watkins in Cape Girardeau County? Only Colonel Pierre Menard, you will recall, said that he had "never heard of a trader of the name of Colonel Watkins among the Osages." "Who is he?" asked Neal. "Is there such a man? was there ever such a man?" His questions were to the point, for why indeed did Colonel Watkins not step forward and demonstrate his willingness to certify upon oath that Hunter had saved him from "inevitable destruction"? On the basis of evidence which he did not produce, Neal recorded his belief that Watkins had never existed or, if he did, "that he ever had anything to do with our hero, in the shape related."

Yet Thomas Jefferson had evidently been confident that Colonel Watkins did exist and that he had had a great deal to do with our hero. Doctor David Hosack, Hunter's friend and patron, who was vice-president of the College of Physicians and Surgeons in New York City, sent a letter to Peter Stephen Duponceau of Philadelphia in which he noted that

the circumstance which of all others satisfied my mind that he was not an impostor was the letter of Col. Watkins referring to his miraculous

38. *Memoirs*, pp. 131–32.
39. Flora Lowrey, "Peter Ellis Bean: A Typical Filibuster of Early Texas History" (unpubl. M.A. thesis, Southern Methodist University, 1945), places her subject on Smackover Creek, Arkansas, from the spring of 1818 until after the Mexican Revolution in 1821 (p. 23). Since the name usually given was Ellis P. Bean, though his son insisted that his real given names were Peter Ellis, Watkins may have understandably rendered the Ellis as *L*.

deliverance by the instrumentality of Hunter—this is the only source of doubt with me—Have you seen that letter?—The genuineness of it can readily be established or disproved—but I want to see the [Cass] review and am anxious to become acquainted with the facts.—Mr. Jefferson as you know is also among his friends and I believe considered the deliverance of Watkins to be an ascertained truth.[40]

Jefferson could no longer speak for himself: he died the month Neal's article was published.

Jefferson had been periodically unwell for some time. One of his correspondents during these last years was I. J. Chapman, an English or Scottish traveler, who provided him with information relevant to a code of regulations for the projected university at Charlottesville, Virginia.[41] In one of his letters Chapman referred to "Hunter, about whom I spoke to you when at Monticello," discussed the enthusiastic reception of the narrative abroad, and continued:

I am anxious to mention this, because I believe it will not only gratify you and Mr. [Thomas Jefferson] Randolph, but I consider it an act of duty to state, that in consequence of the prejudice which I have met with against Mr. Hunter, which I have met with not only in Philadelphia but in New York, I have been induced to mention the favourable testimony which not only Mr. Randolph and you yourself had towards him, but that which I received from those persons in Charlottesville of whom I made enquiry at your suggestion.[42]

Chapman concluded by hoping that, if he had been guilty "of a breach of that confidence you have placed in me," Jefferson would forgive him and understand he had been actuated only "by a desire to defend the absent and to protect the character of one who has no other dependence than that character."

Chapman's letter had the great misfortune, for us, of arriving when Jefferson was suffering from a fever which lingered on for three weeks. When he did reply, he borrowed "the pen of another," probably that of his grandson Thomas Jefferson Randolph, "to thank Capt. Chapman for the kind interest he appears to take in the university & is indebted to

40. Hosack to Duponceau, January 28, 1826, Duponceau Papers, American Philosophical Society.

41. Chapman to Jefferson, May 14, 1823; Jefferson to Chapman, May 28, 1823, Jefferson Papers, Library of Congress.

42. Chapman to Jefferson, July 20, 1823, Jefferson Papers, Library of Congress.

him for many useful ideas." [43] The aged sage can hardly be blamed for falling ill just when we needed him most, just when the issue of Hunter had been fairly raised, nor can we be blamed for thinking the fevers of that summer as particularly damnable.

Nevertheless, there can be little argument about Jefferson's trust in Hunter. Norgate reproduced a letter from Elliott Cresson, Quaker and scion of the well-known family of Philadelphia merchants, who wrote from Paris:

> The subject to which your letter of the 10th of March relates gives me much pain, especially as the charges against Hunter are so unexpected to me. The opinion of our late President, Thomas Jefferson, Esq. as expressed to myself was certainly free from all doubt, and for his opinion I have much respect. . . . I may add, that no family in the United States saw Hunter so frequently as ours, at all times and under all circumstances; his conduct was thus more liable to close scrutiny at our house than at any other; and, during the whole period of our intimacy, *no one circumstance* occurred to alter the opinion we had formed.[44]

Neal predictably dismissed Cresson, who was all of three years younger than he, as "a very worthy young man whose opinion I should care very little for, even in a matter which he might happen to understand."

And so what if Jefferson had no doubts about Hunter's authenticity, Neal observed, for

> Mr. Jefferson could not know, and did not know whether our hero's story was true or not. Mr. Jefferson knows very little of the Indian

43. Jefferson to Chapman, August 1, 1823, Jefferson Papers, Library of Congress.

44. Norgate, *Mr. John Dunn Hunter Defended* (London: John Miller, 1826), pp. 34–35. Though the testimony of Hosack, Chapman, and Cresson is persuasive, one still misses Jefferson's own words. I am much obliged to Mr. Frederick R. Goff of the Library of Congress for pointing out that Millicent Sowerby's unpublished catalog of his last library places a copy of Hunter's *Manners and Customs . . .* at Monticello. No doubt this was a presentation copy of the Philadelphia edition of 1823. Originally bequeathed to the University of Virginia, it was probably one of the volumes in this collection, which, following the demand of creditors on Jefferson's estate, was dispersed in Washington through an auction sale on February 27, 1829. A circular letter to the eighty present owners of Hunter's narrative, listed in Richard H. Shoemaker's *Checklist of American Imprints for 1823* (New York: Scarecrow Press, 1968), elicited useful information but did not lead to evidence which would have established the identity of Jefferson's copy. Some rich annotations in his hand would have been a lovely (and decisive) discovery.

character, and less of the Indian language—of any Indian language. There could be no better proof than the speech of Logan, which is repeated here on his authority, Logan the Mingo chief. It was altogether a humbug, that speech, and Mr. Jefferson is now aware of it; nay, I am not sure that he may not be charged with part of it.

On the contrary, Jefferson could have known about one proof of Hunter's authenticity, namely the Watkins letter.

Long before the Lewis and Clark expedition, Jefferson had demonstrated a vital interest in the country stretching toward the Stony Mountains, as he called them, and beyond. Through Clark, Pierre Chouteau, and others, he learned about the Osage country when he was in the White House. He visited with delegations of Osages when they were in Washington. And he had numerous informants in the region across the Mississippi. One of the agents he sent to spy out the Spanish country in the Southwest, according to some sources, was Colonel Peter Ellis Bean.[45] Conceivably Jefferson learned about Watkins and Hunter from Bean or someone else in the area. It is more likely that he learned about Watkins from someone who knew the latter's family. In the summer of 1823 Jefferson wrote a letter of introduction to William H. Crawford, Secretary of the Treasury, for Dr. Thomas G. Watkins, "an esteemed neighbor of mine and our family physician." [46] Watkins' letters to Jefferson were sometimes dated at Jonesboro and showed him to be involved in Tennessee politics on the anti-Jackson side. In addition to being the family physician, he was a long-time political ally.[47] Though there is no evidence which shows this to be so, Dr. Watkins could have had a kinsman who had traded among the Osages. And though this is scarcely more than informed conjecture, I find it interesting that visitors to Washington in November 1824 met there a "Dr. Watkins and son who called on Mr. Hunter." [48] Might not this Dr. Watkins have been one of those persons in Charlottesville of whom Chapman made inquiry at Jefferson's suggestion? In any event, Jefferson might have received from a number of sources evidence sufficient to persuade him to consider "the deliverance of Watkins to be an ascertained truth."

45. Lowrey, "Bean," p. 11.
46. Jefferson to Crawford, August 23, 1823, Jefferson Papers, Library of Congress.
47. For example, see Watkins to Jefferson, April 30, 1824, Jefferson Papers, Library of Congress.
48. Hiatt, ed., "Diary of William Owen," p. 41; see also p. 45; "Diaries of Donald Macdonald," pp. 215–16.

Though not a professional linguist, Jefferson had a youthful enthusiasm for Indian eloquence. He collected vocabularies and studied all the materials he could come by, and was certainly qualified as an intelligent amateur student of Indian languages. The controversy over Logan's speech, which Jefferson included in his *Notes on the State of Virginia* (1787) and which he believed deserved to be ranked with the best of Demosthenes or Cicero, had instructive parallels with the attempts to discredit Hunter's account of Tecumseh's oratory.

As every schoolboy knew, Logan was a famous Mingo chief. Though a friend of the Pennsylvania authorities, his family had been murdered in 1774 by white men. In reproducing Logan's sad reproaches—"Who is there to mourn for Logan?"—Jefferson took occasion to refer to Captain Michael Cresap as having been a leader of the murderers. In 1797 Luther Martin, Attorney General of Maryland and Cresap's son-in-law, charged Jefferson with having maligned the Indian-fighter and branded the Logan speech a fabrication. There was compelling evidence that Cresap had committed two of the murders, however, and equally persuasive testimony on the authenticity of Logan's speech.

As it happened, George Rogers Clark entered the controversy with a strong letter exculpating Cresap of any wrongdoing. His letter was to Dr. Samuel Brown of Lexington, Kentucky, who then forwarded it to Jefferson. Clark attempted to exculpate Cresap of any wrongdoing, but Brown's comments were to the point: "There were two parties on the frontier: By the one Capt. Cresap was considered as a wanton violator of treaties [and] as a man of cruel and inhuman disposition; by the other he was esteemed as an intrepid warrior and a just avenger of savage barbarities." Clark had apparently joined Cresap in the frontier pastime of killing Indians and by implication was a member of the second party. Despite Brown's recommendation Jefferson did not publish Clark's letter, reasons Dumas Malone, for he may have concluded that the old frontier hero, "who was personally involved in all this business, was trying to apply a coat of whitewash to it." [49] Now William Clark was the brother of George Rogers Clark; if they were both members of this generic second party on the frontier, then the former's actions in Hunter's case become less surprising.

Another ostensible reason for thinking the Logan speech a fabrication was the frequency with which it was coupled with extracts from James

49. Dumas Malone, *Jefferson and His Time* (London: Eyre and Spottiswoode, 1948, 1951, 1962), I, 385–87; II, 101–2; III, 346–56.

Macpherson's supposed translations of Ossian, the legendary Irish bard. In the 1770s Dr. Johnson had charged Macpherson, a Scottish schoolmaster as well as a man of letters, with having forged *Fingal* (1762) and other Ossianic poems. When Macpherson did not produce the originals or reply, claims for the eloquence of primitive peoples somehow generally became suspect. But it was dangerous to reason from literature to life in this fashion: merely because *Fingal* was discredited was no good reason to hold Logan's speech a fraud or to reject the possibility that native Americans like Tecumseh were surpassingly eloquent in their use of natural metaphors and in their expression of deep emotion.[50]

In any event, Neal was much too quick to pronounce the Logan speech "altogether a humbug" and altogether without warrant for denying Jefferson competence to evaluate Hunter's claims.

5

"The question must have already suggested itself to every reader," Norgate had written: "What was Hunter's motive in publishing his book, if he be an impostor? What has he gained, or what did he expect to gain by it? Was it money? Certainly not. The whole sum that the publication of his book produced him in this country was barely sufficient to pay his expences during his residence here; and that he refused the proffered offers of money from persons of highest respectability, I know as a positive fact." Neal retorted that Hunter had, "while here, and after his return to America, obtained money to a large amount, I fear; to a considerable amount, I *know*."

Proof that money was Hunter's object was slim, though Neal asserted that *"Mr. Norgate himself was done out of fifty pounds before my face."* Norgate's report that Hunter had refused offers of money was in accord with Coke's testimony. Before Hunter left for America, Coke apparently persuaded him to accept some agricultural implements, and the Duke of Sussex presented him with a watch which had a platina watch guard— Neal found this outlandish, for it was "probably one of the first watchguards ever seen or heard of in America; where a pocket is not picked

50. Behen, "Captivity Story," pp. 330–34, discusses Ossian, Logan, and Hunter's account of Tecumseh's speech. Timothy Flint believed Hunter's recollections of Indian eloquence showed that he had read Ossian: Flint to Sparks, September 12, 1826, Sparks Mss., Houghton.

of any thing, perhaps, once in five years—nor of a watch, ever." Neal's disclosure of Hunter's debt to Norgate could hardly have come as a surprise to the latter. Surely Norgate might be expected to know about his own financial transactions with his friend. Finally, Neal unwittingly contradicted himself: one reason he gave for his refusal to take part in the plans to help the Indians was Hunter's statement that he had no money and "shall have no need of money."

The truth was that Neal had no evidence whatever. His technique was to scatter charges with a generous hand and hope that some doubts would take root. If a mercenary motive could not be attributed to Hunter, then perhaps he could be made into an instrument of a sinister plot: "I know this," Neal wrote, "I know that he was ready to engage, at a day's warning, in a sort of scheme, proposed by a young, rattle-headed British officer, who had five thousand pounds more than he well knew what to do with." A fascinating charge—but the careful reader was disappointed to discover that Neal said not one word about the identity of the British officer, the nature of the scheme, or how he knew about it.

The grain of Neal's sensibility was revealed by one of his jokes.

"How come you to be so black?" said a friend of mine to another friend, who was very, very dark, to be sure. "My mother was chased by an Indian," said he. "Chased—umph!—he overtook her, I guess." Even so with our hero. If he was ever *carried off* by an Indian, it was probably by a female Indian—his own mother, in pursuit of his father.

The humorist was severely infected with the racial virus.[51] His real feelings about the American savages, in spite of some protestations of friendship, came out in his explanation of why Hunter's narrative had not excited much interest among the folks at Cape Girardeau or elsewhere in the neighborhood of Indians. "Those who have grown up among rattle-snakes, the plague, or the yellow-fever, do not buy books which profess

51. The level of his virulence was illustrated by this story and by his comment, quoted in Ch. III above, that Hunter's carryings-on with women had a character "of which a real Hottentot would have been ashamed." Winthrop Jordan, *White over Black: American Attitudes Toward the Negro, 1550–1812* (Chapel Hill: University of North Carolina Press, 1968), p. 227, points out that, if the Negro was at the lowest rung of mankind, somehow "the Hottentot was generally re-garded as more bestial than the Negro."

to describe, as any body on earth may describe, what they are familiar with—rattle-snakes, the plague, or the yellow-fever."

John Neal's racism and his personal feeling of having been neglected while Hunter was being lionized were joined to a nationalism as intense as that of Cass or our ballad writer–adventurer "Jackson Johonnet." Neal was no more pleased than Cass with Hunter's " '*plans*' for bringing about a coalition of the savages in a part of North America," and he rejected just as angrily "Hunter's heavy charge against the *government* of the United States—a charge I know to be false." Despite his verbal fireworks and posturings, Neal was a thoroughly conventional American who was appalled by what seemed to him the subversive character of Hunter's ideas. Though he did not use the word, he demonstrably regarded Hunter as a sort of anarchist: "He has no knowledge of the first principles of political association," Neal charged. "He would live without law; and he would have the Indians live without law, *after they have been civilized.*"

Though Neal provided valuable additional evidence on the reactions of white Americans and an opportunity for exploring some of the outstanding questions regarding the narrative, his case against Hunter was no more than the froth of his ill-will. He handled ideas as though he were still putting off bad bills in his mother's store or as if he were acting out one of his favorite sayings: "It is better not to speak the truth always, for it too often appears improbable." [52]

The truth content of Neal's article would never make it seem improbable. On the contrary, with so many charges aloft simultaneously, many readers must have assumed that Hunter was being exposed over and over. Coming as it did shortly after Cass's attack, Neal's article caught Hunter in a vicious crossfire.

52. Bessy Walker, one of Neal's correspondents, remarked on his saying in a letter to him: See Richards, "Neal," IV, April 10, 1825. On Neal as a deservedly neglected novelist, given his sensibility and mind, see H. C. M. Martin, "The Colloquial Tradition in the Novel: John Neal," *New England Quarterly*, XXXII (1959), 455–75.

Peter Stephen Duponceau, 6
George Catlin,
and the Reasonable Doubt

> No two languages are ever sufficiently similar to be con-
> sidered as representing the same social reality. The worlds
> in which different societies live are distinct worlds, not
> merely the same world with different labels attached.
>
> EDWARD SAPIR,
> "Linguistics," *Language*, V, 1929

One day after lunch in 1826, America's foremost philologist sat down
to write John Pickering: "This morning I at last received the North
American Review for January," he informed his friend and colleague,
"& my morning was *loungingly* spent in reading Governor Cass's review
of Hunter's book." It was his finding that Cass had largely absorbed the
frontier prejudices against the Indians:

> It is with these poor people as with Negroes, two opposite sentiments
> prevail respecting them in different parts of our Country. The Caro-
> linian and Louisianian will hardly allow the blacks to be human crea-
> tures; indeed, some go so far as to maintain that they are an inter-
> mediate race between man and monkey. Similar feelings prevail as to
> the Indians, and I am sorry to say, produced by similar causes. And in
> this as in every human controversy, both sides are too much disposed
> to exaggerate.[1]

The style was the man, Pierre Étienne Du Ponceau, or, as anglicized,
Peter Stephen Duponceau. He had a supple, probing mind capable of
working through layers of prejudice and of then gently regretting their
existence. Never could he bring himself personally to hate blacks or
Indians. On the other hand, he would never take an adamant stand

1. Duponceau to Pickering, January 23, 1826, Duponceau Papers, Historical
Society of Pennsylvania (hereafter, HSP).

against those who did. From the tone of his graceful, leisurely sentences, so unlike the staccato bursts of John Neal, you would never guess that he had himself been attacked in Cass's article.

Though Jared Sparks's editorial efforts made the writer of the article say of Duponceau and Pickering that they were "philologists of whom the country may be justly proud" and other tributes Cass did not mean, the major lines of the latter's attack remained.[2] He regretted, for example, that Duponceau had fallen into so many errors and found ludicrous his high opinion of the harmony and music of the Wyandot language: "Of all the languages spoken by man, since the confusion of tongues at the tower of Babel," Cass held, "it least deserves this character." And Duponceau had to be pained by Cass's manhandling of *Wulamalessohalian*, a Delaware word which fascinated him and which meant "thou who makest me happy": "The word should be written and pronounced, *Walemulsoohauleun,* or *Walemulsoo hauleun,*" Cass noted sharply, "for we are strongly inclined to think, that liberties have been taken in these combinations, not wholly justified by the Delaware language."[3] Contempt for "that quack D.," as Cass called Duponceau in a letter to Schoolcraft, slipped out from behind Sparks's good words.[4] Yet Duponceau would no more have thought of calling Cass names in return, even in a letter to a friend, than he would think of adopting the general's hectoring tone. When he made no direct response at all, he was congratulated by Albert Gallatin for his decision "to pursue a wise and generous course towards Gen. Cass."[5]

Duponceau differed from Cass in almost every respect—in background, in temperament, in talent. He was born in France, became a Benedictine monk, left clerical life to come to America, served as Baron Steuben's aide-de-camp during the Revolution, and afterward settled in Philadelphia. He became an American citizen, was admitted to the bar, founded the Law Academy of Pennsylvania, and achieved distinction as an authority on constitutional and international law. Translation of David Zeisberger's manuscript grammar of the Delawares heightened his interest in Indian languages. He collaborated with the missionary John Hecke-

2. Cass to Schoolcraft, February 6, 1826, in Clarence Edward Carter, *The Territorial Papers of the United States* (Washington: Government Printing Office [hereafter, GPO], 1943), XI, 945.

3. Cass, "Indians of North America," *North American Review,* XXII (January 1826), 74, 75, 83, 93n.

4. Henry Rowe Schoolcraft, *Personal Memoirs* (Philadelphia: Lippincott, Grambo, 1851), p. 237.

5. Gallatin to Duponceau, May 17, 1826, Duponceau Papers, HSP.

welder and pursued his own studies of vocabularies and grammars, especially of the Algonkian.[6] In 1819 he made his first important report to the American Philosophical Society on the "wonderful organization, which distinguishes the languages of the aborigines of this country from all other idioms of the known world" and gave the name "polysynthesis" to the unique phenomenon. This work led to his later essay, awarded a prize by the Royal Institute of France, entitled *Mémoire sur le système grammatical des langues de quelques nations indiennes de l'Amérique du nord* (Paris, 1838).[7]

When Duponceau and Hunter met, the former was anxious to pursue his study of Indian languages: "I recollect distinctly the evening when I introduced to you at my house Mr. Hunter," David Hosack later wrote his friend, "and the eagerness with which you entered into conversation with him." But Duponceau had some doubts and arranged a second meeting with Hunter in Philadelphia. Afterward, Hosack continued, "you informed me you were now convinced that he was not the character he represented himself to be, that he knew not the languages he professed, and that he occasionally had involved himself in contradictions, making use of the same word to signify different and opposite things [and] at the same time acknowledging he had been mistaken in his translation of certain terms."[8] In a letter to M. A. Julien, editor of the *Révue encyclopédique,* Duponceau himelf recalled: "I exposed him in 1822. He had so much public support, however, I merely reported my findings to friends. I avoided giving more publicity to his imposture, for my assertions might easily have been disputed and may have been difficult to prove."[9]

Avoiding publicity and the sentiment in favor of the "soi-disant élève parmis les sauvages," Duponceau limited himself to alerting a few friends

6. Robley Dunglison, *A Public Discourse in Commemoration of Peter S. Duponceau* (Philadelphia: American Philosophical Society, 1844); Hampton L. Carson, *A History of the Historical Society of Pennsylvania* (Philadelphia: Historical Society, 1940), I, 146–55; Pliny Earle Goddard, "The Present Condition of Our Knowledge of North American Languages," *American Anthropologist*, XVI (1914), 557; Fred A. Crane, "The Noble Savage in America" (unpubl. Ph.D. diss., Yale University, 1952), pp. 102–7.

7. Mary R. Haas, "Grammar or Lexicon? The American Indian Side of the Question from Duponceau to Powell," *International Journal of American Linguistics* (hereafter, *IJAL*), XXXV (July 1969), 239–41.

8. Hosack to Duponceau, January 28, 1826, American Philosophical Society. Hosack was not then convinced, though he "became more measured" in his intercourse with Hunter.

9. Duponceau to Julien, January 13, 1826, American Philosophical Society (my translation).

not to be deceived by any communications they might receive from
Hunter. On August 26, 1822, for instance, he sent the following warning
to someone, probably to John Pickering:

> I have discovered that this J. D. Hunter is an arrant impostor, and that
> he knows none of the Indian languages to which he pretends. He de-
> ceived me at New York, because he told me a few Osage words which
> I knew from memory to be correct; but unfortunately for him he called
> to see me at Philadelphia, where having my materials at hand, I con-
> victed him of ignorance, and he left me not a little ashamed . . . and
> had I not been able to detect him by my long study of Indian lan-
> guages, I should have been, and I was in fact for a while, deceived by
> his apparently innocent manner and the glibness with which he forged
> Indian words when they were wanted.[10]

In October 1823 the narrative received favorable notice in the *Révue
encyclopédique:* "The style is simple," read one sentence, "the events
probable, the observations sensible, one might even say philosophical." [11]
Though disturbed to think that Hunter was being so received in Europe,
Duponceau waited until after Cass's article to write to France that he
had been the first to detect the impostor.

Squeezing what comfort he could from the discrediting of his former
friend, Robert Walsh declared in the *American Quarterly Review,* which
he also edited, that the initial discovery of Hunter's tissue of falsehoods
had been a triumph of American scholarship. It meant that theoretical
men were finally advanced enough in their studies to deal effectively
with those who argued that the only way to find out about Indian life
was to live in wigwams and smoke the calumet at the great council of
warriors: "It led to a satisfactory conviction of the soundness of those
philological studies which have engaged some of our profoundest
scholars; and to a perfect assurance that our theoretical men, as they
have been termed, had at least made sufficient progress in their studies,
to protect them against those errors into which the majority of their
countrymen had fallen." [12]

On the contrary, the assurance was less than perfect that Duponceau

10. Duponceau to Pickering?, August 26, 1822. The letter was later published
in *Paulson's American Daily Advertiser,* January 10, 1826.
11. *Révue encyclopédique,* XX (October 1823), 128.
12. "Tanner's Indian Narrative," *American Quarterly Review,* VIII (September
1830), 113–15.

had not fallen into honest errors in his findings on Hunter. The very nature of his progress in philological studies made this probable.

Though a transplanted European, Duponceau developed a nationalism as intense as that of Cass or Neal. On every occasion, his memorialist wrote, "where circumstances called for the expression of his sentiments, he exhibited that he was sincerely and ardently an American; and was proud that his adopted country should reap the credit and advantage of his intellectual efforts." [13] But when Cass spoke of "the poverty of these [Indian] languages," Duponceau was pained by such short-sightedness. As he had observed to Heckewelder a decade earlier: "Who cares for the poor American Indians? They are savages and barbarians and live in the woods; must not their languages be savage and barbarous like them?" [14] But Duponceau's studies of the Delaware language had convinced him of its beauty and of the wisdom of regarding it and the other Indian languages as among the most precious assets of the New World.

The character and number of native languages raised another, scarcely less important question. In his *Notes on the State of Virginia*, Jefferson had argued that the great number of radically different languages in America indicated the passage of an immense course of time since they had commenced to recede from their common origin, "perhaps not less than many people give to the age of the earth." [15] Decades later he was still of this opinion, as one of his letters to John Pickering showed:

> European nations have so long had intercourse with one another as to have approximated their complex expressions much towards one another, but I believe we shall find it impossible to translate our language into any of the Indian or any of theirs into ours. I am persuaded that among the tribes on our two continents a great number of languages, radically different will be found [and] it will be curious to consider how so many radically different have been preserved by such small tribes in coterminous settlements of moderate extent.[16]

But Pickering could not accept such an inference "in contradiction of the

13. "A more patriotic heart never beat in an American bosom," observed Dunglison in the same passage, *Duponceau*, pp. 29–30.

14. Quoted in Crane, "Noble Savage," p. 105.

15. *Notes on Virginia* (New York: Harper & Row, 1964), p. 97.

16. Jefferson to Pickering, February 20, 1825, Jefferson Papers, Library of Congress.

received opinion of the Christian world as to the age of the earth." He was confident that the number of languages in America would be found "to be very few in number." [17]

At one stroke Duponceau's discovery of the polysynthetic construction of Indian languages established their peculiarly American characteristics and also protected the received Mosaic chronology. As he explained in 1819, the construction was that "in which the greatest number of ideas are comprised in the least number of words." This was primarily accomplished by "compounding locutions . . . not confined to joining two words together . . . but by interweaving together the most significant sounds or syllables of each simple word"; it was also achieved "by an analogous combination [of] the various parts of speech, particularly by means of the verb." This was the "wonderful organization" Duponceau had found in Indian speech. It was also a genuine contribution to linguistics.

Duponceau's term "polysynthesis" has been widely used since. In his structural classification of languages, for example, Edward Sapir distinguished between those which are *isolating,* like Chinese, *weakly synthetic,* like English, *fully synthetic,* like Arabic, and *polysynthetic,* like many Indian languages in which a number of logically distinct, concrete ideas are arranged within the confines of a single word.[18] The principle of classification rests on the degree to which the various parts of a word are welded together. In polysynthetic languages the words are made up, generally, of what linguists call "bound morphemes," like the *in-* in "inactive" or the *-er* in "brother." An example of one of these so-called sentence words is the Delaware *Wulamalessohalian,* "thou who makest me happy."

In his 1819 essay Duponceau held that the languages of America were polysynthetic from Greenland to Cape Horn. When he met Hunter in 1822 he believed that he had discovered the key to Indian languages, that this established their historical unity, and that there was not a single exception to the polysynthetic type in the New World. With so much at stake, he inevitably found Hunter a fraud.

The Osage language was in the Dhegiha subdivision of the Siouan

17. Quoted in Haas, "Grammar or Lexicon?" *IJAL,* XXXV, 241–42.
18. Sapir, *Culture, Language and Personality* (Berkeley: University of California Press, 1956), pp. 20–22. See also Floyd G. Lounsbury, "One Hundred Years of Anthropological Linguistics," in *One Hundred Years of Anthropology,* ed. J. O. Brew (Cambridge: Harvard University Press, 1968), pp. 195–97.

language group.[19] Osage was in fact less polysynthetic, in the sense of being incorporative of bound morphemes, than it was agglutinative, in the sense of being characterized by the combination of free morphemes or independent words. Unaware of the language diversity in the country, especially in the area west of the Mississippi, and unaware in particular that his discovery did not fully apply to the Siouan stock, Duponceau would have suspected any Osage-speaking person of being an impostor.

Aside from speaking to an Iroquois Indian on one occasion, Duponceau's actual investigations were like those of other linguists of his time. He read and translated grammars, collected vocabularies, and made brief grammatical notes.[20] Not only did Jefferson guess more correctly than Duponceau and Pickering about the number of radically different languages in America; he also had a more acute sense of the extreme difficulty of translating from an Indian language into English or the other way around. As his letter to Pickering shows, Jefferson came close to realizing that different cultures are reflected in different languages and that these languages cannot be translanted precisely into one another. Indeed Hunter's difficulty with trying to fix labels from one distinct world, in Sapir's words, on different objects in another may have been completely misinterpreted by Duponceau.

After all, Hunter was not a professional student of Indian speech. He had learned Osage by daily usage and not by the translation method. As Mary R. Haas, a modern anthropological linguist, writes:

> Again and again in my work with Indians I have known them to correct themselves, not because they don't know their own language, but because they can't find the right English equivalent. Many times the same English word will have many translations and vice versa. Since Hunter could scarcely have had the knowledge or the training to investigate the niceties of the intertranslation of Osage and English, the fact that he acknowledged "he had been mistaken in his translation of certain terms" is as much in his favor as against him.[21]

19. Dhegiha is one of the seven subdivisions of the Siouan group; it includes the Osage, Kansas, Quapaw, Omaha, and Ponca.
20. Franz Boas, "Introduction," *IJAL*, I (1917), 1.
21. Letter of April 25, 1969, quoted by permission of the writer. Emphasizing that she has not read Hunter's *Memoirs* or investigated Duponceau's knowledge of Osage in any depth, Professor Haas still states that she doubts very much that Duponceau was equipped to determine whether or not Hunter knew Osage. I am indebted to her for her extraordinarily generous responses to my queries.

Ironies abound. Hunter's hesitations and contradictions may have been direct measures of his sincerity. Duponceau's imaginative contribution to American linguistics and his seriousness as a scholar may have been precisely what led him astray. Duponceau was, in any event, very unlike Cass and Neal. And for Hunter to have been the victim of unjust accusations of hoax because he did not illustrate the "wonderful organization" of the Indian languages would have been the richest irony of all. It would have made him the victim of yet another form of American nationalism.

2

Duponceau did not establish with perfect assurance or even beyond a reasonable doubt that Hunter was guilty of imposture. But let us suppose the reverse. For the sake of play and inquiry, let us assume that his competence in philology had enabled him to prove Hunter an "arrant impostor." This assumption presents a number of appealing problems.

1. "He deceived me at New York," Duponceau wrote, "because he told me a few Osage words which I knew from memory to be correct." But how did Hunter know the few words or a few of the words of Osage that Duponceau had memorized? Had Duponceau subjected the narrative to scholarly analysis, the results might have been suprising. Of the languages of the Indians west of the Mississippi, for instance, Hunter observed that "it has been supposed by some, that all the Indian nations speak different dialects of the same language; but the case is far otherwise. There are scarcely two nations, between whom no intercourse exists, whose languages are so similar as to be mutually understood by the respective individuals of each; indeed, I believe there are none. . . . They maintain their claims to distinctiveness with as much force perhaps as do the English, French, German, and Russian languages." Some sense of this diversity might well have proved helpful to Duponceau.

As for Osage words, since there was no reason to assume that his editor, Edward Clark, had any knowledge in this area, those in the narrative had to come from Hunter or some other source, perhaps from travel books. The only real prospect, to my knowledge, was John Bradbury's *Travels,* which did include a small Osage vocabulary and which was published in 1817. The words in the left column are from Bradbury's list and those in the right from Hunter's section on Osage materia medica:

No-ne-agh, tobacco

Has-ka-ke-da, soldier

Was-saw-ba tonga, male bear

Sha-ba, beaver

No-ne-aw, tobacco

Has-hak-a-da-ton-ga, black root or, literally, strong soldier

Was-saw-bape-sha, bear's fright

Sha-ba-wa-nem-bra, beaver root or, literally, beavers eat it [22]

After due allowances are made for differences in phonetics and orthography, the two lists show that Hunter knew words Bradbury reported but went beyond them to compound stems freely, a characteristic of the Siouan language group.

Difficulties in setting down Osage words were great. The attempts of Bradbury and Hunter to represent the word "tobacco" may be contrasted with that of Francis La Flesche in "A Dictionary of the Osage Language," where it was rendered as No-ni'-hi. La Flesche translated To^n-ga as "big, large." Notwithstanding these difficulties, some of Hunter's Osage words, in the right column below, may be compared with La Flesche's:

Mo^n-shti^n-ge, rabbit

She'-ki, rattlesnake

Sha-be, black

Zhi^n-ga', baby, small

Mi-ka'-k'e, star

Mas-tin-jay, rabbit

Shak-kee, rattlesnake

Saw-ba, black

Shin-ga, young Osage

Me-ka-a, star [23]

In his discussion of polygamy, Hunter mentioned Was-saw-be-ton-ga, a distinguished Osage warrior with four wives. La Flesche listed Wa'-tse-to^n-ga as a personal name meaning "big star." Wa'tse was another word for "star," To^n-ga meant "big," and the -be- in Hunter's name was listed by La Flesche as a ritual term meaning "any one of them."

Hunter related the story of an Osage named Shin-ga-was-sa. While young, he had visited the Kansas and became involved with the wife of one of their leading warriors. A young Kansas helped him make his escape from the woman's infuriated spouse. Years later, during a battle between the two tribes, Shin-ga-was-sa was able to return the favor by

22. John Bradbury, *Travels in the Interior of America in the Years 1809, 1810 and 1811,* in *Early Western Travels,* ed. Reuben Gold Thwaites (Cleveland: Arthur H. Clark, 1904), V, 216–20; Hunter, *Memoirs,* pp. 403, 404, 424.

23. Francis La Flesche, "A Dictionary of the Osage Language," *Bulletin 109 of the Bureau of American Ethnology* (Washington: GPO, 1932); Hunter, *Memoirs,* pp. 326, 343, 409, 413, 422.

saving the life of his Kansas friend. The daring Osage was apparently a man of honor and of magnificent physique. When George Catlin painted his portrait in 1834, he recorded his name as "Shin-ga-wás-sa, the Handsome Bird; a splendid-looking fellow, 6 feet 8 inches high; with war club and quiver." [24]

All this does not establish, of course, that Hunter was fluent in Osage. It does establish his knowledge of some of their words. His narrative would certainly have supplied Duponceau with additions to his meager stock. And, unless he had lived with the Osages, *how could he possibly have known a splendid-looking fellow named Shin-ga-was-sa?*

2. A genuine impostor would have been embarrassed when confronted with Hunter's knowledge of Osage manners and customs. Had Duponceau, who was a fair-minded man, studied his names of the herbs and remedies in Osage materia medica, he might have puzzled over how Hunter could have fabricated the name *Ton-ga-shin-ga* for the Gentian-wild plant, have plausibly translated it as "it-gives-strength-to-a-child," and then have sensibly discussed its use. Surely he would have been driven to ask: How could an impostor have come by Hunter's extensive information and obviously genuine enthusiasm for Indian medicinal practices?

Hunter knew that the Osages observed constellations and directed their way by them—by the Pleiades, for example—but could perhaps have derived this information from Thomas Nuttall's *Journal*.[25] Hunter knew about the Osage veneration for old people and this admiration for the beaver, but could perhaps have obtained their information from Louis Bringier, another traveler.[26] But he knew some things for which there was no other known source. Take, for example, Hunter's account of buffalo-hair weaving:

> The hair of the buffalo and other animals is sometimes manufactured into blankets; the hair is first twisted, by hand and wound into balls. The warp is then laid of a length to answer the size of the intended blanket, crossed by three small smooth rods alternately beneath the threads, and secured at each end to stronger rods supported on forks, at a short distance above the ground. Thus prepared, the woof is filled

24. Hunter, *Memoirs*, p. 326; Thomas Donaldson, "The George Catlin Indian Gallery," *Smithsonian Report of 1885* (Washington: GPO, 1887), Part II, 44.

25. Nuttall, *Travels*, in *Early Western Travels*, XIII, 175–76; Hunter, *Memoirs*, p. 202.

26. Louis Houck, *A History of Missouri* (Chicago: R. R. Donnelley & Sons, 1908), I, 187; Hunter, *Memoirs*, pp. 251, 273, 281–82.

in thread by thread, and pressed closely together, by means of a long flattened wooden needle. When the weaving is finished, the ends of the warp and woof are tied into knots, and the blanket is ready for use. In the same manner they construct mats from flags and rushes, on which, particularly in warm weather, they sleep and sit.[27]

Anthropologists studying the aboriginal culture of the Mississippi Valley and the Southwest have found this paragraph sound and of extraordinary interest.

In the 1890s William H. Holmes used Hunter's description for his account of prehistoric textile art. In 1908 Frank Russell discussed a loom of the Pima Indians which resembled that described by Hunter, though his sources were an old Pima friend and the account of a traveler in the 1850s. The following year David I. Bushnell, Jr., pointed out that little was known about the use of buffalo hair, since the traders' introduction of wool had caused Indians to stop weaving with it: some of the early work of the Cherokees, for example, assumed to have been made of wool, may possibly have been of buffalo hair. Of the early accounts Bushnell discovered, Hunter's was the most graphic and detailed.[28] Finally, in *Navaho Weaving*, which Frederick Webb Hodge described as a résumé of our archeological knowledge of the loom, Charles Avery Amsden quoted Hunter's paragraph and noted that the process described therein was somewhat similar to the archeological evidence on "the loom of early Tiahuanaco times in Peru. . . . But Hunter's description fits Pima weaving more closely still. These people were true-loom weavers of long standing, using native cotton in a horizontal loom . . . the Peruvians sometimes staked out their looms horizontally. There may be a connection; we do not know, for our historic chain has many broad gaps the archeologist must fill." [29] *How could an impostor have supplied one important link for this historic chain?*

---

27. *Memoirs*, pp. 289–90.

28. Holmes, "Prehistoric Textile Art of the Eastern United States," *Thirteenth Annual Report of the Bureau of American Ethnology* (Washington: GPO, 1896), pp. 25–26; Russell, "The Pima Indians," *Twenty-sixth Annual Report of the Bureau of American Ethnology* (Washington: GPO, 1908), pp. 148–49; Bushnell, "The Various Uses of Buffalo Hair by the North American Indians," *American Anthropologist*, XI (1909), 401–25.

29. Amsden, *Navaho Weaving: Its Technic and History* (Albuquerque: University of New Mexico Press, 1949), p. 20. Hunter's reference to "a long flattened wooden needle," Amsden notes, "may be ancestral, technologically, to the batten." Hunter was thus accurately discussing what was used as a kind of shuttle in Peru and part of what was close to the true loom, the "only machine aboriginal America ever produced."

3. Unlike anthropologists, historians have gone to great lengths to avoid Hunter. If the former have sometimes gratefully turned to the narrative as a source, without recognizing that its validity has been challenged, the latter tend never to use it willingly, failing to recognize that its ethnological content has frequently proved sound and valuable. When it is the only source, as in the case of the Osage weaving of buffalo-hair blankets, the historian has been in a bind.

One ploy has been to draw on Hunter extensively and then evade responsibility for using a suspect source with a skeptical shrug: "Hunter, who claims that he was a captive among the Osages, says that . . ." A variant has been to cite "that curious book" for a long quotation which clearly illustrates the writer's point. The most desperate stratagem of all, however, has been to use the *Memoirs* for indispensable evidence and in the same breath attack its validity.[30] What is most curious, however, has been the general disinclination to pursue a simple question: *How is it that Hunter's narrative so frequently provides the only valid evidence?*

4. When Hunter's narrative was reproduced a few years ago, a reviewer in *Nebraska History* (XXXIX [1958], 75–77) justifiably complained that there was "no indication on the jacket blurb or by editorial note that Hunter had often been called an impostor and his captivity tale called a fake. This is the case, however, and the accusations are unquestionably justified." The reviewer readily accepted at face value the charges of Cass, Clark, Biddle, and others, but had read the narrative carefully and raised pertinent questions about the soundness of its Osage history and ethnology: "For example, White Hair's village, where Hunter allegedly lived, is located on the Arkansas River although it was then on the upper Osage River; buffalo are described as having small heads and long necks; Osage oranges are praised for their succulence. The wedding ceremony, modeled on that of the white man, is particularly amusing."

In the course of a discussion of the size, possibilities for domestication,

---

30. Examples are to be found in Houck, *Missouri*, I, 189; Harrison Clifford Dale, *The Ashley-Smith Explorations and the Discovery of a Central Route to the Pacific, 1822–29* (Glendale, Calif.: Arthur H. Clark, 1941), p. 113; Richard Edward Oglesby, *Manuel Lisa and the Opening of the Missouri Fur Trade* (Norman: University of Oklahoma Press, 1963), pp. 160–61. Glen Tucker's *Tecumseh: Vision of Glory* (Indianapolis: Bobbs-Merrill, 1956), pp. 159, 214–17, 348n, 353n, 374, provides an honorable exception to this curious historiography. Still believing that the art of testing documents is a point of departure for the historian, Tucker analyzes Cass's charges carefully before dismissing them and using Tecumseh's speech as reported by Hunter.

and herding patterns and migrations of the buffalo, Hunter had indeed written: "Its greatest girth is just back of the fore legs, from which the body gradually tapers, and also diminishes in height. Its neck is long, and slender, head and eyes small, structure calculated for speed, and its general aspect fierce and terrible; though, except when wounded, or closely pressed, it is harmless and timid." [31] This was an extraordinary description for someone who had discussed in detail how the Osages wove buffalo-hair blankets and who had certainly seen buffalo in the trans-Mississippi West. Could Hunter's description of buffalo have been the result of wayward impulse? Of a prank? Of Southwest humor? Of Edward Clark's rewriting? Of plain blunder? What? I admit to being baffled and willingly grant that, standing alone, the passage would suggest that Hunter was a most careless impostor.

Hunter reported correctly that the wood of the Osage orange was held in high esteem "by the Indians, on account of its great elastic properties. They manufacture it into bows, which become articles of commerce, and are sometimes exchanged for peltries, &c." Had he praised the fruit for its *succulence,* that would not have been incorrect. As he noted, "the rind, when wounded, especially before ripe, emits a milky juice." What Hunter actually said was that it had value for many of the Indians as an *esculent.* In fact, partial confirmation of his statement was published concurrently. In his account of the Long expedition, Edwin James, who served as the party's botanist, included a long discussion of "the bow-wood or osage orange." He noted that Thomas Nuttall had identified it as *Maclura aurantiaca* in *Genera of North American Plants* (1818; II, 233), that its wood was "uncommonly fine and elastic, affording the material most used for bows by all the savages from the Mississippi to the Rocky Mountains," and that its "bark, fruit, &c. when cut into, exude a copious, milky sap." But James could not agree with Nuttall's description of the pulp of the fruit as being " 'nearly as succulent as that of an orange; sweetish, and perhaps agreeable when fully ripe.' In our opinion, the whole of it is as disagreeable to the taste, and as unfit to be eaten as the fruit of the sycamore." [32] Hunter never discussed the succulence of the Osage orange; but James may have been wrong about its unfitness to be

31. *Memoirs,* pp. 164–67.
32. *Memoirs,* pp. 172–74. Since James's *Account of an Expedition from Pittsburgh to the Rocky Mountains, Performed in the Years 1819, 1820* was published in 1823, I am assuming that Hunter could not have used it as a source. For convenience, the reference to Osage orange may be found in Thwaites, ed., *Early Western Travels,* XVI, 170–71; see also XVII, 123–24.

eaten: a number of barks, nuts, seeds, berries, and plants, which seemed strange and unpleasant to whites were victuals to the Indians.[33]

Hunter's description of an Osage wedding had distinctly Christian aspects:

> On this occasion, after the guests are assembled, the young Indian takes his intended by the wrist; occupies a central situation in regard to the party, and, in a standing position, candidly proclaims the affectionate attachments he entertains for her, promises to protect her and provide her with game, and at the same time presents her with some comparatively imperishable part of a buffalo, elk, deer, &c. as a pledge of his faithful performance. The female, on her part, makes a similar declaration of attachment; promises to cultivate the corn, &c.; transact the other offices of her station, and pledges the faithful performance, by presenting her husband an ear of corn, or some other article to which it becomes her province to attend. The new married couple are now greeted with the kind wishes of all present; and the remainder of the day, and a part, or the whole of the following night, is passed in feasting, mirth, and festivity.[34]

The reviewer was amused by the unmistakable overtones here of the love-and-honor pledges of white couples. One can reasonably conclude that the passage was concocted by someone who had never seen the Osages. Still, this conclusion raises some problems.

How was it that Hunter demonstrably knew a great deal about the role of marriage among the Indians? His horrified reaction to the mercenary motives of marriage in England, quoted in an earlier chapter, accords with the observation of a recent student of the Osages: "Mating among them was not for social status based on property or for political balance, without the least concern for eugenics as in Europe and England, where social ascendancy had to be maintained through the merging of property among patricians, and international political balance had to be maintained through the royal matings." Hunter stressed love and did not mention eugenics, of course, but his point was essentially the same. His understanding of the role of women in bearing brave and

33. See, for example, George F. Carter, *Plant Geography and Culture History in the American Southwest* (New York: Johnson Reprint, 1945), p. 29; Jeanette May Lucas, *Indian Harvest: Wild Food Plants of America* (Philadelphia: J. B. Lippincott, 1945), pp. 16, 20, 89, 101.

34. For Hunter's discussion of this ceremony in the larger context of marriage, divorce, adoptions, and Indian names, see *Memoirs*, pp. 231–52.

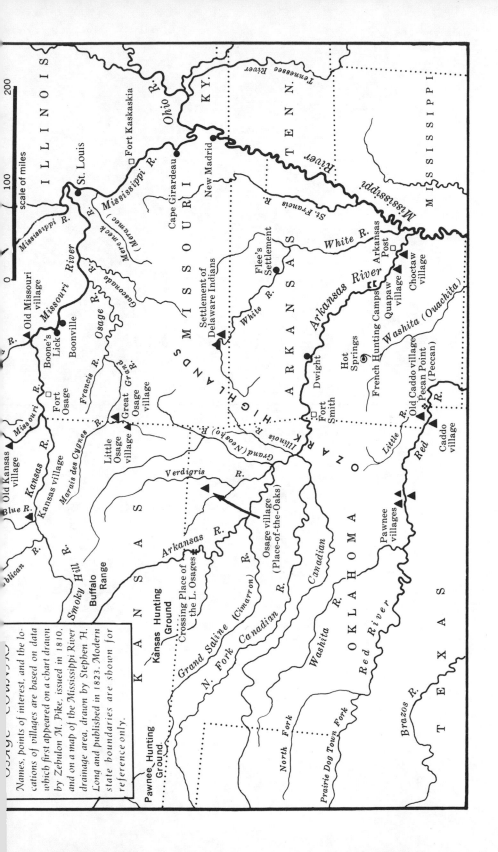

Names, points of interest, and the locations of villages are based on data which first appeared on a chart drawn by Zebulon M. Pike, issued in 1810, and on a map of the Mississippi River drainage area, drawn by Stephen H. Long and published in 1823. Modern state boundaries are shown for reference only.

virtuous children was right in line with the Osage belief that they "are the carriers of the warriors of the future. The girls of the present had in their bodies the warriors yet in Spiritland."

And how did he know that a young Osage could not hope to marry until he had won war honors or had distinguished himself as a hunter? How did he know that the preliminary negotiations were carried out by the maternal relatives of the couple, and how did he know that the wedding ceremony and feast took place in the lodge of the girl's family? To be sure, he had the mothers commence negotiations and failed to mention the maternal uncles, who customarily made most of the arrangements; he also had the couple stand and speak their mutual pledges in the ceremony itself. But grant a minimum of missionary influence and his description was not unlike that of a recent reconstruction of an Osage marriage before the tribal culture began to disintegrate.[35] It even appears that the husband was expected to give his wife a comparatively imperishable part of the buffalo: he gave her a burden strap made from its uncured hide, which was used like a trumpline and which "was a mark of the woman who lived in the traditional manner and symbolized the virtues and prerogatives of the woman."

The most important of the reviewer's points was her first: Hunter had switched the Osage villages around, incorrectly placing White Hair's on the Arkansas and Clermont's on the banks of the Osage in present-day Missouri. On one trip Hunter and his party were said to have gone up the Arkansas, "thence across the highlands, till we struck the head waters of the Grand Osage river, which we descended, to the village belonging to Clermont, or the Builder of Towns, a celebrated Osage chief." But contemporary sources were in general agreement that this village "belonged" to White Hair. Hunter or Clark put a note at the foot of the page which attempted to explain all this: "It should be borne in mind that a part of the Osages, not long since, with the chiefs Big Track and White Hair for their leaders, had separated from the Grand Osage nation, settled on the Arkansas river, and sustained their independence." [36] As stated, this was a serious error, though just close enough to the facts to make it perplexing.

An early and relatively reliable source on the splitting of the tribe was a letter from Lieutenant James B. Wilkinson, Pike's associate. On

35. John Joseph Mathews, "Marriage of Bloody Hands and The Light," *The Osages* (Norman: University of Oklahoma Press, 1961), pp. 312–26.
36. *Memoirs*, p. 42.

April 6, 1807, Wilkinson wrote to his father in New Orleans that he had descended the Arkansas some months earlier in a storm of hail and snow to the winter camp of "Cashesegra, or Big Track, Chief of the Osages who reside on the Verdigris river":

> This band some four or five years since, were led by the chief Cashe-segra, to the waters of the Arkansaw, at the request of Pierre Chouteau, for the purpose of securing their trade; the exclusive trade of the Osage river having at that time been purchased from the Spanish governor by Manuel Liza, of St. Louis. But though Cashesegra be the national leader, Clermont, or the Builder of Towns, is the greatest warrior, and the most influential man. . . . He is the lawful sovereign of the Grand Osage, but his hereditary right was usurped by Pahuska, or White Hair, while Clermont was yet an infant. White Hair is, in fact, a chief of Chouteau's creating, as well as Cashesegra, and neither has the power, nor disposition, to restrain their young men from the perpetration of an improper act, fearing lest they should render themselves unpopular.[37]

Hence there were parallel structures of authority: the traditional chief-tainship and that which whites like Chouteau had established. This breach in tribal organization produced dual chiefs and the continual re-moval and quarreling reported by observers.

Hunter knew that the tribe had three subdivisions, the Great Osage with about 500 warriors, the Little Osage with about 350, and the Osages of the Arkansas with about 450—figures which were in substantial agree-ment with George Sibley's 1817 estimates of 400, 250, and 600.[38] He knew the names of the chiefs, the location of the villages, and the trails or traces in between. Had he lifted his material from Pike's *Exploratory Travels,* as Timothy Flint charged, he would still have needed informa-tion from some other source and could scarcely have missed the fact that Pike encountered White Hair on the Osage River. The mystery re-mains why he repeatedly placed the latter on the Arkansas, unless his final attempt at an explanation offers a clue: "They separated from the Grand Osages, about twenty years since," he reported, "under the osten-sible direction of Big-track, though White-hair instigated the measure, and virtually exercised the duties of chief." [39] So much hinges on what

37. Zebulon Montgomery Pike, *Exploratory Travels through the Western Terri-tories* (London: Longman, 1811), pp. 415–16.
38. Houck, *Missouri,* I, 179–82; Hunter, *Memoirs,* p. 212.
39. *Memoirs,* p. 212.

he meant by "ostensible": Did he mean that White Hair exercised his duties as chief from the old location on the Osage, though Big Track was ostensibly running things on the Arkansas? This would account for White Hair's remaining behind in the trade territory of Manuel Lisa: he could look after Chouteau interests in both villages. And it would account for Hunter's thinking of those who broke away as really White Hair's people and for his continuing to regard Clermont as the true chief of the Great Osages.

But, one can argue, this is not a genuine muddle and attempts to account for it are exercises in special pleading. How then can we account for what Hunter did know? How could he have known that Clermont had four wives? How did he know about baby boards and accurately discuss their use? Hunter knew how the Osages built and placed their lodges, made their skin canoes, and dressed their skins. He discussed the Wolf family and Panther family of the Kansas tribe, thereby demonstrating knowledge of what anthropologists call gentes. He knew of the importance of dreams, the existence of death songs, painted posts, medicine bags. He knew of the practice of abortions, knew how Osage men plucked out their hair, except for "a small tuft that covers the crown of their head or scalp," and knew that they plucked out the hair on the rest of their body. Cass and his mentor, William Robertson, notwithstanding, he knew that the temperament of the Indians "may be as ardent as is common to any particular race of the human family."

Or take Hunter's account of how Indians prepared for war by painting themselves:

> In war, they usually paint themselves red back of the ears, and in stripes of red and black on their faces. Sometimes they paint their faces wholly black, which indicates that no quarter is to be given to their enemies; black being understood by them as emblematical of death, and red merely of war. Their black paints are prepared from pulverized charcoal and bears' grease. . . . The practice of painting is universal among all the tribes, but less dispensable with some than others: with the Osages, an Indian who neglects it, humbles himself very much in the estimation of the rest of the nation: instances of this kind, however, rarely occur; and, when they do, the delinquents are not permitted to join in the ceremonials, or, in other words, are totally neglected.[40]

40. *Memoirs*, pp. 337–38. For Hunter's discussion of the items listed in the preceding paragraph, see pp. 243; 263; 200, 287–88, 291, 292; 302, 320; 225, 228, 328–29, 343; 191, 195; 299.

It was almost as if Hunter had got his information directly from Francis La Flesche's "War Ceremony and Peace Ceremony of the Osage Indians," which was published over a century later:

> When he is about to join an attack upon the enemy he must blacken his face with the "Mysterious Charcoal," thus indicating his determination to show no mercy toward the foe. Should he neglect to put upon his face this symbol he will not be permitted to count $o\text{-}do^{n'}$ (war honors), even if he were to perform all the deeds necessary for the winning of individual $o\text{-}do^{n'}$, nor will he be entitled to count his share of the $o\text{-}do^{n'}$ won by the war party as a body.[41]

How could an impostor have been such a superb field observer?

5. Perhaps the most improbable section in the narrative had to do with Hunter's trip to the Pacific. In company with thirty-six Osage and Kansas Indians, Hunter claimed to have gone up the Arkansas, across to the Kansas and La Platte and up the latter nearly to its source, across the Rocky Mountains, and down the Columbia to its mouth; he returned up the Columbia to the Willamette, up the latter to its source, across several ranges of hills to the borders of a very large lake, thence to a winter camp in "the neighbourhood of the Great Mountains," across these that spring, at a place where "they did not appear so high, numerous, or difficult to pass," and down the Arkansas to home. The exploration took sixteen moons, from the early spring of 1813 or, more probably, 1814, to the autumn of the following year.

Hunter did not mention Astoria at the mouth of the Columbia, the Northwest Company posts, or, in fact, any buildings or parties of whites. His account had the predictable grizzly-bear attacks and near escapes from strange, hostile Indians. Most if not all of his ethnological data on the transmontane tribes reads very much like that in the 1814 Biddle edition of the report of Lewis and Clark.[42] Given these omissions and seeming dependence on an earlier, more detailed source, the expedition to the Pacific may reasonably be rejected as another Dripping Fork incident, added for the titillation of his readers.

Yet this abrupt dismissal creates problems. Hunter's failure to mention

41. La Flesche, "War Ceremony . . . ," *Bulletin 101 of the Bureau of American Ethnology* (Washington: GPO, 1939), p. 54.
42. Hunter's account, *Memoirs*, pp. 56–83, may be compared with Paul Allen, ed., *History of the Expedition under the Command of Captains Lewis and Clark . . .* (Philadelphia: Bradford & Inskeep, 1814), II, 32, 125–39.

Astoria was not necessarily damning, for he rarely mentioned forts in areas he almost certainly knew very well: he never mentioned Fort Osage, for example, from which, according to one of his exposers, he had deserted. Since he kept no journal, he or his editor might very well have picked up the report of Lewis and Clark to flesh out skeletal recollections.

On the face of it, such an overland trek was not improbable for thirty-seven Osages and Kansas. Earlier, Wilson Price Hunt, a St. Louis clerk, made it to Astoria on the Pacific and Robert Stuart led a party of six men back. In 1807 David Thompson crossed the Canadian Rockies with a large party that included his wife and three children; in 1810–11 he made a midwinter crossing at Athabasca Pass. Some Indians had crossed the continent even before Lewis and Clark: there were three in Alexander Mackenzie's eleven-man party that crossed the mountains by way of the Peace River in 1793.[43] Hence the expedition was by no means physically improbable. Nor, given its timing, could Hunter have hoped, as one Philadelphian asserted, "to deprive the celebrated travellers, Lewis and Clarke, of the honour of having been the first explorers who crossed the Rocky Mountains, from the sources of the Missouri, and descended the Columbia River to the shores of the Pacific Ocean." [44]

I have no difficulty in believing that a party of Osages and Kansas might have attempted to cross the Great Mountains. As Hunter related the origins of their journey, they met an Omaha or Maha Indian on the upper Platte:

> This Maha was probably fifty years of age, when I saw him: he spoke the Kansas language so as with some difficulty to be understood. He had been once across the Rocky Mountains, and much among the neighboring tribes and nations; by whom, as well as by his own people, he was held in high estimation. They even supposed him to be more under the immediate protection of the Great Spirit, than the generality of the Indians: hence his influence was great. . . . The description this old man gave of his excursion to the great hills of the west, excited

43. Philip Ashton Rollins, ed., *The Oregon Trail: Robert Stuart's Narratives of His Overland Trip Eastward from Astoria in 1812–13* (New York: Charles Scribner's Sons, 1935); William H. Goetzmann, *Exploration and Empire* (New York: Alfred A. Knopf, 1966), pp. 10–12; Milo Milton Quaife, ed., *Alexander MacKenzie's Voyage to the Pacific Ocean in 1793* (Chicago: R. R. Donnelley & Sons, 1931).
44. George Ord to Waterton, October 20, 1861, American Philosophical Society.

the curiosity and ambition of our whole party, and was the primary
cause that led us to the execution of a similar expedition.[45]

The Maha may very well havé crossed the mountains, and his account
may very well have provoked them to emulate his exploit. May very
well, that is, unless we assume with General Cass that Indians were not
persons, with their own desire for excitement and for exploring the unknown.[46] And, after all, Columbus did not discover America, and Robert
Stuart did not discover the South Pass on Friday, October 23, 1812: a
Shoshone on the Owyhee River in present-day Idaho had directed him to
this "shorter trace" across the mountains, just as in 1824 some Crow
Indians helped Jedediah Smith "rediscover" the same trail.[47]

Summary rejection of Hunter's Pacific trip raises still more specific
problems. On November 3, 1805, Lewis and Clark first used the name
Mulknomah. In April 1806 they referred to the principal southern tributary of the Columbia as the Multnomah, and this spelling was used on
their maps which showed the sources of the present-day Willamette rising in the vicinity of what is now known as Great Salt Lake. Clark entered the river on April 2, and judging "from its appearance and courses,
it [is not] rash to believe that the Multnomah and its tributary streams
water the vast extent of country between the western mountains and
those of the seacoast, as far perhaps as the waters of the gulf of California." Two decades later Clark's famous map, which he constantly
revised as it hung on the wall of his office in St. Louis, showed the Great
Salt Lake as the source of the Multnomah.[48] No one then or since seemed
to realize that Hunter's narrative called this erroneous geography into
question.

45. *Memoirs,* pp. 61–62.
46. For the Osages, as for the ancient Greeks and their descendants, the West
was always associated with mystery: see Mathews, *Osages,* pp. 163, 393. Mathews
notes that tribal memory indicates it is quite likely the Osages made their way
into the Rockies through La Veta Pass and possibly continued across the Continental Divide at Wolf Creek Pass (pp. 149–50); to explore this unknown would
have been especially appealing at a time of crisis and breakdown in tribal lines
of authority.
47. Rollins, *Oregon Trail,* pp. 84, 101; Goetzmann, *Exploration,* p. 116. For a
discussion of the Plains Indians and the South Pass, which includes consideration
of Hunter's trip, see Agnes R. Wright, "A Place in Wyoming Worthy of a Monu-
ment: South Pass," *Annals of Wyoming,* I (July 15, 1923), 3.
48. Allen, *Lewis and Clark,* II, 220; Lewis A. McArthur, *Oregon Geographic
Names,* 3d ed. (Portland: Oregon Historical Society, 1952), pp. 433–34; Goetzmann, *Exploration,* pp. 24–27, 125–26.

"At the entrance of the Mult-no-mah (River of much game)," Hunter related, his party took the advice of Indians there and followed it nearly to its source. Hunter knew the river had several falls, "one of which was very considerable, and appeared at some distance, curtained with a semi-halo of the most brilliant colors," but this probable reference to Willamette Falls, at the site of present-day Oregon City, he or Edward Clark might have pulled out of the report of Lewis and Clark or, though most unlikely, from Robert Stuart's traveling memoranda.[49] At the headwaters of the river, which were not so remote, some Indians "put us on the route eastwardly, across several ranges of hills. Passing these, we found, as we had been told we should, considerable game on the borders of a very large lake." Proceeding on, the party wintered somewhere in the foothills, where they found nearby "several springs of water; one of which was of a temperature nearly sufficient to have cooked food, though we made no particular use of it." After resuming their journey in the spring, they made a relatively easy crossing of the Rockies.

Hypothetically, then, Hunter and his party ascended the Willamette, took the Salt Creek Pass through the Cascades, crossed over Oregon via the headwaters of the Deschutes, and found in Malheur their very large lake. His discussion of hot springs near their winter camp suggests that it was somewhere near the area of the thermal waters in Yellowstone Park, perhaps not far from the route Stuart followed through present-day Idaho. The ease of crossing the Continental Divide suggests they too "discovered" the South Pass. All this, given the sparseness of Hunter's details, is conjectural. What is not is the fact that, had he been taken seriously, the source of the Willamette would not have been placed so far south and it definitely would not have been placed at a saltwater lake—the Great Salt Lake was "discovered" in 1824–25.

Following the Platte east in March 1813, the Robert Stuart party stopped, felled some trees, made canoes, and tried to return to the Missouri by water. After several unsuccessful attempts, the Astorians were forced to give up and resume their overland journey: "Stuart's abortive undertaking to canoe on the North Platte has been sharply criticized by various writers who perhaps were not familiar with the general aspect of

---

49. Allen, *Lewis and Clark*, II, 226–27; Rollins, *Oregon Trail*, pp. 32, 43n. Part of Stuart's traveling memoranda was published in *Nouvelles Annales* (Paris, 1821), but this source was most probably not available to Hunter and Edward Clark. The journals of Stuart and Hunt became "Astor's personal property and like a good businessman he shared very little of his 'inside' information with the outside world," Goetzmann, *Exploration*, p. 35.

the stream," observes Philip Ashton Rollins. "Though in many stretches this river is ordinarily very shallow, its broad waters in numerous other stretches are so turgid as to have drowned countless cattle. Its appearance, which deceived Stuart, deluded also sundry other fur traders in the two and a half decades after his attempt, and thus history records not a few endeavors at its navigation." [50] But Hunter was not deceived by the river:

> The river La Platte rises in the Rocky mountains, runs nearly east, is about one thousand six hundred miles in length, broad, shoal, and not navigable. . . . The route of the Missouri is widely circuitous, the river of difficult ascent, and the mountains next to impassable for loaded teams, even though human art and means should be exhausted in the construction of roads. That of the La Platte from the seat of government, is perhaps the most direct communication; but then, as before remarked, this river is not navigable, nor can it be made so for any expense at present justifiable by the object in view.

The passage was quoted by Harrison Clifford Dale, editor of the *Ashley-Smith Explorations*, to illustrate why the Platte remained so long unused as a central route to the Pacific. The impossibility of navigating the river, Dale noted, was "clearly pointed out in that curious book, *Memoir of a captivity* . . . published in London the year of Ashley's successful utilization of this route (1824)." [51] *Was it not curious that Hunter avoided Stuart's error and that of all those who had attempted to navigate the Platte since?* That in 1823 he was able to provide the best available account of the river and of the route that was to become the Oregon Trail?

Finally, there is the problem of Hunter and the myth of the Great American Desert. The same year his narrative was published, Major Stephen H. Long, leader of the recent expedition to the Rocky Mountains, published his discouraging findings on the area west of Council Bluffs:

> In regard to this extensive section of country, I do not hesitate in giving the opinion, that it is almost wholly unfit for cultivation, and of course uninhabitable by a people depending upon agriculture for their

50. Rollins, *Oregon Trail*, pp. 207, 223.
51. Dale, *Ashley-Smith Explorations*, pp. 112–13; *Memoirs*, pp. 157, 159.

subsistence. Although tracts of fertile land considerably extensive are occasionally to be met with, yet the scarcity of wood and water, almost uniformly prevalent, will prove an insuperable obstacle in the way of settling the country.[52]

His famous map labeled the area between the mountains and the Missouri the GREAT DESERT. The notion of an uninhabitable American Sahara stretching eastward from the Rockies has been traced back by William H. Goetzmann to Pike, who reported seeing "tracts of many leagues where the wind had thrown up the sand in all the fanciful form of the ocean's rolling wave; and on which not a speck of vegetable matter existed." [53] Yet, though Pike was probably the originator of the desert imagery, the view of the whole area as a barren waste goes back further still, to Lewis and Clark. As Long himself recognized in his discussion of the Great Desert, "inferences deducible from the account given by Lewis and Clarke of the country situated between the Missouri and the Rocky Mountains above the river Platte . . . [indicate that it] is throughout of a similar character." [54]

Compared with these prevailing views, Hunter's were both more accurate and more prophetic:

> On account of the scarcity of wood and water, it is not probable that any attempts to settle the central prairies will be made till the lands better adapted to cultivation are first improved. But the many thousand square miles so situated, will finally become of too great value and importance in a national view to be suffered to remain a wilderness, as many now suppose they forever must. The want of wood and water is not however the only barrier to their settlement: another very formidable one is presented in their liability to fires.

Still, he believed the prairie grasses could be plowed as protection against fires, clay was available for bricks, timber could be procured by "cultivating forests" or wood lots, and for fences "nothing can surpass living hedges." Furthermore, "To obtain a supply of water, will in general be more difficult; but as one is in the earth, it may be procured. But apart from this source, I am persuaded it may be conveyed in canals, through

52. *Early Western Travels*, XVII, 147.
53. Pike, *Exploratory Travels*, p. 249.
54. *Early Western Travels*, XVII, 147–48.

some extensive districts of country, which the consequent increased value of the neighbouring lands will eventually justify." [55]

Here we must not tarry to savor the irony of Hunter's optimistic prediction of a process of settlement which in other contexts he knew very well threatened his red sisters and brothers with extermination, nor to wonder at his speculation about drawing water out of the earth—the light windmill was not invented until the 1850s—nor even to marvel at his near fabulous prediction of the irrigation ditches which before long were indeed conveying the waters of the Platte and other western streams to the region. Here the question to be pursued is how Hunter knew that what many supposed must remain a barren wilderness was in fact habitable: *How did he know there was no Great American Desert?*

3

In 1838 Peter Stephen Duponceau invited George Catlin to meet with him and some friends over breakfast. By then nearly blind and quite feeble, the linguist was still anxious to meet with travelers from the Indian country and delighted at the prospect of talking to the painter and pioneer ethnologist who had visited some two-score tribes across the Mississippi in the preceding eight years. After their meal, Duponceau opened his notebook on the table and presented Catlin with a list of two or three hundred English words for which he wanted equivalents in Blackfoot, Mandan, Pawnee, Pict, and so on. Exclaiming over the treat in prospect and fortified by a pinch of snuff, Duponceau was moved to reminisce:

> "In this identical place and on this very table it was, gentlemen, that I detected the imposture of that rascal, Hunter! Do you know that fellow, Mr. Catlin?" "Yes, I have seen him." "Well," said he, "I was the first to detect him; I published him to the world and put a stop to his impostures. I invited him to take breakfast with me as I have invited you, and in this same book wrote down the Indian translation of a list of words and sentences that I had prepared, as he gave them to me; and the next day when I invited him again, he gave me for one-third at least of those words a different translation. I asked for the translation of a number of words in languages that were familiar

55. *Memoirs*, pp. 145–46.

to me and which he told me he understood, and he gave them in words of other tribes. I now discovered his ignorance, and at once pronounced him an impostor, and closed my book."

No doubt Catlin's response came as a surprise, for he asked Duponceau to close his book again: "I am quite sure I should prove myself under your examination just as ignorant as Mr. Hunter, and subject myself to the same reproach which is following him through the world, emanating from so high an authority. Mr. Hunter and myself did not go into the Indian countries to study the Indian languages, nor do we come into the civilized world to publish them, and to be made responsible for errors in writing them." He declined to translate a single word and hoped that Duponceau would leave "a repentant word" of his own in one of his last works "to remove the censure you say you were the first to cast upon Hunter, and which is calculated to follow him to the grave." [56]

Catlin later told this story over another breakfast. Shortly before his death in 1843, the Duke of Sussex visited Catlin's Indian Gallery, then being exhibited in Egyptian Hall on Picadilly, and impressed the painter by his perceptive, sympathetic views of the Indians. When the duke learned that Catlin had known Hunter, he invited him to Kensington Palace. During the course of their conversation the next morning, the old man showed Catlin his Harding portrait of Hunter and remarked that he had learned with deep regret that a learned French gentleman, M. Duponceau, and others had held his friend up to the public as an impostor: "'This to me,' said the duke, 'you can easily see, has been a subject of much pain (as I took more pains to introduce him and his works in this country than any one else), and it explains to you the cause of my anxiety to learn something more of his true history.'" Catlin then told his appreciative host of his confrontation with Duponceau, and the two men agreed that linguists should really go to the wigwams of Indians to fill their notebooks rather than depend for their vocabularies on the ignorant jargon of traders, trappers, and casual tourists.

Catlin added that he too had been pained at hearing the reports of imposture and

that my acquaintance with Hunter had not been familiar enough to enable me wholly to refute them. I stated that I had been introduced to

56. Catlin, *Notes of Eight Years' Travels and Residence in Europe, with His North American Indian Collection* (New York: George Catlin, 1848), I, 79–85.

Mr. Hunter in New Orleans, where he was well known to many, and that I had met him in two or three other parts of the United States, and since reading his work I had visited many of the Indian villages in which he lived, and had conversed with chiefs and others named in his work, who spoke familiarly of him. I felt assured, therefore, that he had spent the Indian life that he describes in his work; and yet that he might have had the indiscretion to have made some of the misrepresentations attributed to him, I was not able positively to deny. His work, as far as it treats on the manners and customs of the American Indians, and which could not have been written or dictated by any other than a person who had lived that familiar life with them, is decidedly the most descriptive and best work yet published on their every-day domestic habits and superstitions; and, of itself, goes a great way, in my opinion, to establish the fact that his early life was identified with that of the Indians.

He concluded by saying Hunter's character "had been cruelly and unjustly libeled," an overall evaluation of Hunter and his narrative which squares in every significant respect with the evidence presented in these pages.

Few white men in America were as well qualified as George Catlin to pass on Hunter's account of Indian manners and customs. He grew up in Pennsylvania with a keen interest in Indian legends and stories and later attended Tapping Reeve's law school in Connecticut, but after practicing briefly, gave up that profession for painting. Like his contemporary Chester Harding, by 1824 Catlin was in danger of becoming merely a successful portraitist of the wealthy, a future guaranteed by his election that year to the Pennsylvania Academy of Fine Arts.[57]

Happily for American art and ethnography, Catlin found his purpose in life when a delegation of Indians passed through Philadelphia on their way to Washington: "The history and customs of such a people are themes worthy of the lifetime of one man," he decided, "and nothing short of the loss of my life, shall prevent me from visiting their country, and of becoming their historian." From 1830 to 1838 Catlin roamed through the upper Mississippi Valley, the Central Plains, and the Southwest, painting a still neolithic world with a few lovely colors. In addition to his hundreds of portaits and paintings of ceremonies, hunts, and wil-

57. My biographical data are drawn from Lloyd Haberly, *Pursuit of the Horizon: A Life of George Catlin, Painter & Recorder of the American Indian* (New York: Macmillan, 1948), still the best modern source; also Harold McCracken, *George Catlin and the Old Frontier* (New York: Dial Press, 1959); Thomas Donaldson, "The George Catlin Indian Gallery"; and Van Wyck Brooks, "George Catlin," in *Fenollosa and His Circle* (New York: E. P. Dutton, 1962), pp. 157–96.

derness scenes, Catlin filled his notebooks with closely observed details of tribal life. Though he was careless with dates and sometimes expanded on a good yarn, he was an exact and painstaking field observer. For the great Indian painter and ethnologist to speak as he did of the narrative, therefore, was for Hunter to receive high marks indeed.

Aside from their personal meetings, Catlin's explorations and connections gave him ample opportunity to hear about Hunter from others. His brother Julius Catlin had been stationed at Cantonment Gibson in the Arkansas Territory after his graduation from West Point and did not leave that post until 1826: the younger Catlin was thus presumably present when Hunter passed through in the spring of 1825 in time to be "exposed" by Major Davenport. Catlin became well acquainted with William Clark and accompanied him on one of his official trips to visit the Kansas Indians. In 1832 he went up the Missouri with Pierre Chouteau in the *Yellow Stone,* the first steamboat to make the trip Hunter had made so much more laboriously with Manuel Lisa years earlier. In 1834 he himself visited what had become Fort Gibson and spent two months in the area painting Indians. Among his Osage subjects were Clermont, White Hair the younger, and, of course, Shin-ga-was-sa. Before the eight years were over, Catlin had visited most of the area Hunter mentioned in his narrative, most of the tribes, and some of the men. If he said that chiefs and others mentioned in the narrative spoke familiarly of Hunter, then they must have done so. On important matters Catlin's integrity was beyond question.

Catlin stood to lose personally by publishing a defense of Hunter in the year 1848. For years he had wanted to sell his Indian Gallery to the United States so that it would become the property of the people. Now he was broke and desperate to have Congress pass the necessary act of purchase. But it happened that the nominee of the Democratic party for the presidency in that election year was General Lewis Cass, most recently a senator from Michigan. A campaign biography listed, among the accomplishments of the man running for the first office in the nation, his role in Winning the West. "The general pacification of the whole west, however, allowed General Cass an opportunity to attend to literary pursuits." Heading the list of the general's literary accomplishments was the exposure of "a person called John Hunter":

> The book has since been acknowledged as a palpable forgery, but at the time it made a great impression on the popular mind. Governor Cass,

from his great intercourse and familiarity with the Indian character, was not to be imposed upon, and at once detected its many errors. These he exposed in an article . . . which at the time attracted universal attention from its peculiarly eloquent style and the engrossing interest of its subject.[58]

With such claims on the confidence of the electorate, Cass could hardly have welcomed Catlin's charge that Hunter "had been cruelly and unjustly libeled."

Nor could Henry Rowe Schoolcraft, Cass's lieutenant and author of the campaign biography quoted above. Catlin's caution in not specifying the "some others" who in addition to Duponceau had held Hunter up as an impostor was not sufficient to avert the wrath of Cass and Schoolcraft.[59] Moreover, Catlin's outspoken defense of the Indians had already earned him the distinction of being "quietly ignored" in Schoolcraft's works. And two years previously, in the summer of 1846, Schoolcraft had crossed the Atlantic to secure permission to use Catlin's pictures in his projected encyclopedia of the American Indians. Though he came armed with a letter from Lewis Cass, Catlin turned him down decisively on the grounds he preferred to publish his own work. Schoolcraft returned to the United States in anger, successfully worked to block the purchase of Catlin's paintings and artifacts for the National Museum—later known as the Smithsonian Institution—and, with Cass's help, secured the passage of a bill funding his own project. At a cost to the government of over $150,000, Schoolcraft's "masterwork"—or his "immense scrap book," as Baron von Humboldt more correctly called it—was published in six folio volumes between 1851 and 1857 under the impressive title *Historical and Statistical Information Respecting the History, Condition and Prospects of the Indian Tribes of the United States.*[60] The study will stand forever as a memorial to the bigotry of the age.

58. *Life of General Lewis Cass: Comprising an Account of His Military Services in the North-West During the War with Great Britain, His Diplomatic Career and Civil History* . . . (Philadelphia: G. B. Zieber, 1848), pp. 85–86. "Pacification" was already an ominous word.

59. Catlin was not unaware of the dangers of speaking directly about such matters. He once remarked, for example, that "his life would not be safe in the Far West if he told all he knew"—Haberly, *Pursuit of the Horizon*, p. 47.

60. Though the six volumes contained valuable data, the scrapbook characterization was apt. It has recently been made more usable by Frances S. Nichols' *Index to Schoolcraft's Indian Tribes of the United States* (Washington: GPO, 1954). For some of the basic documents on the Catlin–Schoolcraft controversy and a sensible discussion of them, see Thomas Donaldson, "Catlin's Indian Gallery," 374–83.

John Halkett's important *Historical Notes Respecting the Indians of North America* (1825), which drew so heavily on Hunter, was contemptuously dismissed by Schoolcraft:

> It is not the United States, but the aborigines, who have been their own worst enemies, at all stages of their history. Their general idleness and dissipation are sufficient to account for their declension, without imputing the decline to political systems. Travellers of the John Dunn Hunter or Psalmanazer [sic] school, continued to pour out their vapid descriptions and ill-digested theories to a late period. Mr. George Catlin, in his letters, gives a spirited view of hunting scenes.

Catlin did not find himself in this company by accident. In an earlier volume, Schoolcraft had seized upon the occasion to challenge the authenticity of Catlin's account of O-kee-pa, the Mandan religious ceremony of self-torture: "This, together with the general account of the Mandan religion, by the same author, is contrary to the facts as understood here." He followed this charge with a letter from Colonel D. D. Mitchell, Superintendent of Indian Affairs, wherein the latter stated baldly: "The scenes described by Catlin existed almost entirely in the fertile imagination of that gentleman." [61] Like the charges against Hunter, these were calculated to follow Catlin to the grave. Shortly before his death he was perhaps comforted by his friend Joseph Henry, the scientist and first secretary of the Smithsonian Institution, who assured him: "Truth, however, is mighty and will prevail, whether Congress intervenes in the matter or not." [62]

It was tragic but somehow fitting that Catlin found himself sharing the fate of the man he had vainly attempted to defend. They had much in common. Both were literally obsessed with the full-scale tragedy of the past and the impending destruction of the Indian peoples and their cultures. Both dared to suggest alternatives to this "inevitable" process. Catlin proposed his "magnificent park," a strip of country along the eastern edge of the Rockies where the Indians and the buffaloes could

61. Schoolcraft, *Indian Tribes of the United States* (Philadelphia: Lippincott, Grambo, 1851–57), V, 53–54; III, 254.
62. Quoted in the recent Centennial Edition of Catlin's *O-kee-pa* (New Haven: Yale University Press, 1967), p. 26. Catlin was in error about the Madoc or Welsh origins of the Mandans, of course, and in his belief that the tribe was totally wiped out by the smallpox epidemic of 1837. For an excellent discussion of the controversy, see John C. Ewers' "Introduction," pp. 1–33.

find refuge from Progress. Hunter proposed and worked for his "red country," with consequences we shall consider shortly. But perhaps their initial blunder, in the eyes of their accusers, was their "sentimentality": they both spoke of themselves as "friends of the Indians" and considered them persons; both tried to portray their looks, manners, and customs with fidelity. "The proud and free character of these free men," which Baudelaire saw in Catlin's Indian portraits, emerged also in Hunter's *Memoirs*. Such depictions understandably affronted Cass, Schoolcraft, and the great majority of their countrymen, for they reminded them that they were destroying admirable men, women, and children.

If truth be mighty, it is frequently mighty slow. Still, Joseph Henry may have been right. Catlin's book *O-kee-pa* is now seen as a classic in the ethnology of North America. The more modest claims of Hunter's *Memoirs* may yet be recognized. Meanwhile, anthropology, if not history, has already passed a verdict of sorts. Schoolcraft missed the honor Hunter received in having his book included in a bibliography of sources Clark Wissler found "immediately serviceable" in the writing of *The American Indian* (1938).

PART THREE

CHILD OF THE FORESTS

WRITTEN AFTER READING THE MEMOIRS '
OF JOHN HUNTER

Is not thy heart far off amidst the woods,
   Where the Red Indian lays his father's dust?
.   .   .   .

For thou art mingling with the city's throng,
   And thou hast thrown thine Indian bow aside;
Child of the forests! thou art borne along,
   E'en as ourselves, by life's tempestuous tide.
But will this be? and canst thou *here* find rest?
   Thou hadst thy nurture on the desert's breast.

.   .   .   .

Hear'st thou not murmurs which none else may hear?
   Is not the forest's shadow on thy dreams?
They call—wild voices call thee o'er the main,
Back to thy free and boundless woods again.

Hear them not! hear them not!—thou canst not find
   In the far wilderness what once was thine!
Thou hast quaff'd knowledge from the founts of mind,
   And gather'd loftier aims and hopes divine.
Thou knowest the soaring thought, the immortal strain—
Seek not the deserts and woods again!

FELICIA DOROTHEA HEMANS, "The Child of the Forests"
New Monthly Magazine, 1824

Back to the Free and Boundless Woods Again

7

The forests of the United States were so aged and vast that, pleased to hear Hunter describe them, they long haunted my fancy. . . . Now in conversation with Hunter, I found that [a] kind of exhilaration was . . . what he felt at awaking, and moving about in the freshness of the morning.

CYRUS REDDING,
Personal Reminiscences of Eminent Men, 1867

In England, remember, the anonymous warning had already been voiced: "The American people are his worst enemies." As Hunter readied himself to go home in the spring of 1824, he showed little sign of having heard this prediction. To be sure, the storm of denunciation was still over the horizon, months away, but there were already reports of abusive Americans in London, New York, Philadelphia. Yet, had some friend informed him of these attacks, he would have refused to give them public notice. He had a truly savage contempt for "back-biting, or talking ill of those not present." Slander, he had written, "is beneath the notice even of Indian women, without reference to the men, whose notions of propriety are still more elevated. This noble trait in their character is highly worthy to be imitated by many of both sexes who pretend to much higher claims in the scale of human beings." [1] Even though other good reasons would keep him from answering his accusers, he still almost certainly would not have replied in kind. All his acculturation had left him unprepared for this facet of civilized intercourse.

Hunter left England with joy to be embarking on his great project. His mood danced down the sentences of a letter to Coke:

I am delighted with your opinion of the President's Message to Congress. They may have to act up to its tone, in opposition to tyrants

1. *Memoirs,* p. 272.

and in support of the Rights and Liberties of South America. Should that event occur, I am confident they will act worthy of the friends of freedom and defenders of the oppressed. O how I long in America to drink your health among them! [2]

He saw himself returning not to enemies, therefore, but to the friends of freedom and defenders of the oppressed. By the time he could again visit Jefferson, in the late summer or fall of 1824, his optimistic assessment of the Monroe Doctrine had already been put to the test. In August Colombia had asked for a treaty of alliance "to save America from the calamities of a despotic system," only to be informed by Secretary of State John Quincy Adams that the United States had no intention of pledging active support of the rights and liberties of the new republics. Like the Latin Americans, Hunter still had much to learn about Presidential messages and the unselfishness of his countrymen.

Elias Norgate provided the sole account of Hunter's return to Monticello:

> The last visit Hunter paid to the venerable Ex-President was in the autumn of 1824, when he remained some time at his house, after having had an interview with the Cherokee and Choctau chiefs at Washington; and it was upon this occasion that Mr. Jefferson dissuaded him from pursuing the plan he has adopted for the amelioration of the condition of the Indians, to which Hunter merely remarks in a letter, which I have now before me, "I know of nothing which would induce me to do so." [3]

The letter *now* lies before him—it would be a breach of scholarly decorum, no doubt, to snatch it off his writing table before it is lost in time. But what else did Hunter say in it?

No doubt Jefferson and Hunter talked about the native Americans and again found large areas of agreement. In his second Inaugural Address, for example, Jefferson had observed that, with the reduction of the lands of the aboriginal inhabitants, "humanity enjoins us to teach them agriculture and the domestic arts." Hunter's own plan to induce the Indians

2. Hunter to Coke, February 15, 1824, in A. M. W. Stirling, *Coke of Norfolk and His Friends* (London: John Lane, 1908), II, 321–22. An item in the *New York Religious Chronicle* revealed that he had returned by June 26, 1824.

3. Norgate, *Mr. John Dunn Hunter Defended* (London: John Miller, 1826), p. 33.

to become farmers probably had its origin in this or comparable statements. Jefferson's sympathetic approach to Logan and other Indians as human beings had to appeal to Hunter, as did his famous pledge "to live in perpetual peace with the Indians, to cultivate an affectionate attachment from them, by everything just and liberal which we can do for them within the bounds of reason."

A white savage could hardly have known that reason's bounds frequently become remarkably cramped. In any event, Jefferson's consummate artistry in the use of political rhetoric, and Hunter's relative innocence, guaranteed that their discussion would flow pleasantly and smoothly. It might have taken some awkward turns had Hunter been knowledgeable enough to inquire into the great gap between Jefferson's words and his deeds. Jefferson had initiated the removal policy through his energetic efforts to "obtain from the native proprietors the whole left bank of the Mississippi."[4] One major reason the lands of the aboriginal inhabitants had been so drastically reduced was Jefferson's acquisition of some one hundred million acres in treaties shot through with fraud, bribery, and intimidation. And when Indians interfered with national interests, as did the "backward" tribes of the Northwest in 1812, Jefferson's humanitarianism hardened: "These will relapse into barbarism and misery, lose numbers by war and want," he grimly predicted to John Adams, "and we shall be obliged to drive them, with the beasts of the forests into the Stony mountains."[5]

No doubt Jefferson and Hunter discussed freedom as well. In the background correspondence leading up to the President's "Monroe Doctrine" message of December 2, 1823, Jefferson reminded his former protégé that European governments were essentially different from that of the United States:

> I have ever deemed it fundamental for the U.S. never to take active part in the quarrels of Europe. Their political interests are entirely distinct from ours. Their mutual jealousies, their balances of power, their complicated alliances, their forms and principles of government,

4. James D. Richardson, ed., *A Compilation of the Messages and Papers of the Presidents, 1798–1908* (Washington: Bureau of National Literature and Art, 1909), I, 368, 422–23. For Jefferson's Indian policy, see George Dewey Harmon, *Sixty Years of Indian Affairs: Political, Economic and Diplomatic, 1789–1850* (Chapel Hill: University of North Carolina Press, 1941), pp. 59–93.

5. Lester J. Cappon, ed., *The Adams-Jefferson Letters* (Chapel Hill: University of North Carolina Press, 1959), II, 307–8.

are all foreign to us. They are nations of eternal war. All their energies are expended in the destruction of labor, property and lives of their people. On our part, never had a people so favorable a chance of trying the opposite system of peace and fraternity with mankind.

Since Hunter's primary desire was to promote the fraternity of mankind —especially the fraternity of reds and whites—his response must have been enthusiastic to this line of discussion. But his sense of the depth of Jefferson's commitment to fraternity and peace would have been shaken had he been able to peruse the latter's letter to Monroe. Jefferson had added that Cuba alone was a problem, that the United States should not go to war over it, "but the first war on other accounts will give it to us, or the Island will give itself to us, when able to do so." Jefferson's principle of two spheres was not so much a matter of the contrast between European despotism and American freedom, then, as it was a declaration of hemispheric imperialism.[6] In operational terms the primary difference was that the United States and only the United States was free to expand in the Western Hemisphere. It wanted, along with other places, Cuba and Texas. It refused to enter into any self-denying ordinance with England. And in Monroe's Message to Congress, which Hunter so grievously misinterpreted, there was precious little room, as we shall see, for fraternity with reds, browns, and blacks on the North American continent.

But why did Jefferson try to dissuade Hunter from pursuing his plan? He may have been apprehensive that Hunter's advocacy of an Indian coalition would interfere in some small way with United States interests in the Southwest. Perhaps more important, his humanitarian side may have made him concerned for the safety of his young guest, whom he found interesting and likable. As one who had done everything he could for those brawny pioneers who were following the setting sun, he had reason to know the dangers confronting anyone who got in their way. Whatever Jefferson's motives, in any event, the conversation of the white savage and the great liberal statesman would have been worth hearing.

6. Jefferson to Monroe, June 11, 1823, Jefferson Papers, Library of Congress. The best discussion I have seen of the Monroe Doctrine and Western expansionism is Richard Rollin Stenberg, "American Imperialism in the Southwest, 1800–1837" (unpubl. Ph.D. diss., University of Texas, 1932), pp. 146–69. Richard W. Van Alstyne's excellent *The Rising American Empire* (Chicago: Quadrangle, 1965) is an independent statement and extension of the same thesis.

In October Hunter wrote to James Madison that he had been in Virginia during the late summer but had been unable to call on him. He inquired whether a copy of his narrative had ever arrived and noted that he had some seeds Coke had given him: "Will you accept from me a few? Will you remember me kindly to Your Lady? I never forget people who treat me kindly. I have [a] new machine for dressing flax without watering and other valuable mechanic improvements. I hope to embark for the Western Country in a few weeks." Madison replied courteously that the turnip seeds had come "safely to hand and will be attended to" and that he had received the book, for which "I can only offer my best thanks. The book will give pleasure to every reader who takes an interest in the subject of it." He wished Hunter success in his future efforts, applauded his not forgetting those who had treated him kindly, and noted he would be glad to see him whenever his movements made it convenient.[7] This rather banal, pleasant exchange is comment enough on the charges that Hunter lied about or exploited his acquaintance with two of America's founding fathers.

Hunter had written to Madison from Philadelphia, where he had taken lodgings in a house on South Third Street. In another letter he remarked that he would have been off sooner "but for the fever which has afflicted New Orleans for months past." He planned to go by sea to the mouth of the Mississippi and then up that river to the Arkansas.[8] But before he could set sail he fell ill and had to stay on another month. This delay made possible an unexpected and thoroughly welcome reunion with Robert Owen.

2

By the time of Hunter's departure from England, Owen had already decided that his mill and factory village provided an inadequate base for launching cooperative communities. Friction with his partners over his antireligious views increased his dissatisfaction with the prospects at New Lanark. His interest in America and the Indians, heightened if not awakened by Hunter, must also have made him psychologically

7. Hunter to Madison, October 15, 1824; Madison to Hunter, October 20, 1824, Madison Papers, Library of Congress.

8. Hunter to John Neal, October 15, 1824, in Irving T. Richards, "The Life and Works of John Neal" (unpubl. Ph.D. diss., Harvard, 1932), IV.

ready for a major change. At this point, in mid-August 1824, he suddenly had an opportunity to buy an entire American town—church, woolen factory, boardinghouses, tavern, and all—along with some twenty thousand acres of partially cleared land. This was the communitarian village of Harmonie (later changed to Harmony) on the Wabash River in southern Indiana, which had been established by Father George Rapp and his followers.[9] Within seven weeks Owen was ready to sail from Liverpool to negotiate for the property. He traveled with his son William and one of his supporters, Captain Donald Macdonald of the Royal Engineers.

The rapidity with which he moved made his arrival in the United States a surprise to many. Exactly when he informed Hunter of his coming is unclear: the latter's letters of mid-October contained no mention of it. Shortly after his ship docked, in any case, he deputized his son to write Hunter that he would arrive in Philadelphia in three or four days.[10] Actually, it took the Owen party a fortnight to get away from New York. Owen attended one of the Saturday soirées at David Hosack's, where he explained his plans for a new society to some of the most distinguished men of the city. James Buchanan, the British consul, sought him out, explaining that it was not customary for His Majesty's officials to make the first call but, since he had long entertained the highest opinion of him and of the benevolence of his views, he considered it a duty to step forward to receive him. Macdonald liked their guest, describing him as "an Irishman [with] a strong head and enthusiastic heart . . . [who] has some plans for civilizing the Indians." Later Buchanan read from the manuscript of his book, which contained quotations from Hunter's narrative and other signs of his influence, and earned Owen's warm praise.[11] Macdonald also recorded a conversation with Dr. Hosack's son, who told him "that on Hunter's return from Europe, he was not so much at his ease in society as before he crossed the Atlantic. He had the peculiar habit of the Indians of never keeping his eyes fixed, but wandering with them from object to object." When the Owen party

9. Robert Dale Owen, *Threading My Way* (New York: G. W. Carleton, 1874), pp. 239–42; Arthur Eugene Bestor, Jr., *Backwoods Utopias: The Sectarian and Owenite Phases of Communitarian Socialism in America* (Philadelphia: University of Pennsylvania Press, 1950), pp. 101–3.

10. Caroline Dale Snedeker, "The Diaries of Donald Macdonald, 1824–1826," *Indiana Historical Society Publications*, XIV (1942), 182; hereafter Macdonald, "Diaries."

11. It was published under the title *Sketches of the History, Manners, and Customs of the North American Indians* (London: Black, Young, & Young, 1824).

finally arrived in Philadelphia on November 19, Macdonald met Hunter for the first time: "He gave me much the idea of an officer of the Navy. He was delighted to see Mr. Owen and gave us all a hearty welcome."

Hunter's introductions were hardly necessary, for Owen's stay quickly became another personal triumph. Owen visited Robert Walsh, the editor, breakfasted with Mathew Carey, the political economist and publisher, lectured at the Franklin Institute, and explained his plans to the members of the Athenaeum. Elliott Cresson took Owen to see the waterworks; Colonel Edward Clark, the "eminent civil engineer," examined Owen's drawings for a socialist community and pledged that "he would himself be an active co-operator"; and another of Hunter's friends, who was leaving for England, carried Owen's letters with him on the packet *Algonquin*. Though Hunter had apparently still thought of going by sea to New Orleans, he must have been persuaded to change his mind, for he joined Owen and his party when they left for the national capital on November 23.

While Owen presented his letters of introduction to President Monroe, John Quincy Adams, John C. Calhoun, and others, Hunter joined William Owen and Captain Macdonald in sightseeing. They walked from the Indian Queen Hotel, where Hunter was staying, to the Capitol and found the front unfinished and men still working on the inside. Strolling down Pennsylvania Avenue to the "palace" of the President, they stopped to admire the fine view of the wooded hills across the Potomac. In the evening they had tea at the Indian Queen and met there "Dr. Watkins and son who called on Mr. Hunter." The next day Owen saw Monroe, "whom he said was a plain and intelligent man. He observed to Mr. Owen that this country gave more scope for improvements of every sort than any other." Macdonald and William Owen meanwhile went to look for Hunter in order to bring him to visit the Choctaw and Chickasaw chiefs who were in town to see the President. "We found him just returned from a dentist, where he had got three teeth drawn, which had pained him. He thought he had better remain at the Indian Queen at present, as the Doctor advised him not to go out." Hunter thus missed Owen's meeting with the chiefs.

In a council circle at the Dennison Hotel, Owen and his companions sat down with the nine or ten Indians present. One of the Indians, dressed in military uniform, with gold epaulets, red sash, and feathered hat, introduced himself as General Pushmataha and said "with a good deal of gestures that he was happy to see us and shake hands with his white brethren." Owen replied that he was anxious to see all united, white and red, "and that he thought the Indians were superior to the whites in many respects; in sincerity, friendship, and honest dealings, tho' the whites certainly possessed many advantages over them." He asked a question he must have discussed often with Hunter: "whether the Indians would prefer amalgamating with the whites or forming a separate body quite distinct from them." The chief's reply made it unclear whether he had ever considered this Tecumseh-like alternative to integration (or extinction): through their interpreter he said "he was aware that the whites were so superior to them that they could only cope with them by imitating them." Owen concluded with a warning which suggested that one of his purposes in coming to America may well have been to join his plan to Hunter's:

> Mr. Owen cautioned them against adopting what had been found injurious in civilized life, and said that he had come more than three thousand miles to promote plans, by which he hoped to make the red brethren superior to the whites. He said Indians taken when young amongst white[s], would become like whites, and vice versa and he concluded that it would be possible to unite the good in the Indian and in the civilized lives, so as to make a being superior to both.[12]

Meanwhile Hunter had started to feel better or had decided he simply could not stay away, for he arrived at the council just as Owen and the other whites were leaving. He could not speak the language of the chiefs but learned through their interpreter, he later informed Macdonald, that they had been pleased with what Owen said. He also reported that seeing them had "produced an anxious feeling in his breast. . . . He added that he had never felt so pleasantly at home as with them, since he left his own people."

On November 28 the Owen party rode out of Washington in three hackney coaches hired for the first leg of their trip across the mountains. "Capt. Macdonald, Hunter and I who were together in one carriage," William Owen wrote in his diary, "had a very interesting conversation regarding the Indians, and past recollections, and future anticipations, more particularly regarding a new state of society." The entry revealed

12. Macdonald, "Diaries," 181–84, 203–11, 217–18; Joel W. Hiatt, ed., "The Diary of William Owen from November 10, 1824, to April 20, 1825," *Indiana Historical Society Publications*, IV (1906), 28–38, 143–45; hereafter Owen, "Diary."

the rather prosaic mind of the younger Owen. Just twenty-two years old and said by friends of the family to be the only Owen with business sense, he wrote a matter-of-fact prose which carefully recorded the temperature and the number of miles traveled each day, but which said very little about his inner itinerary. At thirty-three, Macdonald had a greater fund of experience to draw on as a veteran of the Napoleonic Wars and a survivor as well of the Owenite battles with the clergy. He had become interested in communitarian ideas when he was stationed in Edinburgh in 1821 and had just retired on half pay from the Royal Engineers so he could accompany Owen to the United States. His diary showed him to have a wide-ranging, inquisitive mind and a remarkable capacity for pleasure in his companions and the new country.

At Hagerstown the party changed to a stagecoach, which carried them along the National Road toward Wheeling as far as Washington, Pennsylvania, where they proposed to cross over to Pittsburgh. The weather was fine and the big oaks, hickory, and other hardwoods were red and brown, with a sprinkling of pines for green contrast. As their horses strained to pull the loaded coach up the steep hills, Hunter and Macdonald got out to walk ahead

and often stood admiring the beautiful scenery entirely the work of Nature's hand. Accustomed as he had been to the Indian's life amidst the luxuriance of natural vegetation, and far removed from the artificial arrangements and habits of our white brethren, and taught as I had been among the highlands of my native country to admire their sublime but simple beauties; our sentiments mutually accorded, and we felt no want of farms & the uncouth habitations, architecture & habits of what is vaguely styled civilization to stiffen the charming landscape, or check our flow of spirits. On the side of these hills, Hunter pointed out to me a variety of plants and named the trees.

Along the way they met droves of hogs, sometimes as many as six hundred in a single company, amiably marching to eastern markets. They met a stage going east with some senators in it who called out to ask how the election was going on. They overtook wagons pulled by four, five, or six horses, with men, women and children on foot, all emigrating to the Ohio country. After crossing Mount Savage, they walked into the small village of Allegany a few minutes ahead of the stage. The inn was a farmhouse, where they all sat down to "a good breakfast of coffee, &

tea, made from the sassefras root which Hunter had got during our walk, wheat bread and rye bread, broiled chickens, preserved pears and apricots, wild honey, venison steaks, & sausages." Appetite gives the palate fond memories: their morning jaunt gave Macdonald a keen recollection of this splendid meal and of the sassafras tea with its "high & delightful flavour."

On December 1 they stopped outside the Smithfield Village Inn, where they saw another traveler, General Andrew Jackson, standing at the door surrounded by a crowd "of almost twenty of the people. He is an elderly healthy looking, thin person, with a high forehead, grey hair and stern but pleasing expressive countenance." Owen had a letter from DeWitt Clinton which he presented to Jackson, and introduced Macdonald, Hunter, and his son to the man who had just received, they learned, more electoral-college votes for the Presidency than any of the other candidates. What Hunter was thinking as he shook hands with the renowned Indian-killer and burner of Seminole and Creek villages we shall never learn.

At Washington they caught the mail stage for Pittsburgh, a town they found "enveloped in smoke, looks dirty, and the inhabitants do not seem to enjoy either a healthy or comfortable existence." It was a relief to make a side trip to see George Rapp's new community of Economy, eighteen miles downriver. Hunter and Macdonald rode ahead on borrowed horses. At a house which had a sign marking it as a tavern, they stopped for a drink of cider. Their host joined them in conversation: "He was a jocular politician & had his hits at the governments of the world. He spoke very severely of the British government using the Savage Indians to attack the inhabitants of the U. States. This he styled a barbarous proceeding." And this must have been only one of the many conversations Hunter had to turn a deaf ear to. They arrived at the Rapp settlement after dark, but in time for a supper of buckwheat cakes and honey and a conversation with Rapp. Owen and their host discovered that they had many shared opinions. Rapp "spoke of his having set mankind an example of the advantages of union in creating abundance with easy labour & of practically teaching friendship to society." Macdonald was bothered by the "quite respectful & submissive" manner of Rapp's followers and presumably Hunter was too, and he must have wondered how all this related to his plans for the most unsubmissive Indians.

Fearing the Ohio would be stopped with ice in a day or two, they gladly took passage on the *Pennsylvania,* said to be "a tried steamboat," and started downriver on December 6. When the boat stopped to take on wood, they visited the inhabitants of some of the isolated cabins along the river; at one, on a high bank behind a row of sycamore trees, Owen was told by three women that "they liked the situation but that it was lonely." At Mayesville, Kentucky, "Hunter and my Father bought mit [ten]s and Mr. Owen had a bantering conversation with the storekeeper regarding money and labor notes." At Louisville Hunter discovered that the *Favorite* was the first steamboat leaving from the other side of the falls and barely managed to book a berth for himself. While there Macdonald and William Owen walked down to Shippingport and on the way "met Hunter who showed us a silk plant, senna, honey locust, etc." Though all the accommodations had already been reserved, the Owen party decided to go aboard the *Favorite* anyway. Among the passengers were Edward George Geoffrey Smith Stanley, the future Earl of Derby and Prime Minister of England, and three friends who were also M.P.s. Besides the over-full complement of such eminent and not so eminent passengers, the crew managed somehow "to stow away 47 slaves, going down to be sold." At night mattresses were put down for cabin passengers who had no sleeping accommodations, and "Hunter gave up his berth to my Father."

December 14 was a crisp, clear day. The loveliness of the morning was enhanced by the wild clamor of geese as a flock raised off the river. At dark, 150 miles closer to their destination, they pulled over to the Kentucky side for wood. Several of the passengers visited a house near the wood yard which belonged "to one Sam Davis, who had no wife, but 2 slaves." About a hundred yards back from the river they built a fire at the foot of a hollow tree which soon was roaring as though the hollow tree were a chimney. When the boat clerk came out to tell the gentlemen their couches were prepared, he was told to have porter, brandy, and beef sent out. "Hunter was quite in his element," recorded William Owen, whose prose soared to very nearly match his spirits. The haughty Stanley, then an energetic, boisterous sportsman in his mid-twenties, his friend Wortley, who would become Baron Wharncliffe, and one or two others joined Macdonald, William Owen, and Hunter in a magnificent frolic:

> Hunter cut some 3 pronged forks with which we roasted the beef and on trial it proved very good. We proposed a raccoon hunt, which is always at night, but for lack of dogs we gave it up. We continued

plying the fire well and waited anxiously for the fall of the tree, occasionally raised the war whoop led on by Hunter. At last, about 2 o'clock,
it fell to our great joy, carrying with it several others in its fall. . . .
We set up a loud yell and came away leaving the proprietor two immense piles of ashes. He was with us all the time and very glad of
our frolic [because of] . . . the ashes we left and the ground we
cleared. . . . On coming away Hunter proposed ducking him, upon
which he took the alarm and kept clear of the water.[13]

The reflection of the great fire on the waters of the river, the smell of
the steaks and taste of the porter, the sound of the war whoops ringing
out over Sam Davis' clearing—it was an unforgettable night and one
that at last revealed Hunter not to have been all high-minded seriousness. He possessed a capacity for gaiety, for letting go, and a feeling of
oneness with his body quite proper in a white savage.

3

Just after sunset the next day they pulled in to Mount Vernon, where
Robert Owen, his son, Macdonald, and others got off to travel the last
few miles to Harmonie by land. Though Hunter must have regretted
being left behind, he had to attend to his own concerns and so stayed
aboard the *Favorite* for the trip on down to New Orleans.

Up to this point the diaries of Macdonald and William Owen contained almost a day-to-day commentary on Hunter. Even the least significant of their unstudied entries provided some sense of the man, of
his character, knowledge of trees and plants, concern for the Indians,
passion for life, sense of humor. Now, with the parting of their ways,
Hunter fell back again into the shadows, from which only bits and
pieces of evidence survive to suggest his movements. There remained,
however, one relevant entry in Macdonald's diary. On December 29 he
noted the arrival of the post and of a newspaper that "contained the
President's message, in which he spoke of civilizing the Indians. It struck
us that should Mr. Owen purchase Harmonie, he should be a good agent
for that purpose between the U. States & the Tribes, and the establish-

13. Owen, "Diary," 68–69, and Macdonald, "Diaries," 242; see the preceding
pages for the trip to Pittsburgh and down the Ohio. In March of that year
Stanley had made his first major speech in the House; in 1852 he became P.M.
with the stated purpose of stemming "the tide of Democracy." In 1824 James
Archibald Stuart-Wortley was M.P. for Yorkshire.

ment of Harmonie [as] a place of interest & attraction to them." Owen thus thought of himself as a possible link between white Americans and Indian tribes organized along lines proposed by Hunter and now, apparently, by Monroe. This consideration probably figured in his decision to buy Harmonie.

On January 2, 1825, Hunter wrote to Owen from New Orleans, noting that he had arrived there six days after they parted at Mount Vernon and that he hoped to send the money he owed him back by Stanley and his party but "the man who owes me the money is not in town yet." If he did not show up, he wished Owen "to call on Elliott Cresson of Philadelphia and if he has received any [money] for me to pay you the amount." He was in any event going ahead with his own plans.

> My disappointment can be no material obstruction to my ultimate proceedings for I can obtain what I want here. My credit is good for any amount I may be in need of. I long very much indeed to hear from you, how you are, what's doing. . . . I do long to know if you have purchased any lands in this country and if you have determined on forming a colony on this side the great waters. I feel anxious on many accounts. I want to hear whether you intend remaining all winter at Washington. . . . Wherever you may be, I hope success will reward all your labours. I feel confident the great cause of humanity is advancing.[14]

This deceptive notion of the advance of humanity might have seemed still more certain to Hunter had he known of the phenomenal success of his friend's tour in the East that winter and spring.

At no time before or since, except perhaps in the very recent past, have Americans shown such an extraordinary openness to communitarian ideas. Owen's tour came at the outset of a period of unparalleled experimentation in community building: Arthur Bestor has identified 130 secular and religious communities in the decades before the Civil War. Poverty in the midst of plenty, the question of whether technological progress was to benefit the millions or the few, the issue of reestablishing community in a fragmented, coercive industrial system—all were issues left untouched by the distant, war-making nation-state. The remarkable public response to Owen was partially a personal tribute, but it was also in some measure a recognition that communitarian proposals at least con-

14. Hunter to Owen, January 2, 1825, Owen Papers, Holyoake House, Manchester.

fronted these major problems. His presence and persuasive exposition of his principles moved men to an excited interest in these hopeful new beginnings.

In Pittsburgh on January 22 the enthusiasm was such that the court suspended its session during Owen's lecture. After his appearance in Philadelphia, Thomas Say and other members of the Academy of Natural Sciences made their preparations to join him at New Harmony (as it was now called). In Washington he was greeted as one who had achieved "effects more extraordinary and rational than any law giver of ancient or modern times." Henry Clay and incoming President John Quincy Adams gave him the use of the Hall of Representatives for two addresses, which were attended by large numbers of leading political figures, including Adams, Monroe, and members of the Cabinet, Supreme Court, and Congress. After swinging down into Virginia to visit Jefferson and Madison, Owen made an even more triumphant return to Philadelphia, went on to meet a recently formed Owenite society in Cincinnati, and arrived back at New Harmony in April.

Owen felt he was on the eve of a new empire of peace and goodwill. As he wrote a friend, "The principle of union & cooperation for the promotion of all the virtues & for the creation of wealth is now universally admitted to be far superior to the individual selfish system & all seem prepared or are rapidly preparing to give up the latter & adopt the former." And, he added, "our operation will soon extend to the blacks & the Indians who by singular circumstances have been prepared in a peculiar manner for the change which I propose." [15]

Humanity was not quite ready, alas, for a great leap forward. In the near future Owen would even be forced to admit his failure to establish his plan at New Harmony. Arthur Bestor and others have properly criticized him for traveling about propagandizing when he should have remained behind for the detailed planning and hard work involved in getting New Harmony established. But Owen had in mind more than a single or even several successful villages of cooperation. He sought no less than a new society of such communities and hence seized the opportunity to address his proposals to all Americans. That he greatly underestimated the obstacles and exaggerated the depth of commitment of those who offered support seemed clear to one of his most able associates. William Maclure, the radical republican, brilliant geologist, and

15. Quoted in Bestor, *Backwoods Utopias*, pp. 113–14; for Owen's tour, see pp. 110–13.

educational innovator, once sadly observed that he had been telling Owen not to take at face value the enthusiastic response of liberal reformers, to think of

> how far his system is in advance of any of theirs, and what an immense chasm . . . lies between his radical cure of all evils and the partial remedy of . . . other reformers. . . . This moral chasm ought to be considered as a physical ditch drawn round the old castle of ancient prejudice . . . fortified by all the instruments of defence invented by all the talent and acumen of both church and state for many centuries.[16]

Owen was of course far too sanguine, far too much the Enlightenment rationalist, and had not begun to come to terms with the way individuals were locked in, both voluntarily and involuntarily, by social and political structures. Yet his were errors of generosity and not of mean-spiritedness or pettiness. He cannot be held responsible for the failure of his audiences to give up the system of inequality of wealth and replace it by "common property, and one of common interest." He invited all men to abandon their narrow self-interest, but most preferred to stay behind and act out their beliefs in the inherent depravity of man. If his plan seemed "a refinement of Godwinism," as the New York *Advertiser* charged, he was guilty of no more than a liberating heresy. He could be fairly charged only with challenging individuals to undertake their own self-government. And it was to his lasting credit that he made room for blacks and Indians in this new view of society.

From the point of view of citizens of the United States, it had long been recognized that blacks could expect no room at the inn or anywhere else in what would be a "White Man's Country." Shortly after the turn of the century, President Jefferson had written James Monroe, then Governor of Virginia, his rhapsodical reflections on a destiny that was manifestly white: Americans would multiply and "cover the whole northern, if not southern continent, with a people speaking the same language, governed in similar forms, and by similar laws; nor can we

16. Quoted in John F. C. Harrison, *Quest for the New Moral World: Robert Owen and the Owenites in Britain and America* (New York: Charles Scribner's Sons, 1969), p. 41. For an able discussion of Maclure's radical humanism, see W. H. G. Armytage, *Heavens Below* (London: Routledge & Kegan Paul, 1961), pp. 113–29.

contemplate with satisfaction either blot or mixture on that surface." [17] Lack of satisfaction came nowhere near describing the great revolutionary's aversion to what would happen if a black were allowed to stain "the blood of his master." No friend of slavery, he proposed to solve the whole problem by "expatriation," by ridding the country of all blacks, those previously freed and those newly emancipated. At one point Africa seemed to offer "the most desirable receptacle" for this inky "description of people," but just before his death Jefferson recommended the West Indies as an entirely practicable receptacle. Wherever they were to be dumped, they had to be "removed." Once they were made to go away, then white people could enjoy with good conscience their own natural rights and the revolutionary promise of their past: We hold these truths to be self-evident . . .

Yet such carefree pleasures were impossible so long as the Indians remained behind. Though the red people represented significantly different obstacles and threats than the black chattels, no more than the latter could they be incorporated into white society without "either blot or mixture on that surface." In 1803, to be sure, Jefferson proposed "to let our settlements and theirs meet and blend together, to intermix, and become one people." But he did everything he could, which was a great deal, to prevent this from happening. His actual policy was "the rapid extinguishment of Indian land titles" east of the Mississippi. As he put it in his second Inaugural Address, the right bank was to be settled "by our own brethren and children." Strangers of another "family" had no right to the land lying ahead of "our" overflowing population—to deny this would be as to deny the right of "our Saxon ancestors" to have settled in England. Despite Jefferson's genuine sympathies for the Indians, which I have discussed in other contexts, he had no doubts about who the people—"the folk"—were: they were white, and not black or red.[18] When the possibility of mixing red and white was put to the test, Jefferson opted for pure whiteness. In 1808, for example, when some

17. Quoted in Winthrop D. Jordan, *White over Black* (Chapel Hill: University of North Carolina Press, 1968), p. 547. Jordan's chapter on "Toward a White Man's Country," pp. 542–69, is most illuminating and relevant for understanding the meaning of Indian removal. But see note 18 below.

18. Richardson, *Messages and Papers of the Presidents,* I, 368. Jordan, *White over Black,* pp. 475–81, argues the case that Jefferson took "a dichotomous view of triracial America," that he really saw only the white and black races, with the red "a degraded yet basically noble brand of white man." Jefferson's actions hardly fit this thesis. Moreover, in *Notes on the State of Virginia,* on which Jordan leans, Jefferson explicitly mentioned "what I have seen of man, white, red, and

Cherokee farmers came to him with the request that their lands be assigned to them in severalty and that they be made citizens, Jefferson put them off and urged them to move across the Mississippi.[19] For both the black and red "problems," therefore, the solution was removal.

Over the decades the demand for Indian removal had become more insistent. About the time Owen and Hunter set off down the Ohio, President Monroe delivered the message on civilizing the Indians that reached Owen after he had arrived at Harmonie. "Experience has shown," Monroe declared, "that unless the tribes be civilized they can never be incorporated into our system in any form whatever." Though he proposed to remove them to the West, he firmly rejected force as "revolting to humanity and utterly unjustifiable." On January 27, 1825, Monroe presented a "Special Message" on the same topic. Since the voice of experience still spoke of the utter impossibility of whites and Indians, "in their present state," becoming one people, he proposed that Congress enact "a well-digested plan" which would give the Indians good title to new lands and shield them from ruin. With their consent, they would have a government in their new territory which would have sufficient power to connect "the several tribes together in a bond of amity and preserve order in each; to prevent intrusions on their property; to teach them by regular instruction the arts of civilized life and make them a civilized people." These considerations should prove sufficiently attractive "to surmount all their prejudices in favor of the soil of their nativity" and make clear to everyone that by removing them, with their consent, "we become in reality their benefactors." Congress in turn would pledge "the faith of the nation" to implement the arrangements entered into.[20]

The plan was in truth indigestible. Its most notable characteristic was the same yawning vagueness that had characterized the African colonization discussions of Jefferson and Monroe. How would officials go about getting the "consent" of the Indians? What about those who clung stubbornly to "the soil of their nativity"? What about the western tribes

---

black," discussed such "varieties in the race" as compared with "races of other animals," and gave further evidence of *not* having turned three races into two— unless the two were white and "colored," with the latter containing both black and red (Thomas Perkins Abernathy, ed., *Notes* [New York: Harper & Row, 1964], pp. 56, 59, 63–64).

19. Harmon, *Indian Affairs,* p. 79.

20. Richardson, *Messages and Papers of the Presidents,* II, 261. His Annual Message was delivered on December 7, 1824. For his Special Message, see II, 280–83.

which might be expected to cling to theirs? If what little the eastern tribes still had was being taken from them, why should they feel secure in their new homes? And was it not presumptuous to ask them to regard those who sent them packing as their benefactors? But such questions fell on the deaf ears of those who believed in ethnic magic: following in Jefferson's footsteps, Monroe merely asked the Native Americans, officially and cordially, to become the Vanishing Americans. Unlike the blacks, who could more fittingly be sent "back" to someplace like Sierra Leone, the Indians should move "on" beyond the horizon of the Great Desert.

Some ironic parallels aside, Hunter's plan was in contrast detailed, and was addressed to the critical question of how to reach and teach someone who was likely to be, with good reason, suspicious and hostile. But time was running out for any plans based on persuasion rather than violence. Monroe's messages were indices of this, of the pressure which would rise to produce Jackson's Removal Bill of May 1830 and, a little later, the "utterly unjustifiable": forcible removal and the Cherokee Trail of Tears. Even this early the overflowing white population had washed many tribes and bands of displaced persons across the Mississippi, where Hunter would find them in such desperate circumstances as to present very real "obstruction[s] to my ultimate proceedings."

In all probability Hunter learned before he left New Orleans that the odds against his plan had shot up while he was away. In a letter to an English friend he revealed a keen sense of the possibility of failure or even disaster:

> I am now about to bid Adieu—perhaps forever! to the kind friends with whom I have been blessed for the last six or seven years of my life. Heaven knows: but human foresight cannot look into futurity, and what may await me in the yet almost trackless wilds, we cannot say; even if every thing turns out to the utmost of my wishes, it is impossible for you to conceive the situation in which I am placed.[21]

With his eagerness and determination tempered now by his misgivings as to what awaited him, he was perhaps better prepared to cope with the frustrations which followed.

21. Bessy Walker to John Neal, April 10, 1825, in Richards, "John Neal," IV. Miss Walker included the excerpt from Hunter's letter to show that their mutual friend was adhering to his plans and not, as Neal evidently suggested, planning a return to England.

According to a journal entry at the Dwight Mission on the Neosho River in Arkansas, Hunter arrived there on February 28, 1825.[22] The account of his visit was probably written by the Reverend Cephus Finney, who recorded that Hunter's purpose was to be useful to the native Americans:

> His efforts for their good are to be commenced with the Quapaws. His ardent friendship for the Indians, his native enterprise, his talents & education & property, which is considerable, & the estimation in which he is held by many men of political influence, all conspire to qualify him for the work he is about to undertake. But, alas, he wants the one thing . . . [faith in God?] needful, & without this very little real good can be hope[d] from him.

The writer found him, nevertheless, a suitable subject for the prayers of all who prayed for the Indian missions and was obviously pleased by Hunter's expression of appreciation for the improvement "he witnessed in our schools & in different parts of the [Cherokee] Nation he visited." Hunter may have merely been polite to his hosts, however, for he could not have been enthusiastic about their goal of making the Indian children over into industrious obedient little Christians or their attempts to secure economic self-sufficiency for the manual labor school through making them work the land in what amounted to a system of labor peonage.[23]

From what Hunter said at the Dwight Mission, he still proposed to settle near the Quapaws. So constantly on the move, he had not apparently heard of the tribe's most recent misfortune. For some time there had been pressure to rid Arkansas of Indians. On occasion the argument against their remaining was refreshingly direct, as a letter in the *National Intelligencer* of May 20, 1824, showed: since "the best portion of our territory is now owned by the Indians," an Arkansas subscriber complained, their title should be simply "extinguished." Six months later it was. When Hunter finally reached his friends, probably in March 1825, he learned that the preceding November they had touched the feather to a treaty by which they ceded all the Quapaw land in Arkansas to the United States. Too late to warn them against such a decisive step—one that

22. American Board of Commissioners for Foreign Mission Papers (18.3.1, VI, 85–91), Houghton Library, Harvard; see also *New York Religious Chronicle,* August 6, 1825.
23. See Robert F. Berkhofer, Jr., *Salvation and the Savage* (Lexington: University of Kentucky Press, 1965), p. 40.

provided perfectly legal means for driving them from their homes—
Hunter no doubt realized that they were about to join other tribes in
the forced migration west. As a forlorn last hope, he probably advised the
Quapaws to throw themselves on the mercy of the Arkansas authorities.

On June 20, 1825, Heckaton and Saracen, their principal chiefs, went to
see Governor George Izard and pleaded with him to modify or suspend
"the late treaty concluded by them, by which they ceded all their lands
to the United States." Izard refused, though he admitted that it was
always painful to give up a country "where the bones of one's ancestors
repose." Unlike the governors of Georgia and Alabama, Izard could
hardly urge Indians in his territory to move across the Mississippi where
they would be forever undisturbed. They were already there. But he
did tell them that their move farther west was "as much for their advantage as from a desire on the part of our government to possess their
lands. We are a numerous and increasing people, and when our countrymen shall cross the great river in crowds, the safety of the Indians might
be endangered." [24] The Quapaw chiefs could hardly challenge this
probability.

Meanwhile Hunter had to rethink what was to be done. For several
months he seems to have wandered through the Indian country seeking
likely areas for relocating the Quapaws and other tribes. There is no
reason to doubt that Major Davenport, Lieutenant Julius Catlin, and
others saw him at Cantonment Gibson in April 1825 or that surveyor
John C. Sullivan saw him at about the same time on the western boundary of the Arkansas Territory. According to Sullivan, Hunter was then
on his way to the Red River "to locate himself on a farm." But if he did
go south then, he had returned to Missouri by late summer, at about
the time Generals Clark and Cass were meeting with the northern Indians at Prairie du Chien—in September, you may recall, he wrote his
last letter to Elias Norgate and sent it from Pulaski County.

In Missouri Hunter learned that the Osages were also being "removed"
farther west, under the treaty negotiated by Clark on June 2, 1825, so
that the Cherokees and others could be "removed" to what had been the
Osage prairies and woodlands. Everywhere he went, Hunter found
tribes being uprooted and driven farther and farther toward Jefferson's
Stony Mountains. These movements of homeless peoples came ironically
close to fulfilling, for the first time since the "discovery" of America, the

24. *National Intelligencer,* August 5, 1825.

white myth about "wandering hordes of savages." If the Indians were not to be crushed by this westward movement—which had, as Tocqueville observed a little later, "the solemnity of a providential event"—they would have to get out of the way.

Hunter may have traveled south from Pulaski Country over the Franquelin Trail, proceeded down to Louisiana, and from Natchitoches followed the Camino Real across the Sabine River into the Province of Texas. However he got there, in the fall of 1825 he showed up at the *ranchería* of the Cherokees twelve miles west of the Sabine and about fifty miles north of Nacogdoches. The "scattered and decaying tribes" he was trying to help just might escape Providence across the border in the Republic of Mexico.

The City of Mexico   8

Hunter is certainly a shrewd active man—talking a great
deal about the rights of the Indians, and as I believe not
very friendly to the interests of the United States. . . . I
do not think it would be politic on the part of the United
States to suffer the emigration and establishment on the
Mexican frontier of so large and powerful a body of
Indian warriors, as it is Hunter's desire to move there.

JOEL R. POINSETT,
Minister to Mexico, to Henry Clay, Secretary of State,
April 30, 1826

Buried deep in the Cherokee tribal memory was the recollection of a
band, under the leadership of Dangerous Man, which had crossed the
great river long ago to avoid having any relations with whites. They
were not heard from again, though a rumor once came from the West
that they were still living near the base of the Rocky Mountains. Historical accounts relate that in 1794 another band, led by Di wa'li, or The
Bowl, fled to the Arkansas country to escape reprisal for killing whites
at Muscle Shoals on the Tennessee.[1] After the Louisiana Purchase, at the
government's urging, an increasing number of Cherokees followed their
brothers and sisters to the West: by 1819 there were about six thousand
settled across the Mississippi. It was this policy of relocating the tribe on
lands claimed by the Osages which had angered Hunter, you will recall,
and led him to denounce "the powers that be" for the bloodshed which
followed. The intertribal raids, retaliations, and conflicts over boundaries
were the direct consequence, he had maintained, of such official cruelty
and injustice.

The Bowl and his band were active in the war with the Osages. In

---

1. James Mooney, "Myths of the Cherokees," *Nineteenth Annual Report of the
Bureau of American Ethnology* (Washington: Government Printing Office [here-
after, GPO], 1900), Part I, 99–145; Charles C. Royce, "The Cherokee Nation of
Indians," *Fifth Annual Report of the Bureau of American Ethnology* (Washington: GPO, 1887), 121–378, esp. 242–49; John P. Brown, *Old Frontiers* (Kings-
port, Tenn.: Southern Publishers, 1938), pp. 403–4, 471.

October 1817, for instance, observers commented on the ferocity of his attack against an old man who came out from the village on the Verdigris as a peace messenger. When the fighting was temporarily halted by a treaty, the boundaries established angered The Bowl and moved him again to flee the jurisdiction of the United States. In the winter of 1819–20 he and about sixty warriors crossed over the Red River into Texas.[2]

Other refugees joined them shortly, and the chain of villages they established on the Trinity, Neches, Angelina, and Sabine rivers came to be known as "The Cherokee and Their Associated Bands." The "Absentee Shawnees," who had split off from their tribe following Tecumseh's death, joined the Cherokees, along with Quapaws, Delawares, Kickapoos, Choctaws, Biloxis, Caddoes, and other tribal fragments. The immigrants formed a loose confederation, as if in anticipation of Hunter's proposals, and many of them turned to farming and cattle raising. The rich "red lands" on which they had settled grew lush crops of corn, beans, pumpkins, squash, and melons. They had plenty of water for their fields and pastures, timber for fuel and building, and game for their table. When the Mexican governor visited them in 1822, he was impressed by what they had done in so short a time: "They work for their living," he reported, "and dress in cotton cloth of their own manufacture. They raise cattle and horses, and use fire arms. Many of them understand the English language."[3]

The one thing these Indians had not been able to do was get an outright grant to the lands they had occupied and improved. Their experience with land-hungry settlers across the border had already taught them an unforgettable lesson about the importance of those pieces of paper which established "property rights" and the certainty of being condemned to homelessness for lacking such near-magical proofs of ownership. After the Mexican Revolution, Richard Fields, one of their principal chiefs, thus petitioned the governor of the province: "I wish to fall at your feet and omblay ask you what must be Dun with us pur Indians[.] we have som Grants that was give to us when we live under the Spanish government and we wish you to send us nuws by the Next mal whether that will be Reverd [reversed?] or Not[.]" Governor Felix

2. John Joseph Mathews, *The Osages* (Norman: University of Oklahoma Press, 1961), p. 423.

3. Quoted in Ernest William Winkler, "The Cherokee Indians in Texas," *Texas State Historical Association Quarterly,* VII (October 1903), 97; the best account of the Texas band is still to be found here.

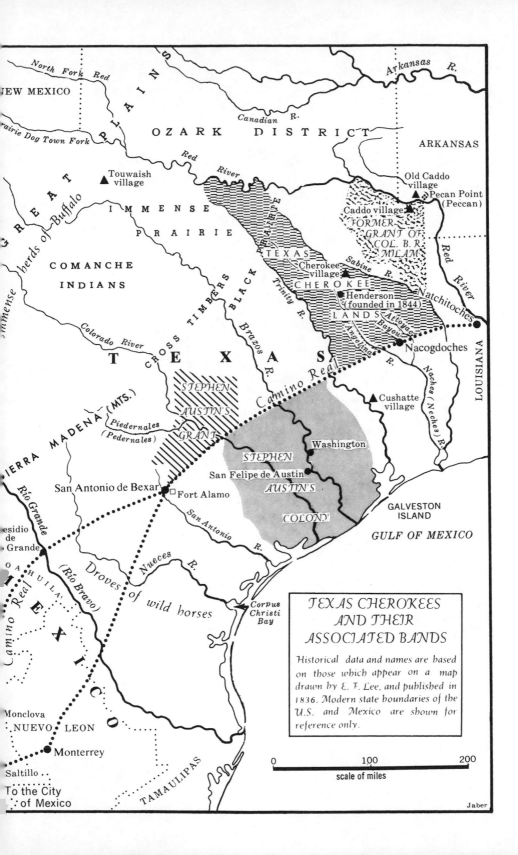

North Fork Red

NEW MEXICO

Prairie Dog Town Fork

GREAT PLAINS

Canadian R.

OZARK DISTRICT

Arkansas R.

ARKANSAS

Touwaish village

IMMENSE

PRAIRIE

Red River

Old Caddo village

Pecan Point (Peccan)

Caddo village

FORMER GRANT OF COL. B. R. MILAM

Immense herds of Buffalo

COMANCHE INDIANS

TEXAS

Cherokee village

Sabine R.

CHEROKEE

Henderson (founded in 1844)

LANDS

Attoyac Bayou

Natchitoches

Red River

LOUISIANA

Colorado River

CROSS TIMBERS

BLACK PRAIRIE

Trinity R.

Angelina R.

Nacogdoches

T E X A S

Brazos R.

Camino Real

Naches (Neches) R.

SIERRA MADENA (MTS.)

Piedernales (Pedernales)

STEPHEN AUSTIN'S GRANT

Cushatte village

Washington

STEPHEN

San Felipe de Austin

AUSTIN'S

COLONY

GALVESTON ISLAND

San Antonio de Bexar

Fort Alamo

San Antonio R.

GULF OF MEXICO

Río Grande

Presidio de Grande

COAHUILA

(Río Bravo)

Droves of wild horses

Nueces R.

Corpus Christi Bay

M E X I C O

Camino Real

Monclova

NUEVO LEON

Monterrey

Saltillo

To the City of Mexico

TAMAULIPAS

TEXAS CHEROKEES AND THEIR ASSOCIATED BANDS

Historical data and names are based on those which appear on a map drawn by E. F. Lee, and published in 1836. Modern state boundaries of the U.S. and Mexico are shown for reference only.

0   100   200

scale of miles

Jaber

Trespalacios signed a paper, which they were pleased to get, that they might continue to cultivate their lands and sow their crops "in free and peaceful possession" till his superiors made some final decision on their claim.

Fields and a delegation of Cherokees, including The Bowl, then journeyed to the City of Mexico and, after some months, secured another piece of paper which showed that the Supreme Executive Power had resolved on April 27, 1823, that their agreement with Trespalacios would remain "provisionally in force" till the passage of a general colonization law.[4] Fields was also said "to have received a verbal promise that his application would be favourably treated, and resting satisfied with this, returned to his tribe." [5] Fields and his tribesmen unfortunately, but forgivably, since they were new to the world of real estate, failed to realize that provisional agreements, even written ones, and verbal promises, no matter how warmly persuasive, did not give them secure possession of one square foot of land.

After the Cherokee delegation returned from the Mexican capital, the Indians had a brief year of security and peace. Fields acted on the promises and concessions he believed they had received, obviously assuming that they had been granted the land they wanted, namely that lying north of the old Camino Real, or the San Antonio Road, south of the Red River, and between the Trinity and the Sabine. And while the Cherokees acknowledged their submission to the laws of Mexico, Fields insisted they were not subject to the authority of local officials.

The end of this Indian idyll came without warning. Before the Cherokees and their allies learned what was happening, the national congress passed a general colonization law and the legislature of Coahuila and Texas passed a state act on March 24, 1825. Less than a month later three claims were granted to settle two thousand families on or near land claimed by the Indians. Fields and his tribesmen were particularly angered by the cession to an American named Haden Edwards, who had received a grant to settle eight hundred families in a district that included the Cherokee village. By late summer the Indians were seemingly preparing for countermeasures. On September 8, 1825, Stephen F. Austin, head of a flourishing colony of whites to the west, passed on a report to his political chief that "Fields is secretly making great efforts to unite all the Indian tribes of Texas in a confederation to destroy the

---

4. *Ibid.*, 99, 105–6. Fields's letter, written for him, was dated February 1, 1822.
5. Henry Stuart Foote, *Texas and the Texans* (Philadelphia: Thomas Cowperthwait, 1841), I, 240.

new settlements, giving for his reasons [1] that if said settlements grow considerably the government can use their militia either to compel the Indians to obey the laws or to destroy them, and [2] that the occupation of the country by the settlers will result in the destruction of the game and the Indians will starve to death." [6]

Just as Hunter arrived in East Texas, then, the affairs of "The Cherokee and Their Associated Bands" had reached a crisis. According to one early historian, a man with Hunter's discernment could hardly have failed to perceive at once "the flimsy and precarious nature of the tenure by which his Aboriginal friends claimed the territory then in their possession"; he thus besought them to grant him a commission to negotiate for a definite title. Another historian credited Hunter with a major role in dissuading the Indians from immediately going on the warpath. Personally opposed to war, especially one of such uncertain prospects, Hunter counseled patience and expressed a willingness "to undertake to secure the long sought titles to their lands." [7] Hunter's own account, which may have deliberately minimized the possibility of Indian hostilities, was somewhat different: at a council held in November 1825, "at which the Deputies of twenty three tribes assisted, it was resolved to abandon for ever their Ancient Homes and to seek beyond the Rocky Mountains or even beyond the shores of the Pacific a refuge from persecution." Before they acted upon this resolution, however, they determined to make one last application for lands and deputed Hunter to undertake the commission. [8]

Hunter had joined the council as a representative of the Quapaws and other Indians still living across the border in the United States, some in the area above the Red River and others in the area between the Sabine and the Mississippi. [9] He quickly assumed a position of prominence in their deliberations and worked closely with Richard Fields.

6. Austin to José Antonio Saucedo, Political Chief of the Department of Texas, September 8, 1825, in Eugene C. Barker, ed., "The Austin Papers," *Annual Report for the American Historical Association for the Year 1919*, Vol. II (Washington: GPO, 1924), 1196; hereafter, "Austin Papers."

7. Foote, *Texas*, I, 247–48; Winkler, "Cherokee Indians," 122–23.

8. Hunter's account of the council appeared in a letter from Henry George Ward to George Canning, British Foreign Secretary, March 19, 1826, Foreign Office (hereafter, FO) Correspondence, Mexico, FO 50/20, No. 20, Public Record Office (hereafter, PRO), London. Since he was talking to an official, a friendly official but still a white representative of a major power, Hunter may have carefully avoided any reference to a possible Indian uprising.

9. Joel R. Poinsett to Henry Clay, Secretary of State, April 30, 1826, Department of State, Dispatches from the U.S. Minister to Mexico, 1823–1873, National Archives, Record Group 59; the microfilm citation, which style will be used hereafter, is M(icro Copy) 97, R(oll) 2, N(ational) A(rchives).

Fields was himself an intelligent man. According to one account "only a quarter-breed Indian" and to another "a half-breed," he fought against the British in the War of 1812, married the daughter of Francis Grapp, a well-known Indian trader at Natchitoches, and, perhaps because he knew how to speak English, replaced The Bowl as principal chief of the Cherokees during the course of the negotiations for land.[10] He could not write, however, and had difficulty in trying to communicate with the Mexican officials and with colonists like Austin. He was not equipped to understand fine distinctions between grants and permits or the difference between verbal and written promises. Hence he understandably welcomed Hunter, who was literate, relatively experienced in dealing with white folks, and no less dedicated to the cause of the Indians. As Fields was reported to have said later in a speech at Nacogdoches:

> In my old Days I travilid 2000 Miles to the City of Mexico to Beg some lands to setel a Poor orfan tribe of Red Peopel that looked up to me for Protasion I was Promisid lands for them after staying one year in Mexico and spending all I had I then came to my Peopel and waited two years and then sent Mr. hunter again after selling my stock to Provide him money for his expenses.[11]

Fields evidently made arrangements immediately to sell his stock, for Hunter was on the road to the Mexican capital in December or shortly after the turn of the year.

No word has survived on his trip. Between San Antonio and Monterrey were great stretches of desolate country which supposedly "swarmed with bandits." But Hunter apparently made it through without incident, for by March 19 he had arrived in the City of Mexico.[12]

10. H. Yoakum, *History of Texas* (New York: Redfield, 1856), I, 250; Hubert Howe Bancroft, *History of the North Mexican States and Texas* (San Francisco: History Publishers, 1889), II, 103; "Austin Papers," 1220–21; Winkler, "Cherokee Indians," 98, 119.

11. Peter Ellis Bean to Stephen F. Austin, December 31, 1826, "Austin Papers," 1554. The spelling was Bean's.

12. Yoakum, *Texas*, I, 237, stated that Hunter "arrived in Mexico on 19 March 1826." The dispatch of the British chargé discussed below, also dated March 19, indicates that Hunter had almost certainly arrived earlier.

2

On that day Henry George Ward, the British chargé d'affaires, wrote two important dispatches to Foreign Secretary George Canning. In the first he reported that he had aided General Arthur G. Wavell, a former English officer who had for some years been active in promoting commercial ventures in Mexico, to secure a valuable grant of land in the vicinity of the border in East Texas. Ward had urged President Guadalupe Victoria to act quickly before the Americans did something to impede the execution of the plan and to show that Mexico was determined "to assert her rights." For once General Victoria had shown "something very like activity and decision," Ward was happy to relate, and had made the grant on condition that Wavell "was not to admit upon it a single North American colonist." [13] In a postscript, dated March 24, he noted that Joel R. Poinsett, the American Minister to Mexico, had officially protested the grant: "The truth is that Mr. Poinsett is determined if possible, to parry a blow, the consequences of which might prove highly injurious to his present schemes." He trusted, however, that the Mexican government would not allow itself to be dictated to by the agent of a foreign power.

Ward's second dispatch announced the arrival of Hunter in Mexico.[14] Hunter had informed him, Ward wrote, that he was commissioned to act for twenty-three tribes of Indians, some of whom were still in the United States, where they "have been so harassed of late by the Backsettlers, whose encroachments, if not positively encouraged, are, at least, not repressed by the Government—that the Chiefs have determined unanimously to seek another home":

> If Hunter's account can be relied upon, nothing can be more nefarious than the means that have been resorted to in order to defraud the Indians of their Lands. Private distilleries have been established upon the Frontier, although prohibited under severe penalties by the laws, and sales made in a moment of intoxication are enforced as bona fide Contracts—which give the Purchaser an undoubted right of possession.

13. Ward to Canning, March 19, 1826, FO 50/20, No. 18, PRO. Ward was a relatively young man, about Hunter's age, who had the reputation of being "an advanced liberal." He had entered the diplomatic service in 1816 and, after posts in various European capitals, first came to Mexico in 1823.

14. Ward to Canning, March 19, 1826, FO 50/20, No. 20, PRO; a copy of Hunter's petition to Victoria, discussed below, was enclosed in this dispatch.

Representation had been made, and redress sought in vain; and yet if the Indians venture to repel force by force, that Power whose authority is denied, when they invoke its protection is the first to claim satisfaction for what is termed unjustifiable violence.

In return for a grant of lands, Hunter offered to bring into Mexico thirty thousand Indians. The Indians would take up farming and defend the frontier against aggressors. Ward suggested to Canning that "a better opportunity would not easily be found of opposing a formidable obstacle to the designs of the United States on Texas." He had, therefore, mentioned the subject to Victoria, "who appeared much pleased at the idea and having thus excited his curiosity, I have taken every means in my power to prepare him to give Hunter a most favourable reception." To avoid appearing too closely involved in the project, Ward introduced Hunter to General Wavell and through him put his application in the hands of "Doctor Cervallos, a Senator, and the Representative of the State of Cohahu'ila and Texas, who appears to take as lively an interest as I could desire."

Ward also drew up a petition for Hunter designed "either to flatter General Victoria's vanity or to work upon his zeal for the interests of religion" and then had Hunter sit down and copy it in his own handwriting. The petition referred to the despair the Indians felt at being "driven from River to River by the advance of the Backsettlers" and pledged that, if Mexico would give them a home, they would renounce their roving habits and become zealous defenders of the rights and territory of their adopted country. The Indians would become Mexican citizens and Christians: "It is thus in Your Excellency's power to confer upon 30,000 souls the inappreciable blessings of civilisation and Religion." There would be a general council of the tribes in May, so if their application were granted, "I shall be welcomed there on my return as the Bearer of most joyful tidings, and Y[our] E[xcellency]'s name will be blessed by thousands to whom you will have given a home." But, Hunter's petition concluded, "should I fail, we shall retire beyond the mountains where neither Mexico nor Whites can penetrate or even come into communication with us again."

Hunter's mission dovetailed nicely with the current definition of British interests in Mexico. After the United States rejected his proposal for a joint declaration of policy on Latin America, George Canning had gone ahead to pledge that England would not take any of the former Spanish colonies for herself or permit any other power to do so. As we have seen, the Monroe Doctrine studiously avoided any such self-denying ordinance for a very good reason: the United States wanted to acquire Spanish-American territory. Canning deliberately exerted British influence in Mexico to counteract these expansionist aims. He quite correctly perceived that the Jeffersonian two-spheres principle would make America a separate world from Europe, as the head of "a general Transatlantic League, of which it would have the sole direction." But if England could link Mexico to Europe through friendship and trade, the "mischief" might be stopped: "I believe we now have the opportunity (but it may not last long) of opposing a powerful barrier to the influence of the US by an amicable connection with Mexico, which from its position must be either subservient to or jealous of the US." [15]

If Canning saw all of Mexico as a barrier to U.S. ambitions, Ward saw Texas as the crucial barrier for Mexico. He repeatedly warned the Mexicans against allowing their powerful neighbors to cross the frontier and take possession of the land. In the autumn of 1825, for instance, he had mentioned these warnings to Canning and noted with some exasperation that "the whole of the lands between the Rivers Sabine and Brazos have been granted away to American settlers, and that the tide of emigration is settling very fast in the direction of the Rio Bravo." The ultimate incorporation of Texas by the United States, Ward held, was "by no means an improbable event." To check the tide of emigration was the only way to hold on, and that could only be done by interposing another population on the frontier. This was exactly what General Wavell had proposed, and now Hunter spoke to the same need: "The establishment of Hunter's Indians will complete this plan by covering the whole line of the Red River beyond the General's Grant," Ward pointed out to Canning, "and this circumstance has been an additional inducement to me to second his views." [16]

15. See William R. Manning, *Early Diplomatic Relations between the United States and Mexico* (Baltimore: Johns Hopkins Press, 1916), p. 71; see pp. 55–88 for a clear and careful discussion of Canning's policy before and after the enunciation of the Monroe Doctrine. See also Arthur P. Whitaker, *The United States and the Independence of Latin America, 1800–1830* (Baltimore: Johns Hopkins Press, 1940).

16. Ward to Canning, September 22, 1825, FO 204/4, Part 2, No. 32, PRO; Ward, *Mexico in 1827* (London: Henry Colburn, 1828), II, 586–87; Ward to Canning, March 19, 1826, FO 50/20, No. 20, PRO. Ward assured his chief that he had "taken the greatest care not to commit myself in any way, and what I have written for Hunter was copied by himself in my sight, so that not only his Petition appears in his own handwriting but no proof exists of my having had anything to do with it."

Even had there been no other reason, support from the British legation was certain to win Hunter the enmity of the first United States
Minister to Mexico. A slave holder in his native South Carolina, Poinsett
still saw himself as an apostle of liberty to Spanish America. While serv-
ing in the diplomatic corps in Chile during the War of 1812, he had
departed from his official duties so far as to participate in an insurgent
campaign. Later in Congress he had spoken out sharply against Spain,
favored early recognition of its former colonies, and supported the
Monroe Doctrine as though it were a divine commandment. As he left
Washington to take up his post in 1825, his friend C. C. Cambreleng had
been only a little playful when he advised him to take the measure of
John Bull, acquire Texas, promote Cuban independence, and stop
Mexican women from smoking.[17] On his arrival Poinsett informed Cambreleng that he had been sent one year too late to stop the rise of British
influence but grimly promised to "do my best to recover the lost
ground."

As Poinsett saw the world, there were two systems, the American and
the European, and all Mexicans, in fact everybody, could be divided into
two classes, those friendly to the United States and those opposed to the
freedom it represented. In the City of Mexico he thought he saw Ward
trying to form a European party composed of monarchists, aristocrats,
and Anglophiles, but took comfort in the fact "there is an American party
in the [Mexican] House of Representatives and in the Senate, in point of
talents much the strongest; but the government have an ascendancy over
both bodies." [18] There followed one of the more bizarre chapters in American diplomacy as Poinsett launched a campaign to change the Mexican
government. Finding that many of the men whom he regarded as re-
actionaries were members of the Scottish Rite Masons, he helped their
opponents form York lodges and then guided the *Yorkinos* into effective
political action. In September 1825 they achieved a kind of "palace revolution" by forcing the leading British sympathizers out of the cabinet.

Though Poinsett always claimed not to have "taken any part in the
internal affairs of Mexico," one of his long cipher dispatches to Clay
showed that he very nearly claimed personal credit for bringing about
this change in government. Others on the scene were quite prepared to

17. J. Fred Rippy, *Joel R. Poinsett* (Durham, N.C.: Duke University Press,
1935), pp. 108, 118.
18. Poinsett to Clay, August 5, 1825, quoted in Manning, *United States and
Mexico,* p. 75.

accept his responsibility. Those politicians who had been ousted were of course furious about his possession of state secrets, his organization of a political party, and his fanning the animosities of their countrymen. Before long, the resentment of Mexicans became widespread. It led the legislature of Vera Cruz to denounce Poinsett as a "sagacious and hypocritical foreign Minister" and eventually moved the Mexican government to request his recall.[19] Ward worked energetically and astutely to this end, persuaded, as he reported to Canning, that there was "no definitive object for Mr. Poinsett's intrigues here unless it is his intention by embroiling [sic] Mexico with England to facilitate the encroachments of the United States in the North." [20]

At this point observe how all this related to Hunter: he had moved into the line of fire between the conflicting interests of England and the United States and the conflicting intrigues of Ward and Poinsett. He had the misfortune, moreover, of coming on his mission to Mexico at a time when Poinsett's influence was temporarily ascendant.

Apart from the diplomatic sparring of Ward and Poinsett was the fact that the very nature of Hunter's plan threw him into opposition to Poinsett, who had been instructed to get Texas for his government.[21] When Hunter arrived, Poinsett was still pursuing negotiations on the Louisiana boundary, negotiations transparently designed to extend American territory at Mexican expense. Not surprisingly, the Mexicans rejected his offer to move the line of 1819 from the Sabine to the Rio Grande or, failing that, at least to the Rio Colorado. According to Ward, Poinsett also intrigued for "the purpose of obtaining such a party in the Mexican congress as would consent to let them have Texas for a certain number of dollars." [22]

19. See Manning, ed., *Diplomatic Correspondence of the United States Concerning the Independence of Latin-American Nations* (New York: Oxford University Press, 1925), III, 1636–40, 1663, 1667. Poinsett to President John Quincy Adams, April 26, 1827, Poinsett Papers, Historical Society of Pennsylvania (hereafter, HSP), contains a revealing explanation of his use of the York Rite Masons to combat jealous men who "view our Republican institutions with abhorrence, being as they are, a practical commentary on their doctrines, and an incontrovertible proof of their falsehood and absurdity."

20. Ward to Canning, March 19, 1826, FO 50/20, No. 20, PRO. Poinsett was not in fact recalled until 1829.

21. Manning, *United States and Mexico*, pp. 289–90, notes that Poinsett once unofficially acknowledged that the United States would like not only Texas but Upper California and New Mexico and parts of Lower California, Sonora, Coahuila, and Nuevo León.

22. Speech in the House of Commons, August 5, 1836, quoted in Richard Rollin Stenberg, "American Imperialism in the Southwest, 1800–1837" (unpubl. Ph.D. diss., University of Texas, 1932), p. 193.

From the first, aware that American settlers might accomplish what negotiations and bribery could not, Poinsett advised the administration in Washington to be patient. One of his dispatches to Clay, for example, proved that Ward's views on the consequence of the tide of emigration were quite precise. "Most of the good land from the Colorado to the Sabine has been granted," Poinsett wrote Clay in July 1825, "and is rapidly peopling with either grantees or squatters from the United States, a population they will find difficult to govern, and perhaps after a short period they will not be so adverse to part with that portion of their territory." The last thing Poinsett wanted was for the Mexicans to make their territory more secure. Word of Hunter's projected settlement on their frontier of thirty thousand Indians had to rouse him to about the same level of enthusiasm he would have shown had someone proposed that he help the British burn the White House again.

Furthermore, Poinsett shared with his countrymen the conviction that neither Hunter's Indians nor any others had rights which white men were bound to respect. A few years after he returned from Mexico, Poinsett delivered a lecture on the "American Race" in which he observed that, "as far as my researches and observations have hitherto extended, the pure and unmixed races of hunters in America have not made any progress in their social condition." For him to make such a statement meant that he had absolutely no idea of the "progress in their social condition" of the Cherokees and their allies. Like Lewis Cass, he regarded the Indians as fixed forever at the hunting "stage," doomed to extermination or to retreat beyond the ever-advancing frontier of the white man. Not by chance did Poinsett succeed Cass as Secretary of War.[23]

Finally, also like Cass, Poinsett had discovered that service in the cause of Progress did not preclude keeping an eye out for the main chance. Shortly after he took up his duties, he wrote Cambreleng that "fortunes will be made and lost in mining—It is gambling—There are still some of the most profitable speculations, more of that anon." Anon, while still an envoy, he became a Texas land *empresario,* in partnership with Lorenzo de Závala, the Mexican liberal who acquired a grant

23. See Frank B. Woodford, *Lewis Cass* (New Brunswick, N.J.: Rutgers University Press, 1950), pp. 193–94; Rippy, *Poinsett,* pp. 167, 181–82. Poinsett therefore had responsibility for carrying out the Indian removal policy initiated under Cass. During his four years in the War Department he moved across the Mississippi some forty thousand Indians, ordered General Winfield Scott to march the Cherokees on their Trail of Tears, and vigorously prosecuted the filthy Seminole war.

stretching along the Sabine just below the Cherokee and Caddo villages.[24]

For Poinsett's schemes, then, personal as well as official, Hunter's application represented a more threatening setback than had General Wavell's. Just what he did to parry the blow sank forever beneath the murky surface of intrigue and counter-intrigue.

At the time of drawing up Hunter's petition, Ward had feared that "at least a month will lapse before the President is worked up into taking a Resolution" and later expressed his disappointment that the Mexican government had suffered "the critical moment to pass without turning it to account." The favorable opportunity had been lost, he concluded, "by that dilatory spirit, which, both in Spain and its dependencies, has been the source of so many evils." But the loss of the opportunity may well have derived from other than the *mañana* syndrome. Victoria had acted with dispatch on Wavell's application and had, Ward reported, "appeared much pleased" at Hunter's proposal. Victoria himself gave Ward

> to understand yesterday morning [February 20, 1827] that . . . after all that has passed between us respecting Texas, some explanation was due with regard to the causes of that Procrastination on the part of Mexico, which had terminated in an event, which I had so often predicted: the blame of this delay he threw entirely upon the Chambers: he assured me that the Executive had never lost sight of the question, nor ceased to press it upon the attention of the Congress . . . he had long known from whence the secret opposition to his plans had proceeded. . . . Of Mr. Poinsett personally, General Victoria spoke with more caution, altho' evident bitterness of feeling.[25]

The evidence, especially Poinsett's dispatches, makes it most likely that Victoria was telling the truth. This truth, so far as it related to Hunter, revealed that he and Ward had been blocked by Poinsett acting through his agents in the congress and possibly the cabinet.

A great, deal depended on when Poinsett first learned of Hunter's mission. Ward had moved quietly and quickly. Further, the first mention of Hunter in the United States legation register was on April 30, well over a month after his arrival. Yet Poinsett had reason to know, as he reported to Rufus King, United States Minister to Great Britain, that

24. Stenberg, "American Imperialism in the Southwest," pp. 194–95.
25. Ward to Canning, March 19, 1826, FO 50/20, No. 20; February 21, 1827, FO 50/31b, No. 34, PRO; Ward, *Mexico in 1827*, II, 588.

"there are no secrets in Mexico." [26] He also knew intrigues are no better than the espionage on which they rely. He saw himself surrounded on all sides by plotters working for Old World interests or by venal souls waiting for an opportunity to sell him out. He accordingly took steps to ensure that he knew what was going on. As he explained in an extraordinary dispatch to Clay, Mexico was "a republic without virtue":

> The state of society here is scarcely to be credited. I hardly know a man however high his rank or office whose word can be relied on and many of the leading members in both houses will receive a bribe to advocate a private claim with as little scruple as you would have received to argue a cause before the Supreme Court; from such men I would have kept aloof had I been permitted to have done so, but they sought me and I found it necessary to form a party out of such elements as the country afforded or to leave the English masters of the field.

Poinsett had his forces in the field, therefore, and if he had not been aware of Hunter's mission soon after he arrived in the capital, he certainly learned of it following Hunter's presentation of his petition to Victoria in March.

Poinsett's dispatch to Clay had said little about his personal actions in bringing about the results he reported. He merely noted that "John D. Hunter, distinguished for his publications and for the account of him by Govr. Cass in the North American Review, has lately been here." [27] He stated without elaboration that "this Government refused to give them [the Indians] a large tract of land, where they might remain united in a body, but offered to settle them in different parts of the Country under Mexican Governors." Now it was most probable, I am suggesting, that Poinsett was really reporting here another of his accomplishments, an ostensible Mexican decision which had been largely shaped by his own hands.

The last best chance for the tens of thousands of displaced Indians to find a home or at least to make a stand against the tide of white settlers

26. Register, April 30, 1826, M97, R1, NA; Poinsett to King, October 10, 1825, and Poinsett to Clay, October 12, 1825, in Manning, *Diplomatic Correspondence,* III, 1635, 1638.

27. Poinsett to Clay, April 30, 1826, M97, R2, NA. Cass's article, remember, was published the preceding January, about the time Hunter set out for the City of Mexico. Poinsett may have read it in the *North American* or he may have received a copy directly from Cass.

disappeared with the rejection of their petition for lands. Hunter would carry no good news back to the council. But there was a certain grim appropriateness in the strong probability that the opportunity had been squashed by the long arm of U.S. interests. It was consistent with the decree that the Indians vanish. Americans did not want the tribes where they were and so launched a policy of removal. Yet the Indians could not remove to where they themselves might go, even if some of them had found a home in what was at the moment foreign territory. So Poinsett suspected Hunter of not being very friendly to the interests of the United States, as the epigraph at the head of this chapter shows, and had the effrontery to write that it would not "be politic on the part of the United States to suffer the emigration of so large and powerful a body of Indian warriors, as it is Hunter's desire to move there." [28] *Suffer* their movements? Was it not a most peculiar Providence that had granted white Americans the right to suffer or not to suffer the emigration of free peoples?

3

No doubt Hunter saw many compatriots in the capital. The American empire was spinning off superfluous men who helped extend its borders at the same time they sought their own fortunes or simply looked for more wilderness to conquer. As Poinsett was patiently to explain to the angry Mexicans at the time of his recall:

> The United States are in a state of progressive aggrandizement, which has no example in the history of the world. Its federal union, instead of dissolving, as had been predicted by European politicians, has strengthened with the progress of time . . . the mass of its population is better educated, and more elevated in its moral and intellectual character, than that of any other. If such is its political condition, is it possible that its progress can be retarded, or its aggrandizement curtailed, by the rising prosperity of Mexico? [29]

28. Poinsett to Clay, April 30, 1826, M97, R2, NA. Later Jackson actually did issue a proclamation forbidding any Indians to cross the Sabine River from the United States. Mooney, "Myths of the Cherokees," 143.

29. "Poinsett's Reply to the Remonstrances of the State of Mexico, 1829," *Niles Weekly Register*, XXXVII, 91–93, quoted in Stenberg, "American Imperialism in the Southwest," p. 167.

Surely this must rank as one of the more remarkable declamations in the history of American expansionism.

Hunter knew, of course, that by coming to the City of Mexico he had followed in the footsteps of Fields and others. He may have heard of Dr. James Long of Natchez, who had recently died there as a captive after trying, through an abortive alliance with the pirate Jean Lafitte, to set up a republic in Nacogdoches. Long had married the niece of James Wilkinson, and the notorious general, erstwhile associate of Aaron Burr and adversary of Manuel Lisa, had also died in the city, about the time Hunter set out from the Cherokee village, still dreaming of a vast western empire. In 1822 Wilkinson had become an adviser to Augustín de Iturbide, the former revolutionary and now Emperor Augustín I, and had urged the emperor to give him a great tract of land so he could transform Texas "from an asylum of pirates and assassins into beautiful settlements, according to modern taste and policy, inhabited by cultured Catholic people." [30]

When the stakes were good lands, the other American applicants who crowded into the capital in the 1820s demonstrated an equally ready versatility in religious and political convictions. Of them all, none was more versatile and successful than Stephen F. Austin, who had grown up as Hunter's neighbor, so to speak, in Missouri. After the death of his father, Moses Austin, the delicately built former clerk took up the family claim in Texas. When he arrived in Mexico, he assured Iturbide of his support and his earnest desire to become, despite his nominal republicanism, a citizen of the empire. When Iturbide dissolved the congress in 1822, Austin sympathized, for he knew the emperor "could not allow the nation to fall into anarchy." When Iturbide was deposed and banished shortly thereafter, Austin understood that too: he established a good working relationship with the new regime and emerged with a concession to establish a colony on the Brazos, a premium for himself of 65,000 acres, some of it on the Pedernales, and legislation which gave effective protection to slave holders in Texas. His biographer attributed these extraordinary acquisitions to Austin's understanding "of Mexican racial qualities." [31] And, though Austin had since returned to Texas to

30. In the fall of 1825 Wilkinson was advertising in Arkansas for "honest & well disposed" Americans to settle on his tract in Texas: *National Intelligencer,* September 7, 1825. His death in December brought his ventures to a close.

31. The biographical data come from Eugene C. Barker, *The Life of Stephen F. Austin, Founder of Texas, 1793–1836* (Nashville: Cokesbury Press, 1926), pp. 1–78.

establish his colony, another former neighbor was still in town in early 1826: Colonel Peter Ellis Bean, also a many-sided expatriate, who recorded Hunter's arrival in his journal.[32]

How Hunter spent his time waiting for word on his petition was not detailed in any of the surviving accounts. While staying in a small village on the outskirts of the city, Poinsett had written Clay that festival days were a round of "early mass and late orgies," with the afternoons and evenings passed in gambling and dancing. Hunter probably enjoyed little of this social life, though he may well have gone to some cockfights, for such was the national passion for the sport that otherwise elusive public figures could be found, along with everybody else, at the side of the cockpit. But Hunter was not in the city on holiday, and wherever he went he must have sought support for the Indian claim to land. And his movements were not unobserved: word got back to Texas that he spent a good deal of his time with General Wavell. James Kerr, a settler on the Rio Guadalupe and one of Austin's agents, later reported to his chief that "it is a well known fact that waval and Hunter were together in Mexico last winter and that Hunter said he was treated with more than ordinary politeness by said waval, and other Englishmen in Mexico." [33]

It was possible that Wavell and Hunter had met before they joined forces in 1826. After lending Austin money and securing his power of attorney to promote their projected company, Wavell sailed from Mexico in 1822. While still in the Gulf, however, pirates overtook his schooner, boarded it, and stripped him of his money and his even more precious documents. As Wavell wrote Austin at the time, "Fate has played me the most scurvy trick I ever yet suffered." Thereafter his voluminous correspondence with his associate—he repeatedly asked for authenticated copies of the stolen documents, while Austin simply ignored his letters—placed Wavell in London when Hunter was there and being made so much of.[34] And recall John Neal's charge that Hunter was ready at a day's notice to join a British officer in some "sort of scheme": it may have been Wavell whom Neal had in mind.

32. Yoakum, *Texas,* I, 237.
33. Kerr to Austin, January 24, 1827, "Austin Papers," 1592.
34. Wavell to Austin, September 10, 1822, "Austin Papers," 544–45; see also 527–29, 572–74, 576–80, *et passim.* Wavell first met Austin in 1822 when both were in the City of Mexico. They joined forces to establish a company for mining and agricultural purposes, but for some reason Austin backed out after Wavell lost his documents. In 1826 the latter finally empowered Colonel Benjamin R. Milam, whose grant Wavell shared, to collect the money Austin owed him.

One of Wavell's letters, preserved in the Foreign Office correspondence, sheds a little light on his relationship with Hunter. On August 20, 1826, Wavell wrote Sir Herbert Taylor seeking official support for his barrier colony. In the course of describing his project, he observed: "I here ought to mention that a person known to many respectable Gentlemen in this Country was lately sent to Mexico by the Chiefs of several Indian tribes . . . in order to solicit for them permission to occupy some of the vacant lands in Texas." This person had come to him for assistance and, after making the kind of stipulations set forth in Hunter's petition, had secured his support: "The President [Victoria] and other persons of the greatest influence with whom we conferred on the subject, were induced to view the proposal in a favourable light." [35] The letter revealed no plot, but merely that Wavell and Hunter were following the course mapped out by Ward. And, though Wavell had obviously overestimated the effectiveness of their conferences with Mexicans "of the greatest influence," he did go on to note that the inhabitants' dread of Indian tribes was such "that a most serious opposition is to be anticipated."

On his trip back to England, Wavell traveled through Texas "and proceeded to the establishment of the Chief of the Cherokees, where the Chiefs of all the tribes were at that period to assemble in order that I might be able to ascertain the real state of those tribes in point of character, habits and civilisation, previously to any arrangement being made for their admission to the lands from the San Saba mountains to the Rivers Red and Arkansas." He had "of late paid much attention to the subject," and his investigations had persuaded him that if Mexico would only take advantage of this opportunity to defeat American schemes, from "30 to possibly 70,000 souls" could be settled on the frontier, "with possibly 10,000 incomparably brave Indian Warriors." He reportedly passed through Nacogdoches and informed Benjamin W. Edwards, brother of the *empresario,* "that *Capt. Hunter,* the Indian agent, appointed by the government for that purpose would be here, about this time, to form treaties with all those tribes for the security of the country." [36]

"About this time" was July 1826, and seemingly Hunter had not yet

35. Wavell to Sir Herbert Taylor, August 20, 1826, FO 50/30, PRO. Lieutenant General Taylor was soon to become Wellington's military secretary and the king's principal aide-de-camp.

36. Edwards to Austin, July 21, 1826, "Austin Papers," 1384–85. References to Hunter as "Captain" or "Dr." had little significance beyond illustrating that from the beginning Texans had a penchant for honorific titles.

returned from his trip. The exact date of his return remains unknown, but he had almost certainly come back "before the end of May," as Ward had reported, "in order to be present at another great council." Ward later related that "Hunter left Mexico without having received any positive answer to his demands; and it is said that, in order to clear himself from the imputation of bad faith before the great council held upon his return, he advised the Indians to cross the frontier, and to occupy the lands, the cession of which they had solicited in vain." Wavell was very likely Ward's informant: he had probably accompanied Hunter back to Texas, was present at the council to judge the feasibility of an attempt to settle Indians on the frontier, and hence was in a position to report on what had happened.[37]

Other evidence on the council is disappointingly sketchy. Fields and Hunter addressed the assembled warriors from a score of tribes. The temper of Fields's remarks may be inferred from what he said a little later in Nacogdoches. This was the speech in which he declared he had spent everything he had in trying to settle the red people and had then sold his stock to send Hunter to the City of Mexico:

> When he got thare he staited his mision to government they said that they New nothing of this Richard fields and treated him with contampt—I am a Red man and aman of onor and cant be emposid on this way we will lift up our tomahauks and fight for land with all those friendly tribes that wishis land also if I am Beaton I then will Resign to fait and if not I will hold lands By the forse of my Red Warriors—[38]

According to Henry Stuart Foote, the pioneer historian of Texas, Hunter spoke to the Indians with "inflammatory eloquence." He had returned

> full of grief and indignation at the cruel treachery which he conceived to have been practised towards Fields, and, through him, upon the Cherokees, and other Indian tribes in alliance with them. These sentiments he announced in full Council, and depictured in strong and glowing language, the gloomy alternative, now plainly presented to the

37. Ward, *Mexico in 1827*, II, 588. After the council Wavell probably proceeded alone to Nacogdoches, where he met B. W. Edwards and spoke to him about the impending arrival of the new "Indian agent."
38. As reported by Peter Ellis Bean to Austin, December 31, 1826, "Austin Papers," 1554.

Indians, of abandoning their present abodes and returning within the limits of the United States—or preparing to defend themselves against the whole power of the Mexican Government by force of arms. The fierce multitude of savage warriors who listened to him, were not long in determining in favour of energetic measures.

Though Foote had not heard the speech and was obviously attempting to put it together from various unnamed sources, his reconstruction for the most part rings true: Hunter must have delivered some such remarks to the Cherokees and their allies.[39]

Sorely missed here, as elsewhere, are Hunter's own words, his discussion of what he thought and how he felt to be bringing back his joyless tidings. Beyond question he had caught a glimpse of his dream in Texas, only to have it disappear behind the persistent refusal to grant the Indians land. Rather than carrying hope to the Indians, he had merely come to share their rising despair. And he well knew that they were no more willing to vanish than were Poinsett and his white countrymen. But was he aware of the similarity in tone and outlook between his speech now at the great council and Tecumseh's speech to the Osages when he was a boy? Had he given up completely on Owen's notion of revolution through benevolence?

Lacking his indispensable answers, we can at least turn to one of Foote's sources for a sense of the intensity of Hunter's feelings about the Indian predicament. In 1827 Herman B. Mayo, a newspaper editor then living in Nacogdoches, wrote a vindicatory article on the white savage. Before they met Mayo had known of his narrative and of the charge "which had so suddenly blighted his fresh fame." Still, little expecting to meet the author in the wilds of Texas, "his countenance and demeanour, before I knew who he was, drew my attention." Mayo pretended to no unusual talent for judging character from external appearance, but "was aware, notwithstanding the plainness of his dress, and the simplicity of his manners, that I was in the society of a highly intelligent man and a gentleman":

His countenance, though far from handsome, was very expressive. The strong lines of a marked character were there, indicating the powerful

39. Foote, *Texas*, I, 248. Foote wrote in 1841 and had at his disposal a manuscript prepared by B. W. Edwards, along with the recollections of others who had lived through the happenings in Nacogdoches fifteen years earlier.

feelings and the glowing enthusiasm that belonged to the man. His manners were, in general, quiet, grave and gentlemanly; but they would burst out into singular vivacity, when his feelings were raised, and then, at times, his high excitement would render him masterless of himself, and, while it made him eloquent in gesticulation, frequently deprived him of all command over words. Any discussion relative to the situation and character of the Indians would rouse the level calm of his ordinary manner into a storm that agitated his entire soul.

Mayo was not ready to believe him an impostor. In the following months the time they spent together led the editor to conclude that Hunter had certainly been long with the Indians: "I went with him last summer to the Cherokee village," he related, "and while there, was informed, by some of that tribe, of a Nottoway Chief who well knew Hunter in his early life, when he lived with that or some neighbouring tribe, and whose account, as far as I learned it, and as my memory now serves, corroborates his own narrative."

During this summer of 1826, however, Hunter was preoccupied with more serious matters. While he had been away in Mexico, Fields had encouraged Indian immigration and at one point had reported to the authorities "that about eight thousand souls of different tribes have crossed the Red River." [40] These and others came into Texas in such numbers as to constitute a large increase in the Indian population. "Bearing in mind Hunter's plan for making an Indian country," explained the historian of the Texas Cherokees, Ernest William Winkler, "it seems that the emigration of those Indians is in line to fulfill that plan; an effort on the part of Fields to furnish the Indians for the lands that Hunter had undertaken to secure." This was close to the mark but left out the probability that Hunter had himself taken a hand in persuading Indians to cross the border. Shortly after his return, in any event, Mexican officials learned "that twelve tribes, four of them large ones, were about to emigrate to Texas."

Fields and Hunter assuredly could draw on a large and growing reservoir of Indian discontent north of the border. As Dr. John Sibley of Natchitoches wrote Austin, "our Gov. is placing above us On the Waters of Red River and Arkansa more than fifty thousand Indians of different and discordant Tribes I do not like the Policy, not for the reason only, that it will hasten their extinction. The Caddos and Quapas,

40. Fields to Political Chief, March 20, 1826, quoted in Winkler, "Cherokee Indians," 130.

are going to settle above you On the same River.—They will be peacable, but unprofitable Neighbours." [41] The chances are good that Hunter traveled north to counsel these Quapaws and other tribes to sidestep extinction by coming to take a stand with their red brothers in Texas. And this probability would account for his activities after his return.

By autumn, however, the growing bitterness and frustration of all these displaced persons had become explosive. According to Foote, the Indians wanted to commence hostilities upon the colonists in Edwards' grant nearby:

> At this crisis, the attitude of Hunter became one of great and painful responsibility: if he ventured to dissuade his tawny associates from this terrible project before their ardour had a little moderated, it was obvious that he must, in a great degree, forfeit their confidence, if he did not draw down their vengeance upon himself; if he coincided in the plan of attack suggested, he must soon witness scenes of devastation and bloodshed which would fill his soul with horror, and render him for ever miserable. Under such circumstances, he adopted a middle course, acquiescing in the proposition of war, but urging the expediency of suspending hostile movements for a week or two, until he could have an opportunity of visiting Nacogdoches, and ascertaining the exact condition of the colony.[42]

The time had clearly passed for falling at the feet of the authorities and humbly begging for land. The need for "energetic measures" was at hand, perhaps even for lifting up the tomahawk. But first Hunter had a few days to scout out the situation in Nacogdoches.

41. Sibley to Austin, September 15, 1826, "Austin Papers," 1456.
42. Foote, *Texas,* I, 248–49.

The Red and White
Republic of Fredonia

9

Accounts have been received from Texas of an insurrection. . . . A half-breed by the name of Fields, a man
by the name of Edwards, to whom the Legislature of
Texas granted a large tract of land, and John Hunter of
notorious memory, are the ring-leaders. They have made
Nacogdoches their Head Quarters—have hoisted a red
and white banner, indicative of the union of the whites
and Indians—and declared that district of the country
as far as the Rio Bravo del Norte independent.

JOEL R. POINSETT
to Henry Clay, February 21, 1827

Nacogdoches lay about fifty miles from the Cherokee village on the
wrong side of the frontier that separated Progress from the rest of the
world. Behind it loomed the West, the Far West, the Wild West, the
meeting place of savagery and civilization. But so much for geographic
reality; in epic truth, it floated in mythological time and space, waiting
for a call into history by Davy Crockett on his way to the Alamo, Wild
Bill Hickok going to take over as marshal in Abilene, Judge Roy Bean
sitting to dispense his law west of the Pecos, Jesse Chisholm riding to
herd his longhorns north into immortality, and for Lyndon Baines Johnson to bring this tradition of strong, hard men down to our own time. It
lay waiting on the far side of the thousand and one Westerns which have
brought it down to our own time. It was fair game for all the dime
novelists, pulp, script, and scenario writers to come, and for the con-
trivers of heroic fictions like Colonel Frank Triplett, whose *Conquering
the Wilderness* was to celebrate in "Picturesque Sketches of Border Life
. . . the Romantic Deeds, Lofty Achievements and Marvelous Adventures"
of Peter Ellis Bean, Jean Lafitte, and a host of other desperadoes, scouts,
and Indian-fighters. Later still the outpost could be regarded by a professional historian, who served on the faculty of the great university

located in Austin, as part of a glorious chapter in the Westward Movement of the Anglo-American People.[1]

Nacogdoches really existed, nevertheless, and had since 1716 when it was established as a barrier against the French. When Peter Ellis Bean and what was left of his party were locked in the Old Stone Fort in 1801 —after having entered Texas, so they claimed, "to engage in the capture of Mustang horses"—the Spanish town was the quiet center of a district inhabited by almost a thousand persons. A few years later, however, the irregular fighting and upheavals of the Mexican Revolution commenced and eventually drove everyone out. After 1821 the old settlers returned and were joined by new neighbors, swarms of American squatters who moved in after hearing the exciting news of the land grant to Moses Austin. One estimate put the population of the district at 1600 by the mid-1820s.[2] Near the border, the town made an easy stopping-off place for drifters, runaways, rootless persons of all nations. Near the principal route for taking stolen horses and mules from Texas to the United States, it also made a convenient meeting place for gamblers, smugglers, thieves, and outlaws. It was infested, that is, by the kind of men the historian Theodore Roosevelt would call scoundrels, notorious bullies, and ruffians. The supply of badmen was more than sufficient to engage the best efforts of a score of posses, had they been called out.

Haden Edwards had the misfortune of having Nacogdoches included in his grant. Said to be "a wealthy and intelligent gentleman from Kentucky," Edwards had recently spent three years in the City of Mexico waiting for his concession and naturally wanted to clear up the question of land titles as quickly as possible.[3] No doubt he proceeded without full realization that his demands for proof of ownership would sound like eviction notices to the old Spanish settlers and squatters, since most of them had no title whatsoever to the land they occupied. There followed an involved, prolonged, and increasingly bitter conflict between Edwards and his supporters and an opposition of squatters and old settlers. The latter were led by Samuel Norris, who succeeded in becoming *alcalde*

1. Colonel Frank Triplett, *Conquering the Wilderness* (New York: N. D. Thompson, 1883); Eugene C. Barker, *The Life of Stephen F. Austin, Founder of Texas, 1793–1836: A Chapter in the Westward Movement of the Anglo-American People* (Nashville: Cokesbury Press, 1926).

2. Lester G. Bugbee, "The Texas Frontier," *Publications of the Southern History Association,* IV (March 1900), 102–21.

3. H. Yoakum, *History of Texas* (New York: Redfield, 1856), I, 215; Homer S. Thrall, *A Pictorial History of Texas* (St. Louis: N. D. Thompson, 1879), pp. 158–62.

(mayor) after a contested election, and his brother-in-law James Gaines, who commanded a local band of Regulators. Fearful of secession, government officials understandably threw their support behind this so-called Mexican party.

Norris and Gaines domineered over and harassed their opponents. Charges were brought against Edwards; rumors were circulated that his grant had been canceled; and discriminatory treatment was meted out to individuals. Moved to indignation by all this, an earlier generation of American historians tended to see the Mexican party as the sole repository of evil. "The shamelessness of Norris—who was, however, controlled by James Gaines," wrote Hubert Howe Bancroft, "was such that these abominable claims were sanctioned by him. A reign of terror followed. American settlers were dispossessed of their homes; were arrested at midnight and dragged before the alcalde to be punished for acts they had never committed; they were fined and imprisoned; and every contumely and vexation that envy and malice could suggest were heaped upon them." [4] Edwards' colonists saw themselves as Bancroft saw them, as embodying the national love of freedom and hatred of oppression. From this point of view, they had exercised remarkable self-restraint in the face of unspeakable outrages.

Yet by the late autumn of 1826 their patience had worn thin. On November 22 a man named Martin Parmer rode into Nacogdoches at the head of thirty-six armed Americans. They arrested the *alcalde,* seized his archives, arrested José Antonio Sepúlveda, the court clerk, and proclaimed a reward of one hundred dollars for James Gaines, "dead or alive." In the official record of their proceedings they explained that when they had emigrated "from their native land, the birthplace of freedom," they carried with them

> the republican ideas which had been instilled into them by their fathers in their own native country. But disdaining to submit any longer to the oppression which has ground them to the dust they now resolve to investigate the causes that have led to these lamentable results, and to punish with exemplary justice their authors, after an impartial and deliberate trial.[5]

4. Bancroft, *History of the North American States and Texas* (San Francisco: History Publishers, 1889), II, 102.
5. From "Minutes of the Court Martial, 23–25 November 1826," reproduced in Eugene C. Barker, ed., "The Austin Papers," *Annual Report for the American Historical Association for the Year 1919,* II (Washington: GPO, 1924), 1511–23; hereafter "Austin Papers."

The prisoners could scarcely have been reassured by such impartiality, or by the charges against them. Among the lighter counts was one against Norris for "imprisoning Leonard Dubois for thirty days for ironically calling Hosea Sepulver an honest man" and one against the latter, Sepúlveda, for "possessing a general character of notorious infamy." Though the men were convicted on these and other charges, ranging from treachery to the people to corruption and forgery, Parmer and his officers unexpectedly demonstrated a capacity to temper justice with mercy. After taking into account Norris' ignorance and "the influence of infamous advisers over him" and figuring in Sepúlveda's general roguery, they found them both "worthy of death" but merely sentenced them to be removed from office and forever barred from holding any position of public trust. They declared Joseph Durst temporary *alcalde* until the people could make a new selection, liberated those imprisoned, and disbanded.

There is good reason to believe that Hunter knew something of the rebellious mood of the Americans before he came to town, for his friend Herman Mayo played a prominent part in the court-martial. Mayo, who had all the makings of a frontier humorist of genius, kept the minutes of the proceedings and was no doubt largely responsible for the parody of legal forms and the straight-faced extravagancies—at the first session he simply listed himself as "Clerk," but by the second day he was "Judge Advocate" and by the third he had risen still farther to "Maj. H. B. Mayo, Judge Advocate." Chief Justice Mayo would have wanted to get word to Hunter.

Yet Hunter probably received the news directly from a man named John Basset, with whom he worked. According to James Kerr, Austin's agent, both men "say they are cherokees by adoption." Observing their friendly association, Kerr rashly concluded: "I have seen Hunter and Basset together and I believe them to be brothers." [6] As an Indian trader, Basset had been forced to obtain a license from Norris, meet demands that he get a new one, and then suffer being fined for noncompliance. Basset reacted angrily, going to Nacogdoches "and taking Dr. Hunter with him entered the house of the prisoner [Norris], and demanded some papers of his in the possession of the prisoner [—] having a very unfavorable impression of the prisoner he thought it prudent to go armed with a pistol for his own Security, but [it] was neither cocked, nor presented, nor used in any hostile manner." Basset's testimony showed that Hunter

6. Kerr to Austin, January 24, 1827, "Austin Papers," 1591.

had some firsthand knowledge of the state of affairs at Nacogdoches and would be promptly informed of these most recent developments when Basset returned to the Indians.

When Hunter did arrive in town, however fully forewarned, he kept his own counsel for a day or two till he could get some sense of things. At length he determined to see the brothers Haden and Benjamin Edwards "and to lay before them a proposition for the formation of *a league offensive and defensive* against the Mexican government." He found them friendly and willing to talk, listened to their grievances, and ventured "by degrees to unfold the object of his visit. He painted to his new acquaintances the exposed condition of the colonists . . . and urged them, in terms replete with affection and reason, to unite with the Indian tribes under the control of himself and Fields, in a war against the common enemy." Amid rumors of a government force marching on Nacogdoches, the Edwards brothers and Hunter worked out the preliminaries of their compact. Hunter returned to the Cherokee village to get sanction for the alliance and to bring back as large a body of warriors as he could "to unite with the colonists in the measures of defence now become necessary." [7]

On December 15, as he returned from a rapid trip to rouse the outlying settlements to resistance, Benjamin Edwards paused to devise a suitable flag: it had two vertical stripes, red and white, symbolizing the union of Indians and colonists, and upon it the words "Independence, Freedom and Justice." [8] The Fredonian Republic was proclaimed the following day.

Hunter returned to Nacogdoches on December 20, accompanied by Richard Fields and other Indians, ready to settle on the terms of the alliance. They joined the settlers in a general council, at which Benjamin Edwards and Mayo were appointed as "Agents of the Committee of Independence" and Fields and Hunter as "Agents of the Red People." These representatives, or "commissioners," as they were called, were given responsibility for drafting a "Declaration of Independence." [9]

7. Henry Stuart Foote, *Texas and the Texans* (Philadelphia: Thomas Cowperthwait, 1841), I, 249, 250.

8. Affidavit of John C. Morrison, "Austin Papers," 1575; Ernest William Winkler, "The Cherokee Indians in Texas," *Texas State Historical Association Quarterly*, VII (October 1903), 139.

9. Foote, *Texas*, I, 253. Ward enclosed a copy of the "Declaration of Independence" in a dispatch to Canning, February 21, 1827, FO 50/31b, No. 34, PRO; it was called the "Treaty of Alliance" in the Natchitoches *Courier*, January 16, 1827.

A most unusual moment in Western history: How many times, before or since, have settlers and natives come together in the realization that liberation for one depended on liberation for both?

2

Anthropology and history, the primitive and the modern, came together in the committee of four. Fields and Hunter, the former more completely than the latter, spoke out of a context of savage thought, "of thought which quite genuinely takes the words it uses seriously," as anthropologist Claude Lévi-Strauss notes, and which was grounded in the primary values of individual freedom and warm communal bonds, whereas Edwards and Mayo carried in their baggage all the complexities of "civilized" expression: "In comparable circumstances we only 'play' on words," Lévi-Strauss observes.[10] Consider the following illustration: in his speech in Nacogdoches, delivered at this time (quoted on pages 183 and 196), Richard Fields stated, with closely entwined thought and emotion, that he had gone to the City of Mexico for lands "to setel a Poor orfan tribe of Red Peopel that looked up to me for Protasion" and had been "Promisid lands for them after staying one year in Mexico and spending all I had. . . . I am a Red man and aman of onor and cant be emposid on this way." In the language of Edwards and Mayo, the emotion was not, as in Fields's plea, integral with the thought; in their document they spoke of the pattern of "repeated insults, treachery and oppression" suffered by "the White and Red emigrants from the United States of North America, now living in the Province of Texas, within the territory of the said Government, into which they have been deluded by promises solemnly made, and most basely broken." Still, though this windy rhetoric made any organic relationship of thought and emotion chancy at best, the Enlightenment tradition out of which they spoke had always been potentially open, as Robert Owen demonstrated, to a union with savage thought. The emphasis on natural law and natural rights presupposed all along an aborigine, a natural man, who was subject to this law and who shared these rights with all other human beings. Jefferson's great Declaration promised this universalism by holding that all men were created equal and then promptly denied the promise by

10. Claude Lévi-Strauss, *The Savage Mind* (University of Chicago Press, 1966), p. 265.

tacitly inserting the word "white" before "men." In inception the Fredonian Declaration denied that denial by explicitly recognizing that red men too had "unalienable rights" and could not "be emposid on this way."

Like the model on which it drew, the finished document showed a decent respect for the opinions of mankind by outlining the injustices which had reduced them "to the dreadful alternative of either submitting their free-born necks to the yoke of an imbecile, faithless, and despotic government, miscalled a Republic; or of taking up arms in defence of their unalienable rights and asserting their Independence." "The White and Red emigrants" chose to espouse "the same Holy Cause"; to bring it to a successful conclusion they bound "themselves by the ligaments of reciprocal interests and obligations" through "a Treaty of Union, League and Confederation." The committee then agreed upon seven articles, three of which undertook to implement the confederation, defend their mutual independence of Mexico, and establish reciprocity of rights for Indians and colonists in their respective territories. The substance of their agreement on the crucial question of lands, dealt with in the other four articles, divided Texas by a line running east to the Sabine and west to the Rio Grande from a point near Nacogdoches, with all the area north of the line to belong to the Indians and all south of it to the colonists. The entire document was then submitted to the general council and ratified on December 21, 1826. Rather than fifty-five signers there were only thirteen, but they included Ne-ko-lake, John Bags, and Cuk-to-keh, names just as impressive as John Hancock's and certainly more unusual in American politics.

At last the Indian country was on paper. Now Hunter and Fields returned to get the approval of the tribes they represented and to gather those who would work to make it Indian country in fact. Back in the villages, however, they ran into obstacles. Though the season was well advanced, a number of the principal warriors were still away on hunting trips. More serious was the old problem which had vexed Indian leaders from Metacom to Tecumseh: if one of the delights of North American Indian life was the absence of empires with coercive centers, the consequent independence and diversity made concerted intertribal action, even against a common foe, most difficult. Events proved that the Cherokees' loose confederation, however creative a response in itself to the problem of political power, had by no means overcome tendencies toward separatism.

The Kickapoos provided a case in point. The Texas band numbered about eight hundred and included some of the strongest and most able of all the warriors. But they had been so alienated by their experiences with Americans—the tribe had been part of the inner circle of Pontiac's "conspiracy" and a mainstay of Tecumseh's movement—that they rejected "any friendly arrangement with the colonists: they cherished sentiments of deadly hostility towards the whole white population, on account of injuries, either real or imaginary, alleged to have been experienced by them during the last war between Great Britain and the United States." [11] Spending precious time in a fruitless effort to persuade this left wing, so to speak, to accept the wisdom of an alliance with whites, Hunter must have felt he had come full circle: as you will recall, he commenced his Indian life as a captive of the Kickapoos or an allied band.

Moreover, even at the tribal level concerted action depended upon the acceptance and support of individuals. In a strict sense, every Indian "army" was volunteer. The absence of rulers, the disdain for superiors, and the impatience with restraints made these tribes resemble the pastoral Nuer of the Sudan, said by E. E. Evans-Pritchard to be organized along lines of "ordered anarchy." [12] Fields and Hunter thus had to do more than win over the weight of opinion at the councils: if they wanted united action, they had to cultivate and convince individuals, including women, whose opinion often carried very considerable weight.

The two revolutionists almost certainly ran into serious opposition among the Cherokees themselves. The names of Big Mush and The Bowl, the peace and war chiefs, respectively, were significantly missing from the roster of those who signed the Fredonian Declaration. Under these circumstances Fields and Hunter decided it was prudent for the former to remain in the villages another week or two. In the last days of December Hunter rode back into Nacogdoches "at the head of thirty chosen warriors." They found their playful white allies in a state of considerable disarray.

Martin Parmer had left his troops alone for a few hours while he made a necessary trip out of town. In his absence they had promptly drunk themselves into an angry quarrel or, as Foote more elegantly put it, they had laid themselves open to the influence of "*Bacchus*, that mischief-loving god, who in all ages has been the arch-promoter of disorder."

11. Foote, *Texas*, I, 256; see also A. M. Gibson, *The Kickapoos* (Norman: University of Oklahoma Press, 1963), pp. 146–48.
12. For Evans-Pritchard's discussion of "ordered anarchy," see *The Nuer* (London: Oxford University Press, 1940), pp. 181–82.

However put, as Hunter and his men reined up at the Old Stone Fort they found themselves in the midst of a drunken brawl:

> When the ferment was allayed, which in truth was the case upon the return of the officer in command, it was found that nearly half of the Cherokee warriors had disappeared, and were then on their way back to the village; upon arriving at which, it may be conjectured, they made a report of what they had witnessed calculated greatly to impede the operations of Fields, and to sustain the Kickapoos in the stand they had taken.[13]

It may not be conjectured safely what Hunter's thoughts were at this moment. Given the intensity of his feelings about the Indians, he probably could not have articulated them anyway.

Both sides of the red and white alliance obviously had an urgent need for additional support. Hunter could hope that Fields would succeed in pulling the Cherokees and at least some of their allies into the campaign for independence. He counted on the tribes which he represented and which were still in the United States to cross the border and, if they arrived in time, to join in the fighting.[14] And, one of Austin's agents reported, Hunter let it be known that he counted on support from other sources as well:

> I was informed by some of the out Laws while at Nachadoches that he Hunter had said, his great dependence, and hopes for assistance to revolutionize the department of Texas was on the British; that he expected in less than four months to be reinforced by 500 englishmen who would land at the mouth of the Brassos under the command of said Waval [General Wavell]; that a Doctor *Somebody* who spoke french, english, and spanish was then in the interior as a spy. that Hunter would act on the frontiers; stimulating to action our red Brethern, while the Brittish would land on the Coast and over power all opposition.[15]

13. Foote, *Texas*, I, 257.
14. Ward to Canning, March 31, 1827, FO 50/31b, No. 49, PRO, referred to the factor of "Time for Hunter's Indians to cross the Frontier, and join Field[s], Edwards and the other Chiefs of the soi-disant Republic of Freedonia."
15. Kerr to Austin, January 24, 1827, "Austin Papers," 1591. Hunter's former friend Robert Walsh showed that the suspicion Hunter was working for or with the English soon reached the United States. "It has been suspected," he wrote, "that his plan either of an Indian or of a white independent government had met with some sanction from the British Ministry; we have however, never seen any evidence of their connexion or acquaintance with it"—"Tanner's Indian Narrative," *American Quarterly Review*, VIII (September 1830), 115.

A formidable international undertaking: if Hunter called it up for the imaginations of his hearers, he did so to frighten the government party. He knew very well that he could count on no support from the British so long as he was allied with American colonists, the very people they wanted out of Texas. As an act of psychological warfare, however, it seems to have reached its target. Early in January, José Antonio Saucedo, the political chief of Texas, said of Hunter: "everyone is persuaded he is an emissary of some European cabinet"; Mateo Ahumada, the military chief, was more specific: "everyone is suspicious of the English Dr. John Hunter." [16]

On their side Benjamin Edwards and Mayo worked to enlist assistance from other colonies and from across the frontier. They dispatched Joseph A. Huber, one of the signers of the Declaration, to raise a force in the United States among the frontiersmen ready to fight oppression at a moment's notice. As the Committee of Correspondence, they also put their case before other colonists, especially those in Austin's key settlement, with a bombardment of letters designed to rally Americans to "this glorious cause with a determination to be freemen or to perish under the flag of liberty." The day after Christmas, for example, Edwards wrote to Captain Aylett C. Buckner at Austin's colony that "the flag of *liberty* now waves in majestic triumph on the heights of Nacogdoches, and despotism stands appalled at the sight." Subject to a perfidious government, they had made a compact with the Indians:

> The treaty was signed by Doctr John D Hunter and Richard Fields as the Representatives of the United Nations of Indians, comprising twenty three tribes—They are now our decided friends, and by compact as well as interest are bound to aid us in effecting the *Independence* of this country.

He was confident that the members of Austin's colony were true Americans, the sons of freemen: "To arms then, our countrymen, and let us no longer submit to the caprice, the treachery, and oppression of such a government as this!—Our friends in the United States are already in arms, and only waiting for the word." [17] Edwards was himself more than a little capricious about the essential distinction between what had hap-

16. Quoted in Winkler, "Cherokee Indians," 139n.
17. "Austin Papers," 1545, 1546–48.

pened and what he wanted to have happen; his call to arms may have been good rhetoric, but it did not meet with the actuality.

The relatively few revolutionists actually under arms soon had occasion to use them. Seeking revenge and an end to the rebellion, Samuel Norris, the deposed *alcalde,* raised a force of ten or twelve Americans and fifty or so Mexicans.[18] On January 4, 1827, Norris received word that not more than fifteen Fredonians were presently in Nacogdoches. Vowing to hang them all, according to Foote, he moved his men into town, "on horseback, with a drum beating, and the National Standard of the Mexican Republic unfurled." Eleven Fredonians, who "scorned to take shelter behind their fortifications" at the Old Stone Fort, took up positions

> in front of the Liberty pole which had been there planted. Being joined, at the instant, by Hunter and eight of his Cherokee warriors, they impetuously rushed upon the enemy with fierce shouts, and, in three minutes, put the Alcalde and his myrmidons to rapid flight. The Fredonians had one of their number only wounded slightly in this encounter; whilst the Mexicans left one man dead upon the ground of conflict, and ten or twelve others wounded in such a manner as to be incapacitated for joining in the retreat. Twenty or thirty of their mules and horses were likewise captured; and even "the spirit-stirring drum," under the inspiration of which they had so pompously challenged the strife of arms, was found too unwieldy to be borne off in such hasty flight as they resorted to, and fell into the hands of the Cherokee warriors; who seized upon it with eagerness, and reserved it as a special trophy of victory.

Were this a Hollywood Western, a fade-out would now be appropriate: the Cherokee warriors would be left standing there, rejoicing on the field of battle not less "than would the Romans of old have done over the earning of *Spolia opima.*" They had earned the victory and the trophy. As a symbol and a portent, however, the drum was a bit overdone. With its resonant inner void, it represented the only tangible gain in store for Hunter and his United Nations of Indians.

18. Foote, *Texas,* I, 258–59; *National Gazette,* February 16, 1827; "Austin Papers," 1576.

3

The Fredonian Committee of Correspondence had no monopoly on the ability to use the language of 1776. Listen to Stephen F. Austin rouse his colonists:

> To arms fellow countrymen! to arms in the cause of liberty, of virtue and justice! to arms in defence of your property, your families, and your honor! to arms in defence of your adopted government; and, hurl back the thunder upon the heads of those base and degraded apostates from the names of Americans, who have dared to invite you by a threatening invitation to join their mad and criminal schemes.[19]

Out of these thunderclaps all the key words came splashing down: Liberty, Justice, Honor, and not least, Property. But beneath the grandiosity was a bedrock fact: Austin did not approve of the course set by the Fredonians.

For a number of reasons which seemed to him compelling, he rejected their confident appeals for aid and instead threw the full weight of his influence against them. A careful, calculating man, notwithstanding oratorical squalls like the one above, he was primarily an administrator concerned with his concession. Rebellion menaced his project and his property: to his mind, the Fredonians were "jeopardising the prospects of hundreds of innocent families who wish to live in peace and quietness in the country." He was especially concerned to protect those colonists who had brought their slaves into Texas. He lobbied and petitioned in behalf of the South's "peculiar institution" and resented the fact that these efforts were endangered by the uprising: "The slave question is now pending in the legislature," he declared angrily, "the constitution now forming. What influence are acts of this outrageous character calculated to have on the minds of the members and on the decision of the slave or any other question involving the interests and prosperity of the new Settlements?"[20]

In style Austin was a pragmatist. "The Mexicans love indirection," asserted his biographer, "and Austin made himself a master of the

19. Natchitoches *Courier*, February 20, 1827.
20. Austin to John A. Williams and B. J. Thompson, December 14, 1826, "Austin Papers," 1532–33; Bancroft, *North American States and Texas*, II, 107; Natchitoches *Courier*, February 20, 1827.

oblique approach." It would be a mistake, however, to regard him as a mere opportunist. His reverence for authority was quite genuine and catholic—it extended, as we have seen, even to the Emperor Augustín de Iturbide. Evil for him was not defined as the oppression, hurting, or killing of other men; it consisted quintessentially in the rejection of authority. Authority was to be revered; rebellion was hateful in equal measure. He was in principle opposed to the Fredonians, therefore, and spoke out of his deepest beliefs when he declared that there were in Nacogdoches "some bad and rebellious men who must be expelled from the Country": to his mind "bad" and "rebellious" were synonyms. It seemed to him quite literally crazy for individuals to reject the supports that kept his world from sinking. As he remonstrated with a former acquaintance for joining the revolt, this "mad business" was totally wrong: "No individuals have or ought to have the power of taking into their hands the authority vested by law in the competent tribunals, for this principle strikes at the root of all Govt and opens the door for anarchy and a Govt of mobs instead of a Govt of laws."

Like so many of his contemporaries, men such as Cass, Neal, and Poinsett, Austin practiced a civil religion based on the sacred authority of government: "For without Government, without law," he rhetorically asked, "what security have we for our persons, our property, our characters, and all that we hold dear and sacred? None, for we at once embark on the stormy ocean of anarchy, subject to be stripped by every wave of faction that rolls along, and must finally sink into the gulf of ruin and infamy." [21] It followed that it was "our duty as *men*, to suppress vice, anarchy and Indian Massacre." The three evils were not accidentally linked. Lacking government, the Indians were not *men*. They were and had been forever sunk in ruin and infamy or were ungoverned children of nature, which came to the same thing.

Upon establishing his colony, Austin had grimly set about clearing out the "natives of the forest" with the determination of a farmer clearing his field of stones. On one occasion, for example, when some Coaques captured and skinned a calf, Austin commenced a campaign of extermination. His men killed five members of the tribe in retaliation. "His colonists," claimed his biographer, "had taught the Indians the first lessons of respect for the white man." The fact that the Fredonian revolt had been staged by a red and white alliance, then, was precisely what most horrified him. His hatred of rebellion was so intensified by his

21. Barker, *Austin*, p. 448; "Austin Papers," 1528, 1539, 1558–59.

racism as to make of his words a torrent: "Great God," he exclaimed, "can it be possible that Americans, high minded free born and honorable Americans will so far forget the country of their birth, so far forget themselves, as to league with barbarians and join a band of savages in a war of murder, massacre and desolation?" [22]

With unfeigned enthusiasm Austin joined the Mexican authorities in preparing to move against the insurgents. While Saucedo and Colonel Ahumada camped at San Felipe de Austin with over a hundred infantry and fifty cavalry, Austin raised a force of several hundred militia to march with them. Before they set out, however, Saucedo and Ahumada wrote Fields, and Austin wrote Hunter, in an effort to break them off from the alliance.

Austin's long letter to Hunter summarized his reasons for opposing the Fredonian Republic and at the same time laid bare with surprising directness the roots of the American response to people of color.[23] He began with the assumption that Hunter's only object was to get lands for the Cherokees, since to suppose his intent was rebellion "would be to suppose you destitute of that intelligence integrity and judgement which you have always manifested on all occasions so far as I have heard of you." Hunter had evidently met Austin on his way to or from the City of Mexico, for Austin went on to observe that "when you was here I expressed myself fully as to the cherokees and unequivocally stated that I was a friend of those Indians and would take an interest in their affairs, so far as my duty to this Government would permit." The reason the Indians had no title to their lands flowed from the usual delays of governmental business and not from a refusal to comply with promises. "If you are the man of talents I believe you to be and are actuated by the benevolent feelings toward the cherokees which you profess, you will see that the favorable moment in the tide of their affairs has arrived." If he brought the Cherokees in to confer immediately, Austin had "no doubt [the Government] will be willing to give them a title to lands at that place." If he did not and the Indians persisted in their rebellion, the government would be satisfied with "*nothing short of extermination or expulsion.*"

"My Dr. Sir, let us examine this subject calmly," Austin proposed, "let us suppose that the Indians over run the whole country and take possession of it for the present as far as the Rio Grande and drive out or

22. Barker, *Austin,* pp. 104, 148; "Austin Papers," 1539.
23. Austin to Hunter, January 4, 1827, "Austin Papers," 1564–68.

massacre all the honest inhabitants. What will they gain?" The Indians
would soon be fighting among themselves, he explained, for they could
not establish *government*: "You know the Indians well enough to know
that so many different tribes of different habits and languages cannot be
organised into any thing like regular government, or government of any
kind, and could not long agree amongst themselves." Hunter's plan to
establish an Indian country was folly, for nothing but confusion and
massacre would be the consequence. But say the Indians did get possession, how would they maintain it?

> The mexican Nation *has* force to subdue you, and even admitting they
> had not, she can procure it from the United States of the North, for
> both nations would unite in crushing a common enemy to both, and
> anihilating so dangerous and troublesome a neighbor as a large com-
> bination of Indians would be—but admitting the Govt. of the United
> States would not furnish troops and this Govt. could not subdue the
> country—*they would cede it to the United States* were it for no other
> reason than to get rid of such neighbors, for the U.S. would soon sweep
> the country of Indians and drive them as they always have driven
> them to ruin and extermination—So that admitting this madness, this
> Independence succeeds to its full extent, the parties concerned have
> nothing but ruin in prospect, and will either cause the country to be
> desolated, or throw it into the hands of the United States and in either
> case the Indians are *lost,* past redemption *lost.*

So did Austin undertake to discuss calmly the prospects of annihilation.
He was right, of course, about one thing: the Indians were lost beyond
redemption if they fell into the hands of the United States. Hunter hardly
needed his pointed reminder: "*You* know the Govt. of the United States
and its policy as respects lands and Indians." He did.

And because he did, he could not have been too surprised by Austin's
underlying message: either the Indians submit to cultural subjugation or
die. If not exterminated by Mexico, they would be by the United States,
which "always have driven them to ruin and extermination."

Now if the modern word "genocide" means the deliberate destruction
of "a part of an ethnic, national or religious group," as it has been defined, then Austin was merely enunciating, as known fact, that American
Indian policy had always been genocidal in intent. He threatened Hunter
and the Cherokees with the same fate unless they were good—unless,

that is, they gave up their mad efforts to be free. Rebellion, especially among natives, had to be shown not to pay.

The letter was more an effort to intimidate than to persuade. It may have confirmed Hunter's worst fears about white attitudes; it did not bring him to heel. He could have reflected that among his Indian friends respect was earned and not obligatory. Evidently he did not bother to reply.

4

Such strenuous opposition from the leading Texas *empresario* hurt the Fredonians badly. Austin scored every time he denounced them as "no longer Americans, for they have forfeited all title to that high name by their unnatural and bloody alliance with Indians." Apparently a citizen's passport was lifted automatically when he joined in an alliance with Indians, which was a remarkably candid definition of Americanism. Austin's colonists unanimously joined him in condemning the perversion of the Fredonians.[24] Ironically, their condemnation weakened the resolve of the white Fredonians for reasons not unconnected with the racism of the rebels. As Foote sympathetically observed, word of Austin's preparation for action against them was "calculated greatly to paralyze the energies and chill the ardour of the Fredonians, who, however devoted they were to the cause in which they were enlisted, and however eager to be avenged upon their Mexican oppressors, naturally felt a strong repugnance to shedding the blood of men of the same race, and complexion, and language, with themselves, who had never heretofore done them the least injury, and among whom they recognized many old and dearly-loved friends."

The Fredonians were also disappointed in their expectation of aid from friends and sympathizers in the United States. As it turned out, very few could be found who were ready to fight oppression at a moment's notice. Their cause was made to seem more disreputable when word of Austin's opposition reached Natchitoches and other towns across the border. And their chances for support from that quarter were destroyed, finally, when their emissary Joseph A. Huber deserted their cause and denounced them.[25]

24. Natchitoches *Courier*, February 20, 1827; "Austin Papers," 1559–61, 1572, 1573–74, 1594–95.
25. Foote, *Texas*, I, 270–71, 277; Yoakum, *Texas*, I, 249.

The only remaining hope for the Fredonian Republic lay in "The Cherokee and Their Associated Bands." Mexican officials and Austin accordingly intensified their efforts to break up the association. On January 6 Saucedo issued a proclamation of amnesty and, with Austin, dispatched James Kerr and two other men to persuade the rebels to lay down their arms. A few days later Kerr and his associates had to report failure "in the hoped for object of our mission." [26] In Nacogdoches they had met with "the principals in private . . . Viz Hayden and Benjamine Edwards on the part of the white people, and one John D. Hunter and ——— [John] Basset on the part of the red people. (This Hunter said he was the representative of twenty three tribes of Indians and further that he was the absolute agent and attorney in fact of Dick fields.)" The commissioners argued that the proclamation of amnesty showed the justice and benevolence "of this our beloved, and adopted Country," but received the answer

> that they would never concede one inch Short of an acknowledgement on the part of the Govt of their entire free and unmolested *Independence* from the Sabine to the Rio Grand. . . .
>
> Fields was in his own village; and we deemed it not only hazardous, but dangerous to attempt to see him; which however is the less to be regreted as we are satisfyed that he is under the influence of Hunter—Two principle war Chiefs (Bowl and Big Mush) have as it is said refused to join fields.

No doubt the commissioners had been informed of the refusal of Big Mush and The Bowl by the man largely responsible for it. Working closely with Austin, Colonel Bean had already made effective use of the time-worn tactics of divide and conquer.

If America has ever had any representative men, then Peter Ellis Bean was one of them. He was of the breed of Ishmael Bush, the violent, remorseless, plundering squatter in Cooper's *Prairie* (1827). He was the embodiment of all of Bush's archetypal qualities as a superfluous man, with no productive place in the society behind him, except that he wandered even farther from home, had the imagination to become a spy and a soldier of fortune, and the audacity to become a bigamist. As Colonel Frank Triplett observed with admiration, "The career of this Texan hero

26. Richard Ellis, James Cummins, and James Kerr to Austin, January 22, 1827, "Austin Papers," 1586–87.

and pioneer is one of the most romantic imaginable. Born of respectable parentage, he was a native of the State of Tennessee and early discovered an inclination for roving and adventure. He was but sixteen years of age when he determined to cut loose from his home moorings and start out for himself on the voyage of life." [27] Starting out alone down the Tennessee River at the turn of the century, he . . . from here on the reader can fill in his own fantasies. Western historians have done so, making him sufficiently fabulous to be the Texas answer to Alexandre Dumas. The late J. Frank Dobie went so far as to say that Bean's adventurous life "almost deserves to be ranked alongside Casanova's accounts of his escape from the leads of Venice." It does, almost.

Bean was a member of that honored group of Bad Men which included James Wilkinson, Aaron Burr, Philip Nolan, and Jean Lafitte. The men were connected in one way or another: General Wilkinson presumably helped raise Nolan and exercised a bad influence on him; Nolan became a friend of Bean's and presumably exercised a bad influence on him. The two men led a party of men to Texas in 1800, and Nolan was killed in a skirmish with the Spanish. Bean wound up in prison at Chihuahua and, finally, at Acapulco. After numerous unsuccessful attempts to escape, he was finally released to serve in the royal army against the revolutionists. Instead, Bean deserted to join General Morelos. "Brave as a lion in action," according to Colonel Triplett, he soon acquired the rank of colonel and a Mexican wife. In 1814 Morelos commissioned him to seek aid and recognition of the revolution in the United States. On the way Bean met the pirate Jean Lafitte, and the two men went together to see Andrew Jackson in New Orleans. Jackson knew Bean well and put him in charge of those guns on the levee which helped stop the redcoats in their tracks on January 8, 1815.

In 1818 Bean returned to Tennessee to get married, moved to Arkansas, where he may have known Hunter, and, after the border opened again, moved on to Texas, where he received a league of land along the Neches. In 1825 he returned to the City of Mexico, resumed relations with his Mexican wife, received an appointment as colonel in the regular army, and was at hand to record Hunter's arrival in the city. On his return to Texas he found the Nacogdoches uprising just getting under way. It was

27. Triplett, *Conquering the Wilderness,* p. 703. The following biographical data come from Triplett, pp. 703–10; Yoakum, *Texas,* I, 236–37; and Flora Lowrey, "Peter Ellis Bean: A Typical Filibuster in Early Texas History" (unpubl. M. A. thesis, Southern Methodist University, 1945).

given a truly romantic dimension, I must add, by Bean's complex matrimonial affairs: while he was away his Texas wife had moved in with Martin Parmer, a leader of the rebels. For personal as well as official reasons, then, Bean took to the field on the government side and promised to "put out the fier."

On December 14 he was still in San Felipe de Austin with about thirty-five troops. On that day Austin sent the following directions to John A. Williams of Nacogdoches: "Col Bean is going on, he is an officer in the mexican army. *Advice with him* and put aside all your ill timed and I must say injudicious and obstinate republican nicity, and allay all your passions and excitements and take prudence for your guide." [28] When Bean did go on as far as the Trinity, where he camped, he found willing instruments in men like Williams who had decided to take prudence and avarice for their guides: the historian Yoakum asserted that Williams and the other agents of Bean each received a league of land for their services.[29] The agents occupied themselves in buying off Indian opposition by promising land to those who would lay down their arms. And their success was a major factor in the opposition Fields and Hunter had encountered upon their return from Nacogdoches. While they and their white allies had busied themselves in drafting the Fredonian Declaration and proclaiming the republic, Bean had undermined their position.

By December 28 he was able to report to Austin major gains against "those Villions":

> I have devided them so that I have now 70. me[n] coming from the Irish Bayu [Ais Bayou] to attack 30 that is in nacodoches and my leters from field [Fields] yet I have had no answer But I am wating howerly for the answer if I Suckseed in Braking him of[f] I then put out the fier instantly and thare is litel Doubt with me in my mind But that I shall suckseed.

Three days later he wrote that "if Mr Sauceda will come as quick as posibel on Perhaps we can make a compremise with the Ingins for they are all that is to be feard they ame at marching to Sn Antonio if some thing is not quickly done." He had also written "to Richard fields and Dr. Hunter fields Did not Rite me But sent me word that I was to late if he

28. "Austin Papers," 1534.
29. Yoakum, *Texas*, I, 250n.

had of saw me one month sooner Perhap we might of come upon tirms that is all the satisfaction he gave me." In Bean's judgment, "the onley way to stop this is to come forward Sor Sauceda and give them lands or the Countrey will [be] entirely lost if we can Brake of[f] the Ingins the thing is setled you will hurry Sausada and let him now what I Right you." On January 4, 1827, he wrote again with the latest intelligence:

> I found out that those Rascals is Braking of[f] from Nacodoches at this time thar is a guard of 12 men onley in the stone house I wish you to hurry on the troop as fast as Posibel for now is our time Before the ingins geather But by aleter that I Recived this Day from samuel Noris I find the Ingins is also Devidid and it apears that they wont be hear bary shortly but the troop must hurry all that they can.[30]

As Bean predicted, this division among the Indians about settled the thing.

Several thousand miles back Hunter had informed Norgate that not Jefferson's dissuasion or anything else would keep him from pursuing his plan for an Indian country: "I know of nothing which would induce me to do so." Now everything put this pledge to the test. As he hurried back to the Cherokee village he had to know that his vision was lost or, as Austin would say, "past redemption, *lost.*" It was too late to bring the Indians together again and too late to turn back. Nevertheless, he and Fields worked desperately to repair the irreparable. "Fields and Hunter," wrote Mayo, "strained every nerve to rouse the faithless Indians to the performance of their reiterated promises, and their solemn obligation by treaty; but in vain." Austin and Bean had done their work too well.[31]

Promised the lands they had contended for, the Indians repudiated their champions:

> Hunter, finding every effort fruitless, for the few who had not been bought over were unwilling to act with so small a force, left them, saying he would go alone and share the fate of his American friends in Nacogdoches. His opposition to their treachery excited their deadly hostility. He proceeded to join the Americans accompanied by two Indians. He stopped at a creek near the Anadagua village, to let his

30. "Austin Papers," 1551, 1554, 1561.
31. Bean to Ahumada, February 7, 1827, reproduced in Lowrey, "Bean," appendix; "Austin Papers," 1592–94.

horse drink, and while thus unguarded in his security, one of his savage companions shot him with a rifle in the shoulder. His horse started and he fell into the creek. The monster raised another fatal weapon, and while the unfortunate Hunter implored him not to fire, for it was hard, he said, to die by the hands of his friends,—sent this extraordinary spirit to appear before an unerring tribunal.[32]

How Mayo knew what the victim said as he was being shot a second time is unknown. But for Hunter to be assassinated under those circumstances implied just such a reaction on his part: it was hard. And if he did not get a chance to say so, he should have.

"It is said that Bowles [The Bowl] was hired to assassinate Fields and Hunter," wrote Yoakum in the 1850s. "Fields was first killed, and shortly afterward Hunter suffered the same fate near the present town of Henderson." Now, fortunately, this rumor can be pinned down. On March 11 Ahumada wrote to General Anastasio Bustamente, Commandant of the Eastern Internal States, to arrange a payoff for Big Mush and The Bowl:

Justice obliges me to inform you that Mohs and Buls—civil and military chiefs of the Cherokees—agreed to and gave orders to kill Hunter and Fields, recovering the papers and [the revolutionary] flag mentioned, and giving me every proof of loyalty to and love for our government, from which they hope for a grant of some land in the district for the settlement of their tribe, which solicitation I commend to your Excellency very particularly.

Bustamente replied on April 7 that he was pleased to support a reward for such valuable services:

The death of those perfidious demagogues Fields and Hunter is certainly a very fortunate circumstance for the happiness of the tribes, who were led astray, and for the preservation of the integrity and peace of that territory which they claimed to rule. On which account I have particularly recommended to the Supreme Government the merits of Mohs and Buls, who commanded a breach of the pledge with said visionaries.[33]

32. Quoted in Foote, *Texas*, I, 280. Hunter was thus killed in late January or early February 1827.
33. Yoakum, *Texas*, I, 250n; Winkler, "Cherokee Indians," 149–50.

Though Hunter was shot by one of his "savage companions," the Indian was simply acting as the agent of his erstwhile compatriots. Austin and Bean may not have pulled the trigger of the weapon that killed Hunter, but they had put his assassin out there on the creek bank.

5

As it turned out, had Hunter been able to get to Nacogdoches, he would have found that his white allies had only been playing on words when they pledged to realize their glorious cause "or perish under the flag of liberty." On January 28 they dissolved their "cabinet," abandoned the Old Stone Fort, and fled across the Sabine to avoid the advancing troops and militia from Austin's colony. A dispatch from one of their pursuers, dated February 1, gleefully declared the Fredonian Republic "totally exploded." [34]

Before word could get to the City of Mexico that "tranquility" had been restored, the revolt created quite a stir. "I have not seen anything excite even amongst the most moderate men, so general a sensation," Ward wrote Canning on February 21. "The Chambers have placed half a million dollars at the disposal of the Government for the first expenses of the Expedition, and have declared their readiness to support the War, be the consequences what they may." On the same day Poinsett wrote Clay an account of the affair, from which comes the epigraph at the head of this chapter, and added that, in the course of the debate in the Congress on how to quell the insurrection, "some of the ignorant members did not hesitate to express their opinion that the Government of the United States was privy to this movement—if indeed it had not encouraged it." [35]

In a curious way the charges were not completely wide of the mark. Had Poinsett not exerted himself to block the Indian claim for land, the chances were that Hunter would have gone back to Texas with good news and there would have been no rebellion. There was thus a measure of retributive justice in the fact that the uprising aroused suspicions about the intentions of the United States. As Poinsett explained to President John Quincy Adams:

34. John A. Williams, who had been brevetted a major by Bean, in the Natchitoches *Courier*, February 20, 1827. See also *National Gazette*, February 27, March 13, April 10, 1827.
35. Ward to Canning, February 21, 1827, FO 50/31b, No. 34, PRO; Poinsett to Clay, February 21, 1827, M97, R3, NA.

When intelligence was received here of the factious movements of Fields & Hunter in the State of Texas, it was at once presumed that they were secret agents of the United States, whose interest it is supposed to be to create dissentions in that country. This belief soon became common to all parties.' . . . The suspicion of the conduct of the govt. of the U.S. was so general & the resentment of our presumed proceedings so great, that we had not a single friend in or out of Congress.

In order to combat this widespread distrust, Poinsett drew up for the Mexican Army, which had ordered ten thousand troops to march on Nacogdoches, a plan of operation "to put down this ill-judged & ill-timed rebellion," which it adopted. Had the Fredonian Republic not already fallen, then, Poinsett would have willingly helped crush Fields and Hunter, "of notorious memory." In Poinsett's mind, the widespread belief that they were American agents was damaging, and an affront: they were the wrong leaders of the wrong rebellion at the wrong time. His additional comment to President Adams made clear that when Texas fell, Poinsett wanted it to fall into the right hands:

No views in my opinion ought to be entertained of acquiring for the United States any territory beyond the line established by you. The state of Texas, must from the nature of things, one day drop off from this confederation, and the policy to be pursued by the United States in such an event ought to be early and deeply meditated.[36]

Which was to say that the right hands would be white American hands.

If Hunter was looked upon as a U.S. agent in the City of Mexico, in Texas he was, as we have seen, thought to be an emissary of Great Britain. Ward's dispatch to Canning made clear he was not:

Amongst the Parties who have signed the Texas Declaration of Independence, I was sorry to see the name of *Hunter,* whose mission here I mentioned. . . . Disappointed in their hopes of attaining a favourable answer from the Mexican Government . . . it appears that the Tribes which Hunter represented have agreed now to accept the Lands which they wished to hold of Mexico as Mexican Citizens and subjects, from

36. Poinsett to Adams, April 26, 1827, Poinsett Papers, Historical Society of Pennsylvania.

> . . . the very men against whom they pledged themselves to defend
> any lands, which Mexico would give them title to call *their own*.

The tribes' alliance with the American colonists was obviously not in the
interest of His Majesty's government or, in Ward's view, in their own.
He held that the white Fredonians had declared independence simply as
a first step:

> I have reason to know that this step was suggested merely in order to
> save appearances in the first instance: it will be followed by a *Second*
> Declaration by which the same Individuals will declare that they are,
> and will be, independent of *Mexico*, but that it is their wish to put
> themselves under the protection of the United States, and to become
> members of that Great Republic.

What reason Ward had for knowing this he did not say: in the conspiratorial atmosphere of the capital, an informed suspicion must have been
given considerable weight in his thinking. But if he did have evidence
to go on, then the white allies of Fields and Hunter had been doing
more than playing on words.

Though Hunter's actions in Texas had deeply disappointed Ward by
dashing his hopes for an Indian buffer colony, he refused to condemn
him. Indeed, he generously rose to his defense against the Americans
who had denounced him in their periodicals "as an adventurer who imposed upon the credulity of the British public, by representing himself
as the hero of a romance of his own creation. To me it appears that his
crime has been the boldness with which he vindicated the rights of an
injured, and persecuted race, to whom he devoted his life, and in whose
service he was at last sacrificed." But this brings us back to where we
came in.

Ward was right about the Fredonian revolt being only the first act of
the drama. For once he and Poinsett were in complete agreement, for
he too thought there now could be little doubt that Texas would ultimately be "thrown into the hands of the United States." But when the
second act was staged a few years later, the moving force in the Texas
revolution was not a red and white alliance. Indeed the ultimate fate
of the Indians in the Lone Star State was also prefigured by the Fredonian revolt.

Once news arrived that the rebels had been dispersed, Ward pointed out to Canning that Austin's role had been central and in part rested on his aversion to Indians:

> This Gentleman, not liking the Neighbourhood of the savage Tribes, whom the Whites of Nacogdoches wished to introduce into Texas, declared himself, at once, against their Projects, and having united the Forces of his Colony . . . with the Mexican Troops under General Bustamente, decided the Contest without allowing Time for Hunter's Indians to cross the Frontier, and join Field, Edwards and the other Chiefs of the soi-disant Republic of Fredonia.[37]

Events proved the acuteness of Ward's observation on Austin's real feelings about Indians as neighbors.

After the occupation of Nacogdoches, Austin wrote his secretary that "things are all settled here and I think tranquility is fully and firmly established." James Gaines and others had been critical, but

> I have a consolation that to me is worth more than the approbation of any man,—in the consciousness that I have done right—Fields and Hunter are certainly killed by the Cherokees and all the other leaders of the party have escaped over the Sabine and I advised a mild course with those who were compromitted in a secondary degree. . . . I hope the people of the colony will be satisfied with me for next to the approbation of my own conscience, *theirs* is worth more to me than all the world beside.

Austin could add to his self-approbation that of the Mexican officials. Ignacio de Arispe, the acting governor, furnished him with a document which certified he had earned "the highest opinion from the Government" for perfect discharge of his duties:

> The same citizen Stephen F. Austin contributed most efficaciously placing himself at the head of his colonists in beating the rebels of Nacogdoches . . . having united his forces to the Mexican troops by which movement their dispersion was obtained, and the death of several of their ringleaders, by which the order and tranquility of the frontier were restored.[38]

37. Ward to Canning, February 21, and March 31, 1827, FO 50/31b, Nos. 34, 49, PRO; Ward, *Mexico in 1827* (London: Henry Colburn, 1828), II, 587.

38. Austin to Samuel M. Williams, March 4, 1827; Ignacio de Arispe to "the interested person," December 21, 1827, "Austin Papers," 1610–11, 1731.

The document made it official: Austin could take major credit for the deaths of Fields and Hunter.

On the other hand, the Cherokee chiefs may well have been more reluctant to give Austin their approbation. When he had wanted their help and appealed to them to drive away the "bad men," he had addressed them as "brothers" and reminded them that "the Cherokees are a civilized and honorable people, and will you unite yourselves with wild savages to murder and plunder helpless women and children"? After the chiefs had killed Hunter and Fields in a civilized way, however, and had helped drive the other bad men away, they seemed to have slipped back somehow into "their pristine savage condition." [39] On July 2, 1827, Austin joined two other *empresarios* in petitioning the Mexican authorities to protest the "forced and unnatural accumulation of Savages" in the adjacent border areas of the United States. The Cherokees were listed with the other barbarians whose immigration should be stopped and who should not be allowed a permanent foothold in Texas:

> And we further present to Your Excellency [Bustamente] the great danger and manifest impolicy of making any promises of concessions of Lands, either temporary or perpetual, and of offering any other rewards or emoluments, whether it be by military appointments or civic honors, to any of the Chiefs or head warriors of these barbarous Tribes —The friendship of savages is always treacherous—it is purchased today and lost tomorrow.

The chiefs might have more justifiably reflected that "civilization" was like an *empresario's* goodwill—here today and gone tomorrow. The truth was that most white Texans shared Austin's dislike for "savage Tribes" in the neighborhood and looked upon the Cherokees, unless they needed them, as savages.

Colonel Bean also had earned the high praise of the Mexican government for putting out the fire at Nacogdoches. As a reward he was appointed Indian agent. But no more than Austin was he willing to stand behind his word to the Cherokees. In 1833 Bean disclosed their "plot" to bring in families once the land question was settled. In his opinion, "if those Indians obtain possession of the tract of land which is

---

39. Austin to Cherokee Chiefs, January 24, 1827; David G. Burnet, Ben R. Milam, and Stephen F. Austin to Bustamente, July 2, 1827, "Austin Papers," 1592–94, 1667–71.

situated about five leagues distant, there can be no doubt that the arrival of those families will fill those lands with a class of barbarous people, and that it will become more and more difficult to cause them to go back." He therefore recommended to his superiors that the Cherokees be relocated on lands next to tribes "with whom we are now at war. In this way and with such provisions, the expenses will be obviated which we have been obliged to make in subjugating our enemies, the Comanches and Tehuacanas." Those lands next to hostile tribes should be given to the Cherokees "as the land which they claim by promise from the government." [40] Too late Bean's "barbarous people" discovered they could not trust the man of many promises: in the words of one Cherokee, "Bean lie heap."

A sad mistake: the Indians had believed Austin and Bean and had killed their friends, not so much because they were themselves "faithless to the performance of their reiterated promises," as Mayo contended, as because they were quite literally seeking some way to survive. After the assassinations, Big Mush and The Bowl spoke to Francisco Ruiz, the Military Commander of Nacogdoches, about the family of Fields:

> The same Chiefs came and said that they had killed Fields as a traitor and rebel; that he left a widow with seven children of a tender age, and unable to support themselves. That Fields left also a very small quantity of Cattle, by means of which his family are living now; but as he had business transactions with several persons, they apprehended he left some debts, perhaps unjust ones, for the payment of which his widow and orphans may be deprived of their scanty inheritance and reduced to starvation. Therefore they pray the Government to act as a father to these children, who should not be held accountable or made to suffer for the sins of their father, and to exonerate them of these debts.[41]

Here spoke no monsters but savages who showed a decent concern for the children of one of the rebels whose heads they had offered up to appease civilized wrath.

Big Mush and The Bowl were nearly as great victims of the settlement of the Fredonian rebellion as the Fields children. By way of expressing

---

40. Quoted in Winkler, "Cherokee Indians," 161; see also Lowery, "Bean," pp. 27, 29.

41. Ruiz to Colonel Ahumada, May 14, 1827, Nacogdoches Archives, Texas State Library.

official gratitude for his services, Mexican officers commissioned Bowl a lieutenant colonel, gave him some presents, and informed him that he was the principal man of the tribes.[42] But Colonel Bowles, as he was known thereafter, and the other Indians wanted the lands they had been promised. Nothing seemed to work to this end, not even being good natives. Then, in 1829, Governor Sam Houston came from Tennessee to live among them and let it be known that he meant to set up a "two-horse republic" in Texas with their help. And here we experience an unsettling sense of *déjà vu* when we learn that some of the details of his filibustering plans came from the lips of "one of his adherents, a young man named Hunter." [43]

When he became president of the Texas republic in 1836, Houston negotiated a treaty with the Cherokees which gave his friends, at long last, title to a tract of land. Still the Indians were not home free: the Texas senate rejected the treaty in 1837 and Houston was succeeded by Mirabeau B. Lamar, no friend of the Cherokees or of any other Indians. In his inaugural message of 1838, Lamar declared that "the sword should mark the boundaries of the republic." [44] It soon did.

The Indians were told they would have to go back across the border. This time Colonel Bowles encouraged his tribesmen and their allies to resist. Several regiments of Texas troops attacked on July 15 and 16, 1839. Colonel Bowles, Big Mush, and a large number of Indians were killed. Some of the surviving Cherokees recrossed the Red River to join their kinsmen in the Indian Territory, so called, "bringing with them the blood-stained cannister containing the patent for their Texas land which Bowl had carried about with him." In the end even the long-sought, near-magical piece of paper had served as no protection.

The white Fredonians had long since scattered and were not likely to be too concerned over the fate of their former allies. Herman B. Mayo was one, however, who had shown some understanding of Hunter and of what was at stake in his attempt to establish an Indian country. He wrote a eulogy which stressed that Hunter was a man of the most rigid integrity. It was obviously rare in his experience of the world to meet someone who meant exactly what he said. Demonstrably he and the

42. Winkler, "Cherokee Indians," 153.
43. Richard Rollin Stenberg, "American Imperialism in the Southwest" (unpubl. Ph.D. diss., University of Texas, 1932), pp. 221, 223. A different Hunter, no doubt—every inquiry must have an end.
44. James B. Mooney, "Myths of the Cherokees," *Nineteenth Annual Report of the Bureau of American Ethnology* (Washington: GPO, 1900), Part I, 144–45.

Edwards brothers had not, but had merely bandied about such fragile words as "Liberty" and "Justice." An uneasy conscience moved him to pay his handsome tribute to "this extraordinary spirit." And one self-reproach he expressed directly. "I shall ever deeply regret," he wrote,

> that a false delicacy withheld me from ever mentioning to Hunter the subject of this odious accusation, for I am convinced that he died profoundly ignorant that any stain rested upon his reputation. He could then, if innocent, have had the opportunity to restore his name to its former purity. He had been, from before the time when he was first stigmatised as an impostor, travelling through Mexico, or living among the Indians. He once mentioned to me that he had not seen a newspaper of the United States, since he had left them. He could not, therefore, have known that such an imputation had an existence.[45]

But Mayo need not have taken himself to task on these grounds, for Hunter could not have wasted time defending his good name during those last few months of his life.

All along the dark shadow on his dreams—Mrs. Hemans' saccharine and complacent "Child of the Forests" notwithstanding—had been the ongoing extermination of the Indians. His heart was far off in the woods and prairies because he knew the Indians were people and liked them and their ways: He knew that real brothers and real sisters were being driven and hunted from river to river, from desperation to despair. Theirs were the wild voices Hunter heard calling him to help them find some way out. This was what he had lived for since coming into the white world, and it was for this that he died.

45. Quoted in Foote, *Texas*, I, 247.

MORAL HERMAPHRODITE

Idolizers of Power have so debauch'd the Minds of Men with false Notions of human Nature, Morals, and Politicks, that some celebrated Writers have supposed Mankind so *ill-made*, that they could not subsist without *Subjection to Power*. Anarchy, or the State of Man without Government, they have represented as Chaos and Confusion; and a *State of Nature* as a continual War of every Man against every Man. Thus human Nature, Truth, Justice, and the Honour of God, are *prostituted* to the Support of *arbitrary Power*.

A State of Nature is, where every Man's allowed to do what he will with his own Person and Property, consistent with other Men's; and those *common Rights* are so easily discerned, that the *Indians* live much better than Men under any *Tyranny* and *arbitrary* Government. Their Virtue and Happiness are owing to their being untaught by those whose *highest Interest* is to *deceive* them.

The great *Inequality of Property* is the source of almost all Murders, Robberies, and other Vices among ourselves, which the *wiser* and *happier* Savages knowing nothing of, are blessed with *Security* and *Ease:* For they *naturally* assent to that divine Truth, *sufficient unto the Day is the Evil, and the Good thereof too;* every Man provides for himself and his Offspring, and, invading no Man's Property, is invaded by no Man; and they are content to die as they live, not worth a Groat; when they have *no Occasion* for it, they have no Occasion for Government: For all Government owes its Necessity to the Inequality of Property.

"Of Tyranny, Anarchy, and Free Governments,"
London Journal, January 6, 1733.

In his famous 1850 "Preface to the Leather-Stocking Tales," James Fenimore Cooper explained that "in a moral sense this man of the forest is purely a creation." He had given him a character natural to a man who possessed "little of civilization but its highest principles as they are exhibited in the uneducated, and all of savage life that is not incompatible with these great rules of conduct." The imagination thus had no great task, Cooper believed, "in portraying to itself a being removed from the every day inducements to err, which abound in civilized life, while he retains the best and simplest of his early impressions." John Dunn Hunter wrote almost as if he had put his imagination to the same task. Could he have drawn on Cooper as a source? As it happened, he could not, for *The Pioneers*, the first of the series, was published in February 1823, the same month and year as the Philadelphia edition of Hunter's narrative. And good evidence exists that the influence was the other way around, from Hunter to Cooper.

Like Hunter, Cooper had been deeply impressed by *la vie quasi-sauvage* of the already legendary Daniel Boone. With the first appearance of Leatherstocking, a reviewer detected that he had "been modelled from the effigies of old Daniel Boone, who abandoned the society of his kindred and built a hut among the Indians." [1] When *The Last of the Mohicans*, the second tale, was published in 1826, an English critic praised the fidelity of its representation of Indian character and thought it extremely probable "that the author has availed himself of the narrative of John Hunter and of the notices of the missionary Heckewelder." [2] Curiously, not one of the hundreds of students of Cooper's Indians has thought to follow up this lead. Susan Cooper's suggestions about her father's reading helped them to demonstrate his reliance on John Heckewelder for much of his Indian lore and to establish his dependence on the narratives of the expeditions of Captains Lewis and Clark and of Major Long for *The Prairie* (1827), the third of his series. [3] But Hunter's narrative also lay within reach. What about it?

The external evidence is very nearly compelling. In 1822, when Hunter was creating a stir in New York, Cooper moved into a house on Broadway

1. "The Pioneers," *Portfolio*, XV (March 1823), 232.
2. *Monthly Review*, II (June 1826), 123.
3. Susan Fenimore Cooper, "Introduction," *The Last of the Mohicans* (Boston: Houghton, Mifflin, 1876, 1898). For a thorough, careful discussion of sources, see Marcel Clavel, *Fenimore Cooper* (Aix-en-Provence: Imprimerie Universitaire de Provence, 1938), pp. 381–86, 567–71.

and participated fully in the intellectual life of the city.[4] Would not the writer, whose novels were to be essentially free adaptations of the Indian captivity chronicles, have shared the general interest in the celebrated captive and sought him out at one of David Hosack's Saturday soirées or at some other gathering? He could have met him in company with the geologist Benjamin Silliman, for his old friend and college tutor was also one of Hunter's patrons. And, according to Susan Cooper, the idea of writing "a romance essentially Indian in character" came to her father when he toured upstate New York with a party of friends in the summer of 1825. While at Lake George they visited the nearby caverns at Glens Falls, and one of their group held that here was the very scene for a romance. Cooper promised to write it. The man to whom he gave the promise was the Honorable Mr. Stanley, later Lord Derby, who had participated with Hunter in the memorable midnight frolic on the banks of the Ohio and who had earlier in the year been with Hunter in New Orleans. I find it inconceivable that Stanley and Wortley did not talk about their trip with the Owen party and heighten or arouse the novelist's interest in Hunter: the Leatherstocking of *The Last of the Mohicans*, which was the novelist's fulfillment of his pledge, bore a closer resemblance to our Hunter than to the sometimes querulous old hunter of the earlier *Pioneers*.

Besides, that Cooper knew about Hunter can be proved by his 1850 "Preface," wherein he replied to one of his critics who, "on the appearance of the first work in which Indian character was portrayed, objected that its characters were Indians of the school of Heckewelder, rather than of the school of nature." Here Cooper at last replied directly to Lewis Cass's *North American* article, which had contained incidental criticism of *The Pioneers* along with the extended exposé of Hunter.[5] Furthermore, Hunter could have been on the novelist's mind when he decided to transport Leatherstocking west of the Mississippi for *The Prairie*. As late as October 1826 one of his letters from Paris, where he had gone to work on the manuscript, suggested he had in mind a plot involving the Osages, though in the final version it was the Pawnees of Hard-Heart, a character modeled after a young chief he had met,

4. Robert E. Spiller, *Fenimore Cooper: Critic of His Time* (New York: Minton, Balch, 1931), p. 76.
5. "Preface," *The Deerslayer* (New York: G. P. Putnam, 1850). Cass had written that " 'the last of the Mohegans' is an Indian of the school of Mr. Heckewelder and not of the school of nature"—"Indians of North America," *North American Review*, XXII (January 1826), 67.

who were in conflict with the Sioux of Mahtoree.[6] Finally, though Hunter had made no claim to such priority, Cooper may have been thinking of his expedition, as well as Lewis and Clark's, when he advanced "the historically improbable claim that Leatherstocking had visited the Pacific coast before the Louisiana Purchase." [7]

The internal evidence that Cooper drew on Hunter is still more conclusive. Consider these few illustrations: In his *Memoirs* Hunter related that when a war party arrives "within the neighbourhood of their enemies, a whispering council is held, which is constituted of the principal and subordinate chiefs." In *The Last of the Mohicans* Cooper had Uncas move a war party through the forest "until they came upon the lairs of their own scouts. Here a halt was ordered, and the chiefs were assembled to hold a 'whispering council.'" [8] So far as I can determine, the novelist must have found his quoted phrase in Hunter's narrative, though the possibility remains that he discovered it elsewhere. The dangers of undertakings of this sort are obvious.

Cooper's erroneous use of a word ironically turns out to be more decisive for our case than the material he used correctly. In *The Last of the Mohicans* he had Leatherstocking explain that the whippoorwill was "the wish-ton-wish . . . well, since you like his whistle, it shall be your signal. Remember, then, when you hear the whip-poor-will's call three times completed, you are to come into the bushes." Yet Hunter had noted clearly that the "Wish-ton-wish of the Indians" was the prairie dog, or barking squirrel.[9] And sure enough, *wishtonwish* is listed in Frederick Webb Hodge's "Handbook of the American Indians" as the name applied to the prairie dog by the Caddoan tribes of Louisiana. Pike's *Sources of the Mississippi* (1810), the only other known source available to Cooper, noted that "as you approach their towns, you are saluted on all sides by the cry 'wishtonwish' (from which they derive their name with the Indians), uttered in a shrill and piercing manner." [10] Now if the novelist ran across the word in Pike or Hunter or both, why did he lift

6. Cooper to Mrs. Peter Augustus Jay, October [1–15?] 1826, in *The Letters and Journals of James Fenimore Cooper*, ed. James Franklin Beard (Cambridge: Harvard University Press, 1960), I, 158–64.

7. Henry Nash Smith, "Introduction," *The Prairie* (New York: Rinehart, 1950), p. vii.

8. *Memoirs*, p. 325; *Last of the Mohicans*, p. 387.

9. *Last of the Mohicans*, p. 271; *Memoirs*, p. 168.

10. Hodge, "Handbook of American Indians North of Mexico," *Bulletin 30 of the Bureau of American Ethnology* (Washington: GPO, 1912), Part II, 965. See also Mitford M. Mathews, *A Dictionary of Americanisms* (University of Chicago Press, 1951), II, 1882.

it out and have his knowledgeable scout misapply it to the whippoor-will?

The question became still more intriguing in 1829 with the publication of *The Wept of Wish-Ton-Wish,* wherein the name was again bestowed on a "bird of night," to a valley along the Connecticut "in commemoration of the first bird that had been seen by the emigrants," and even to an inn with the explanation that the symbol on its sign was the whippoor-will, "a name that the most unlettered traveller in those regions would be likely to know was vulgarly given to the Wish-Ton-Wish, or the American night-hawk." [11] On the contrary, even the most lettered travelers through Cooper's works continue to be puzzled by the reference.[12] Yet, had they read Hunter carefully, they might have cleared up this confusion: Cooper seemingly was fascinated by the word *wish-ton-wish* when he discovered it in the narrative and determined to use it, with the same hyphenation, in *The Last of the Mohicans* as part of his hero's Indian lore. And since the sound of the ax had not yet driven the scout from his beloved forests of the East, he had to use the name for something other than the prairie dog. This Leatherstocking did and at the same time threw pursuers off his creator's trail.

Moreover, the novelist left a clue to his indebtedness to Hunter in the other part of the title in which he used the name. The Wept was mourned because she was a white captive who chose to die by her Indian husband's grave rather than return to her family. She was, to be specific, the fair-haired daughter of the Heathcotes; after her capture by the Narragansetts she was renamed Narra-mattah and became the wife of the great Conanchet. Here Cooper was fairly open in his use of the captivity chronicles and explicit that this was yet another attempt to come to terms with those "seducing pleasures" which led some captives to choose Indian life "in the freedom of the woods." And Metacom, known as King Philip, the Wampanoag statesman who forged an alliance with Conanchet and the Narragansetts, was likened by Cooper "to that Indian hero of our own times, Tecumthé," who had also concluded that the Indians would have to unite and crush the whites or perish.[13]

11. Cooper, *The Wept of Wish-Ton-Wish* (New York: International Book, n.d.), pp. 27, 188, 225, 289, 362.

12. James Franklin Beard, editor of Cooper's letters and journals, writes that "there is much we don't know about this book and one of the unknowns is the source of the title" (letter, October 8, 1970).

13. *Wept,* p. 227; cf. Hunter, *Memoirs,* pp. 46–47. Cooper's dependence on Hunter does not rule out, of course, his possible indebtedness to other captivity stories.

Indeed, Cooper must have composed some of the speeches of his Indian orators and their champions with Hunter's narrative in hand. In *The Wept of Wish-Ton-Wish* the half-witted Whittal Ring, another former captive who preferred Indian life, made boastful and presumably comic statements which came almost directly from the narrative. According to Hunter, Tecumseh had said to the Osages:

> The white people came among us feeble; and now we have made them strong, they wish to kill us, or drive us back, as they would wolves and panthers.
> *Brothers*—The white men are not friends to the Indians; at first they only asked for land sufficient for a wigwam, now, nothing will satisfy them but the whole of our hunting grounds, from the rising to the setting sun.

Whittal said:

> Big canoes came out of the rising sun. . . . At first, the strangers spoke soft and complaining like women. They begged room for a few wigwams. . . . But when they grew stronger they forgot their words. . . . A paleface is a panther. When a-hungered, you can hear him whining in the bushes like a strayed infant; but when you come within his leap beware of tooth and claw!

The metaphor may have been suggested by Tecumseh's reference to panthers. But the Shawnee had earlier used a simile to characterize palefaces: "Brothers, the white people are like poisonous serpents; when chilled, they are feeble and harmless, but invigorate them with warmth, and they sting their benefactors to death." [14]

From the first of his romances "essentially Indian in character" to the last, Cooper evidently drew extensively on Hunter for the themes, imagery and rhythms of Indian oratory. In *The Last of the Mohicans* the aged Tamenund observed sadly that "his arm is withered like the branch of a dead oak"; " 'The hour of Tamenund is nigh!' exclaimed the sage; 'the day is come, at last, to the night!' " Hunter had remembered that a venerable Kansas patriarch said of himself: "Like a decayed prairie tree, I stand alone. . . . My sun is fast descending behind the western hills,

---

14. *Memoirs*, pp. 45–46; *Wept*, p. 222.

and I feel that it will soon be night with me." [15] In *The Oak-Openings* (1848), Scalping Peter, an Indian nationalist explicitly cast in the mold of Tecumseh, addressed a midnight council of chiefs and warriors openly using Tecumseh's call to unity of all red men as children of the same father, his characterization of whites as killers of old men, women, and children, and even his moving repetition of the salutation "Brothers." [16]

Marcel Clavel observes that Cooper's works have made all this rich imagery "partie du patrimoine littéraire de l'humanité." If so, then our literary heritage is indirectly indebted to Hunter.

But enough of the demonstrations of what must now seem obvious. It would have been incomprehensible had Cooper *not* drawn on Hunter to pursue his great themes. Was not the most celebrated and vilified captive of the day particularly well qualified to serve as one of the models for Leatherstocking? The historical and fictional figures both straddled the breach between the races and attempted to present them to each other. Indeed, Cooper's tales were in one sense, in D. H. Lawrence's sense, an attempt to appease the ghosts of the aborigines already slandered and murdered. That brotherhood of red and white which Hunter yearned for in real life ascended to the mythopoeic level in the friendship beyond time of Leatherstocking and Chingachgook. Like Hunter, Cooper's hero posed the question of the subjugation and attempted annihilation of the Indians as a moral problem: How could a system of justice in the clearings be built upon a record of injustice in the wilderness? A society of Christian brotherhood erected upon its denial? Respect for law and order based upon broken treaties, bribery and debauchery, and a thoroughgoing contempt for the natural rights of natives? Finally, there was the singular allure of forest freedom set against the oppressive conformism of the settlements. As Leatherstocking remarked in *The Pioneers:* "I lose myself every day of my life in the clearings." [17]

Both Hunter and Leatherstocking might have readily agreed with Has-hak-a-tonga, or Big Soldier, an Osage who visited Washington and returned to remark in 1822:

15. *Last of the Mohicans*, p. 372; *Memoirs*, p. 22. Cooper drew on Heckewelder for Tamenund's name and tradition of greatness, but could not have used the missionary's work as a source for his oratory. See John Heckewelder, *History, Manners, and Customs of the Indian Nations Who Once Inhabited Pennsylvania and the Neighbouring States* (Philadelphia: Abraham Small, 1819), p. 300, for his discussion of the legendary Delaware chief.

16. *The Oak-Openings* (New York: International Book, n.d.), pp. 294–96, 375; cf. *Memoirs*, pp. 45–48.

17. *The Pioneers* (New York: E. P. Dutton, n.d.), p. 442.

You are surrounded by slaves. Every thing about you is in chains, and you are slaves yourselves; I fear if I should change my pursuits for yours I should become a slave. Talk to my sons; perhaps they may be persuaded to adopt your fashions, at least to recommend them to their sons; but for myself, I was born free! and wish to die free!! [18]

Hunter may well have helped Cooper toward—however ambivalent the actual expression—a yearning to live so free and for release from his government-issue chains. In any event, Hunter had already acted on the anarchistic principles asserted by Leatherstocking in *The Deerslayer* (1841): "When the colony's laws, or even the king's laws, run a'gin the laws of God, they get to be onlawful, and ought not to be obeyed." [19]

In his remarkably perceptive review of *The Pathfinder* (1840), Balzac saw in Leatherstocking "a magnificent moral hermaphrodite, a child of savagery and civilization, who will live as long as literature does." [20] By living his life as just such a moral hermaphrodite, Hunter made his own unintended and unacknowledged contribution to the magnificence of Cooper's moral creation.

2

Small wonder, then, that Lewis Cass became the arch-enemy of Hunter and the arch-critic of Cooper. His reaction to both is important to history precisely because he was not a monster but a benevolent figure, according to current definitions, and because his views were by no means aberrant or his influence marginal.

A portrait painted in his later years, when he was Secretary of State under Buchanan, revealed something of the character of the man. Then in his mid-seventies, Cass's heavy-lidded eyes, balding head, and sagging jowls bespoke advancing old age. His high collar, stock tie, and velvet-trimmed coat gave him a slightly genteel appearance, but he still seemed a fit rival of Thomas Hart Benton for the title "Father of the West." Indeed, he had the preeminent claim, Andrew McLaughlin asserted, for scarcely any other man had been for so many years so closely connected

18. As quoted by George Champlain Sibley in the *Niles Weekly Register*, September 14, 1822.
19. *Deerslayer*, p. 37.
20. Balzac, "Revue parisienne," in *Oeuvres complètes* (Paris: Calmann-Lévy, 1879), XXIII, 584.

with "the rise and progress of the United States." The son of a regular army officer who fought under Washington, Cass had grown up in New Hampshire, gone to Phillips Exeter Academy with Daniel Webster, moved west to take up the study and practice of law in Ohio, become governor of the Michigan Territory in 1813—the office he still occupied when he denounced Hunter—served as Jackson's Secretary of War and later as his Minister to France, returned to become senator from Michigan and a perennial Democratic candidate for the Presidency, and finally accepted a place in Buchanan's Cabinet in 1857. For his portrait Cass struck an imperious, Napoleonic pose, with hand and forearm tucked into his waistcoat, as though he thought of himself as the leader who had carved out an empire for white settlers. But, according to Lewis Einstein, who has written the most penetrating account of his statecraft, Cass was the "kindest of men. . . . His character was without blemish, his personality attractive, his patriotism real, his abilities moderate." [21]

By 1826, when he wrote his article on Hunter, Cass had had over a dozen years of continuous dealings with Indians. He had negotiated almost a score of treaties with the various tribes and ultimately, before assuming national office, extinguished Indian title to many millions of acres, including most of present-day Michigan, Wisconsin, and northern Minnesota. Moreover, he was known for moving the aborigines out for their own good, to help them escape the moral and physical evils brought about by too close contact with whites.

His article exposing Hunter was the first of three in the *North American Review*.[22] These articles established his position as a scholar and gained him an honorary Doctor of Laws degree from Harvard in 1836. No one in the country could hope to challenge his position as the foremost Indian expert. Colonel Thomas L. McKenney, an expert in his own right, once called Cass "the best informed man in the United States on Indian affairs." Or as Jared Sparks put it, "He is allowed to have a better knowledge of the Indians than any well educated man in the country."

In fact Cass demonstrated in these articles a broad and deep ignorance of Indian life. This was true in his attack on Hunter and true when he turned his attack on others. "Of abstract ideas," Cass declared, the In-

21. Einstein, "Lewis Cass," in *American Secretaries of State and Their Diplomacy*, ed. Samuel Flagg Bemis (New York: Alfred A. Knopf, 1928), pp. 295–384; McLaughlin, *Lewis Cass* (Boston: Houghton, Mifflin, 1891), pp. 348–49 *et passim*.
22. The three were "Indians of North America," XXII (January 1826), 53–119; "Heckewelder on the American Indians," XXVI (April 1828), 357–403; and "Removal of the Indians," XXX (January 1830), 62–121.

dians "are almost wholly destitute," and went on to ridicule Hecke-welder's "poetical knowledge" of them and to attack Cooper for drawing his red men from the missionary Heckewelder's ideal instead of from nature. He regretted that Cooper "did not cross the Allegany, instead of the Atlantic, and survey the red man in the forests and prairies. . . . If he would collect his materials from nature instead of the shadowy rep-resentations he has studied, he might give the world a series of works, as popular and interesting as any that adorn the literature of the day." But the novelist had every reason to be apprehensive about this good advice.

Cass shared the widespread and mistaken assumption that a simple people had to possess a simple language, barren of abstractions and rich only in words that related to animal needs. But there was published evidence at the time which refuted some of his charges against Hunter and his other statements about the Indians. Moreover, Americans then had over two centuries of direct experience with them to draw on. How, therefore, could Cass have gained his reputation as the country's leading expert?

Part of the answer lay in the self-assurance with which Cass spoke on Indian affairs. Readers assumed he had to know what he was talking about, especially given the absence of a single sign of an inner hesitancy which might shake their belief that he did. Indeed, there is no evidence that Cass himself suffered a moment of flagging confidence in his abso-lute mastery of the field. In his article on Hunter, he knew beyond question that the Indians were "stationary, in their manners, habits, and opinions." In his attack on Heckewelder in 1828, he again took up the fixed, sensual nature of the Indians. And in his 1830 article "Removal of the Indians," Cass made explicit the body of assumptions on which he was drawing. By way of a grand summary of the characteristics of natives, Cass invited the reader to consider the work of a real expert:

> The faithful portrait of the Indians drawn by Dr. Robertson in the fourth book of his History of America is creditable alike to his industry and sagacity. It evinces the hand of a master, and we are tempted to lay before our readers a few detached extracts from that work. They delineate the red man as we have found him.

The passage had depths of irony which obviously escaped Cass: it showed him, for all his nationalism, turning to a master in the Old World for a faithful portrait of the Indians. On the deepest level, however, it went beyond irony to become fabulous.

William Robertson was a Scot who had never crossed the Atlantic, let alone the Alleghenies, to study the North American natives at first hand. A Calvinist minster, he was nevertheless "an avowed optimist of the eighteenth-century type," as one of his biographers observes, "and none of his contemporaries philosophised upon defective data with greater dignity or complacency." His defective data dovetailed neatly with his grotesque assumptions. Drawing heavily on the French naturalist Buffon, Robertson soberly asserted that the Indians had no body hair, were so feeble as to be "destitute of one sign of manhood and strength," and were, consequently, strangers to sexual passion: they were "mere animals," in short, and puny, frigid ones at that.[23] Robertson conducted generations of willing Americans into mazes of contradictions about creatures who were both migratory yet attached to the land, enfeebled yet "a people whose only business was war and hunting," a people at once both contemptible and formidable. For Cass to accept "the faithful portrait of the Indians drawn by Dr. Robertson" meant that, in all his years of contact with native Americans, he had never *seen* a single one.

His mentor thus identified, Cass's onslaught at last fitted snugly into its larger context. As a leading colonial servant of the policies Hunter indicted, Cass patriotically rose to their defense. But the white savage's insistence that Indians were persons went too far: it threatened *how* the general saw the world. Before Cass unearthed a single one of his "vast multitude of facts," he knew for a certainty what he would prove. Robertson had provided him with a theory into which Hunter's narrative simply would not go. The Scot placed the "wonderfully improvident" savage at the level of "mere animal" and left him there forever. He admiringly watched the white man, on the other hand, as he fulfilled his destiny by climbing from one stage of civilization to the next: "As the individual advances from the ignorance and imbecility of the infant state to vigour and maturity of understanding, something similar to this may be observed in the progress of the species." That Hunter did not write of the Indians as though they were retarded children made him, from this point

23. William Robertson, *The History of the Discovery and Settlement of America* (New York: Harper & Brothers, 1843), pp. 139–96. First published in two volumes in 1777, the work became so enormously popular in the new nation that there were ten editions by 1803. For data on his ideas and a discussion of them, see the *Dictionary of National Biography* and Roy Harvey Pearce, *Savagism and Civilization* (Baltimore: Johns Hopkins Press, 1965), pp. 86–91.

of view, a palpable fraud. If Robertson had said that tribesmen "waste their lives in listless indolence," Cass dutifully referred to the "listless indolence" of the natives and rejected out of hand Hunter's account of their strenuous exertions to cross the Rockies just to see what was on the other side. As Frantz Fanon pointed out, for white settlers the natives have always been "faces bereft of all humanity . . . that laziness stretched out in the sun." [24] These ignorant imbeciles were providentially destined to disappear before the "progress of a new race of men," white Americans, that is, and if Hunter attempted to interfere with this historical imperative, so much the worse for Hunter.

Here a nagging question becomes insistent: Did Cass really believe in his misrepresentations, distortions, and inaccuracies? Not in all of them. Winning the West was a dirty, frequently profitable business, and Cass had his own tough-minded awareness of that fact. In his article on Hunter, he was moved to express the regret that the Indians "have lost so much of what we have gained." But he was keenly conscious of the economic stakes, land and mineral, which gave point to all his treaties and which underlay his rhetoric about the designs of providence for advancing the white man and squashing the red man. His father, as a veteran of the Revolution, received a grant of four thousand acres on the former site of a Shawnee village in Ohio. Cass inherited a share of this estate, adding to his already substantial holdings. And in Detroit he sold off his own five-hundred-acre farm piecemeal, biographer Woodford proudly records, "realizing upwards of three-quarters of a million dollars and providing himself with a substantial fortune." Cass could afford a few insubstantial regrets.

In 1811 the Ohio Indian agent, John Johnston, proposed two assassinations to the Secretary of War: "If it was agreeable to the Government," Johnston wrote, "the Indians could be easily prevailed on to kill the Prophet and his Brother [Tecumseh]." In 1817 Johnston brought several thousand Indians to a council on the Maumee River. Pontiac's sister was among the Ottawas who refused to sign the document drawn up for them. When the whites present learned this, they "took it into their heads that she must sign the Treaty," reported Johnston, "brought her forward, [and] held her hand until she made her mark." Lewis Cass, as it happened, was one of the commissioners present. Afterward Cass remarked that he would not undertake such a task again for any private

24. Fanon, *The Wretched of the Earth* (New York: Grove Press, 1968), p. 151.

consideration: "Nothing but a principle of obedience to the orders of Government," he admitted, "would induce me to do it." [25]

So Cass, "the kindest of men," was quite capable of providing rather direct illustrations of the banality of evil. If he thought he was acting in obedience to the orders of government, as he unquestionably did when he went to St. Louis to get ammunition for use against Hunter, then he was quite capable of conscious misrepresentation and distortion. The likelihood that he so acted becomes stronger in the light of Lewis Einstein's observation that Cass's record as Minister to France was marked "by his discovery of imaginary plots and his continuous attempts to embroil us with Great Britain."

Like his charges against Hunter, however, such countercharges remain unproved, and here they are largely beside the point. At the core of his consciousness Cass believed in his "savages." That is, he believed in the inventions of his imagination and felt free to bend the evidence in whatever way would best protect them.

Of course, more strictly put, Cass's "savages" were collective creations. He gained his reputation as an expert from the vigor and persistence with which he defended projections which were public property. His long career in appointive and elective office had placed him at dead center of mainstream American thought and politics. When he spoke on Indians, therefore, he spoke for the vast majority of citizens who shared his preconceptions and who already believed in his phantoms. The very lack of originality in his thought, its commonplace quality, gave his reaction to Hunter and Cooper its significance.

If the cutting edge of the conquest of the continent was "the metaphysics of Indian hating," to borrow Melville's phrase again, then Cass was truly the "Father of the West," for he was the leading metaphysician.[26] From his and almost everybody's viewpoint, to question the Win-

---

25. Quoted in Robert F. Bauman, "Review of *John Johnston and the Indians* by Leonard U. Hill . . . ," *Ethnohistory*, V (Fall 1958), 392–96.

26. Readers of Melville's *Confidence Man* will recall that he explicitly credits his Indian-hater to James Hall, whose *Sketches of History, Life, and Manners in the West* (1834–1835) pleads for sympathetic understanding of the Indian-killer as the vanguard of Christian Progress. Now by a curious quirk of history, a copy of the Philadelphia edition of Hunter's narrative, inscribed "James Hall," has turned up in the Minneapolis Public Library. Though there are no other annotations, we may be sure of what genial Judge Hall was thinking when he read Hunter's insistence that the Indians were human beings: like Cass, he must have been certain that only an impostor would so foolishly question the inevitability of their extermination. And it was his counterassumption that the Indians were subhuman which gave rise to the metaphysics that Melville slashingly satirized as an apologia for terror and murder.

ning of the West was to threaten the process by which the American eagle did "his wild pinions extend,/ To the ocean that rolls in the west," in the words of Johonnet's prophetic Liberty Tree ballad of the 1790s (see p. 59); it was to endanger the necessity that the continent be settled to the right bank of the Mississippi and beyond by "our own brethren and children," as Jefferson had insisted, and most alarming of all, it menaced the certainty that this was a White Man's Country. John Dunn Hunter came forward to challenge the myth that the United States government was the primary engine of a beneficent Progress. Not by accident was he opposed and put down by two men who became Secretaries of War and by a third who colonized a state. He was first the victim of character assassination and then of physical assassination because he dared speak and act for the Indians. And the attack on him, of course, was merely an incident in the Three Hundred Years' War against the red man.

"It is a dark crime to slander the reputation of a single individual," observed one of Cass's critics in 1830. "But it is one of uncommon malignity to calumniate the character of a whole people." [27] But this writer was exceptional in rising to defend the Indians with the poignant query: "Are they not men—are they not our brethren?" Because some of those in Cooper's novels seemed human, Cass brusquely dismissed them as "beings with feelings and opinions, such as never existed in our forests." Denunciations of Cooper's Indians followed in other quarters and were frequently reiterated over the decades. Still following in Cass's footsteps, John Neal came back into the fray in 1849 with an article which denied the eloquence of Indian speech: "As for the speeches that are generally put forth in America, or published by authority . . . they are positively mere trash and counterfeit." [28] But by then, as if to demonstrate the pervasiveness of American nationalism and racism, Cooper had crossed over to the camp of his critics and seemed to repent his earlier subversive tendencies. In *The Oak-Openings,* his last Indian story, he created a Caliban, a Tecumseh, who became a Good Indian in the end. He was good because he had come to realize the truths of the Gospel of Progress. But Scalping Peter had in fact been scalped by his creator:

> Injin don't own 'arth. 'Arth belong to God, and he send whom he like to live on it. One time he send Injin; now he send pale-face. *His* 'arth,

27. Anon., *The Removal of the Indians. An Article from the American Monthly Magazine; an Examination of an Article in the North American Review* . . . (Boston: Pierce & Williams, 1830), p. 55.
28. Neal, *Godey's Lady's Book,* April 1849, p. 267.

and he do what he please wid it. No body any right to complain. Bad
to find fault wid Great Spirit. All he do, right; nebber do anyt'ing
bad. His blessed Son die for all color, and all color muss bow down
at his holy name.[29]

Whites nebber do anyt'ing bad like kill Injin and take land—this was
welcome news for the aging novelist and his countrymen. It was good
to know that in the end your victims understood you and loved you.

Certainly no ghost of the eloquent Tecumseh lingered on in this
wretched pidgin English of Peter, but historian Francis Parkman still
could not forgive the novelist his other earlier incarnations. After Cooper's death he indicted his Indians as either superficially or falsely drawn
and held him personally responsible "for the fathering of those aboriginal
heroes, lovers, and sages, who have long formed a petty nuisance in our
literature." [30] Parkman's repeated expressions of gratitude to Cass under-
scored his indebtedness to the Dean of the Indian Experts for his own
conception of the Indians as forest beasts, as "man, wolf, and devil, all
in one." [31] Theodore Roosevelt took up this spirited justification of Anglo-
Saxon conquest where Parkman left off: the Indians in *The Winning of
the West* were Parkman's forest wolves and Cass's savages, "fearless, ferocious, treacherous, inconceivably cruel; revengeful and fickle; foul and
unclean in life and thought." [32] And so on down to the most recent glori-
fications of fur trade empires, California's forty-niners, and those airborne
cavalrymen who were still playing Cowboys and Indians in the second
half of the twentieth century, though by then they were fighting away at
Winning the West in Southeast Asia.

Henry David Thoreau attentively followed the controversy over Cooper's Indians, read Cass's attacks with care, and took the measure of the
American historians who followed his lead. On February 3, 1859, he put
his mature reflections in his *Journal:* "It frequently happens that the historian, though he professes more humanity than the trapper, mountain
man, or gold-digger, who shoots one [an Indian] as a wild beast, really

29. *Oak-Openings*, p. 404.
30. Parkman, "Review of the Works of James Fenimore Cooper," *North American
Review*, LXXIV (January 1852), 150.
31. The best discussion of Parkman's Indians is David Levin's *History as Romantic Art* (Stanford, Calif.: Stanford University Press, 1959), pp. 132–41. For
Parkman's expressions of gratitude to Cass, see his *Conspiracy of Pontiac* (Boston:
Little, Brown, 1929), I, xi; II, 362.
32. Roosevelt, *The Winning of the West* (New York: G. P. Putnam's Sons,
1896); see, for example, IV, 137–38, 335.

exhibits and practices a similar inhumanity to him, wielding a pen instead of a rifle." Thoreau was contemptuous of those who spoke slightingly of the Indian "as a race possessing so little skill and wit, so low in the scale of humanity, and so brutish that they hardly deserved to be remembered" and might have been referring directly to Cass in his scorn for those who used "only the terms 'miserable,' 'wretched,' 'pitiful,' and the like." [33] For his own part, Thoreau found the indigenous women and men of America inexhaustibly interesting: "If wild men, so much more like ourselves than they are unlike, have inhabited these shores before us, we wish to know particularly what manner of men they were, how they lived here, their relation to nature, their arts and their customs, their fancies and superstitions."

As he had made clear in *A Week on the Concord and Merrimack Rivers* (1849), Thoreau knew that, like Columbus, "the earnest seeker and hopeful discoverer of this New World always haunts the outskirts of his time, and walks through the densest crowd uninterrupted, and as it were in a straight line." He thereupon walked straight through crowds of Indian-haters to consider the relationship of the captive Alexander Henry with his "brother" Wawatam. Thoreau's discussion of their friendship revealed full awareness that the captivity chronicles gave the earnest seeker means to explore the possibilities of brotherhood in this still undiscovered New World.[34] With such understanding, Thoreau could hardly have passed Hunter by.

In the sixth of his Indian Notebooks, collections of materials which he started in 1851, Thoreau reminded himself that Hunter's narrative, along with the works of Catlin, Heckewelder, Halkett, and others, was to be found "on the first three shelves over the door in the American History Alcove" of the Harvard Library.[35] He checked out the 1823 London edition of *Memoirs of a Captivity* on December 7, 1854.[36] Copious ex-

33. *The Journal of Henry D. Thoreau*, eds. Bradford Torrey and Francis H. Allen (Boston: Houghton, Mifflin, 1949), XI, 437–38.
34. *A Week on the Concord and Merrimack Rivers*, ed. Odell Shepard (New York: Charles Scribner's Sons, 1921), pp. 194, 202–4; Leslie Fiedler advances an interesting interpretation of Thoreau's discussion of Henry and Wawatam in *The Return of the Vanishing American* (New York: Stein and Day, 1968), pp. 109–19.
35. Indian Notebooks, MS MA 596–606, Pierpont Morgan Library, New York. There are eleven notebooks in all, comprising about 2800 pages of extracts, with a few comments and annotations. For a general description of their contents, see Albert Keiser, "Thoreau's Manuscripts on the Indians," *Journal of English and Germanic Philology*, XXXVII (April 1928), 183–99.
36. John Aldrich Christie, *Thoreau as World Traveler* (New York: Columbia University Press, 1965), pp. 29, 322.

tracts from Hunter's work, some thirty-seven pages in all, promptly appeared in the seventh Notebook. Among the topics in the narrative which interested him, he showed a predictably keen interest in Tecumseh's speech, and in Hunter's description of the wanton destruction of game by whites, his account of how the Osages wove buffalo-hair blankets. And he could not pass by the Crèvecoeur-like sentence that "there is in the Indian mode of life something peculiarly fascinating." In September 1856 he promoted Hunter to the *Journal* itself, for upon his return from a trip to Brattleboro, Vermont, he recorded that the most interesting sight had been the skin and skull of a panther and added the reference: "*Vide* Lawson, Hunter, and Jefferson in Book of Facts. Hunter when near the Rocky Mountains says, 'So much were they [cougars] to be apprehended . . . that no one ever ventured to go out alone, even on the most trifling occasion.' He makes two kinds." [37] In the eleventh and last Indian Notebook, for which he was collecting materials shortly after his castigation of American historians, Thoreau copied out long extracts from Cass's *North American* article, laying out the charges much as we did in Chapter 4. Unfortunately he did so largely without comment, except to question Cass's use of English orthography in the name Tecumthé and at one point—in the context of the general's discussion of how the numbers of Indians "have decreased with appalling rapidity"—to challenge his evidence: "V[*ide*] his statistics?" And, since he had already drawn on Hunter extensively, Thoreau must have winced while copying out Cass's assertion that the narrative was "a useless publication." In the same Notebook, a little farther along, he introduced extracts from John Halkett's *Historical Notes Respecting the Indians*. While copying a Halkett statement beginning "I was informed by Mr. Hunter . . . ," he broke off the quotation to exclaim in his own voice: "So he had seen such a person!" [38]

Had he lived, Thoreau's projected work would have deepened our

---

37. *Journal*, IX, September 9, 1856, 74. The cross-reference to the "Book of Facts" was not to the Indian Notebooks but to "Extracts mostly from Natural History," materials which interested Thoreau but for which he had no immediate use in his *Journal*. This extract book is in the Widener Library at Harvard; it contains a long quotation from Hunter's narrative on pp. 302–3.

38. Indian Notebook, MS MA 606, Pierpont Morgan Library, New York. Thoreau was copying a passage from Halkett which read: "I was informed by Mr. Hunter that the Indians can march at night in a direct line through the forests, when they cannot see even a star to guide them, merely by feeling the bark of the trees as they move along," *Historical Notes Respecting the Indians of North America* (London: Archibald Constable, 1825), p. 324n.

understanding of historians who hunt their fellow man wielding a pen rather than a rifle. He would no doubt have discussed Hunter under "Treatment of Captives" and perhaps under other headings in the list of subjects he outlined in his Indian Notebooks. The level of his interest suggests that he seriously considered an attempt to unravel the charges of Cass and others. After reading and laboriously copying from the Harvard copy of the narrative, he apparently decided he should have it in his personal library. Sometime between 1854 and 1856 he acquired a copy of the Philadelphia edition of 1823, *Manners and Customs of Several Indian Tribes;* [39] it became one of the nine books in his very select collection on Indians.[40] On the flyleaf of his copy, which wound up in the Concord Free Public Library, he wrote in neat script: "This is praised in the 61st no. of the London Quarterly Review—but both it & the reviewer are severely handled in Vol. 22 of the N. A. Review (1826) ap[parently] by Cass, who also criticizes severely Heckewelder & refers to Halkett." And in another annotation: "See Catlin's 'Eight Years' Travels,' Vol. 1, p. 83. Lond. 1848. [Also] Schoolcraft's Personal Memoirs, p. 83—(Phil. 1851)." [41] At this stage of his inquiry Thoreau had staked out the perimeters of the topic we have pursued from London to the City of Mexico and back.

It would have been extraordinary had Thoreau not been intrigued by the white savage. For him Hunter's life was an illustration of his abiding conviction that man lived best with a mixture of "civilization" and "wildness." Like Thoreau's Indian friend Joe Polis of the posthumous *Maine Woods* (1863), Hunter had helped himself to the advantages of the settlements without losing his wilderness lore and closeness to nature. But Hunter had more to offer the poet than further evidence on the desirability of the hybrid, half-savage/half-civilized state.

39. The timing of Thoreau's acquisition of *Manners and Customs* can be pinned down with relative certainty. The page references in the seventh Indian Notebook (MS MA 602), Pierpont Morgan Library, New York, were to the London edition, no doubt to the Harvard copy of the *Memoirs* he first checked out in December 1854. His *Journal* entry of September 9, 1856, however, as the references in his Book of Facts (Widener Library, Harvard) make clear, was to the Philadelphia edition, probably to the copy in his personal library. John Aldrich Christie, *Thoreau as World Traveler*, p. 322, erred when he contended that Thoreau must have acquired Hunter's work "*after*" 1856, since his excerpts are all taken from the London ed." Not all: that in the Fact Book was not.

40. Walter Harding, *Thoreau's Library* (Charlottesville: University of Virginia Press, 1957), pp. 19, 21, 61.

41. Sophia Thoreau gave her brother's copy of Hunter's narrative to the Concord Library in 1874. I am indebted to Mrs. Marcia Moss, the Concord reference librarian, for her helpfulness.

When Thoreau wrote of "wild men, so much more like ourselves than they are unlike," he revealed an ongoing process of redefinition which only his death cut short—his last words were said to have been "moose" and "Indian." Thoreau was redefining civilization and savagery, terms badly in need of redefinition then and so desperately needed today as to make literary criticisms of "primitivism" not Parkman's "petty nuisances," but intolerable ones.[42] To say that wild men were fundamentally like ourselves was to announce a radical break from the consensus of Cass and most white Americans. Like other former colonials, the people of the United States had established a society in which non-Europeans were nonpeople.[43] Everywhere the native was subjugated or slaughtered, or he was culturally castrated and herded onto reservations. The pattern in the United States had its own configurations, however, based mainly on the *distance* between its doctrines of universal Christian brotherhood and of Enlightenment natural rights, on the one hand, and its practice of Indian removal or extermination, on the other.

Standing outside this white definition of humanity, Thoreau was one of a handful of men, which included a few other isolated radicals like George Catlin, who gave an attentive hearing to anyone who spoke of the Indians as acquaintances, friends, or family. When Hunter recorded his fond remembrance of tribal life, he offered Thoreau a link not only to the "tawnies" but to the rest of the nonwhite majority of mankind. He had lived what was to Thoreau still an intellectual and moral possibility —the possibility, that is, of transcending an inhuman perspective. Hunter was bound to have importance, therefore, to a man whose writings showed him to be interested in natives everywhere, in Asia, Africa, and the New World, with a particular interest in those closer to home, like the fugitive slaves, the Mexican prisoners, and the Indians. In 1859 he noted bitterly that it was the fashion in California and Oregon "to treat men exactly like deer which are hunted, and I read from time to time in Christian newspapers how many 'bucks,' that is, Indian men, their sportsmen have killed." [44]

42. On the still more urgent need today for redefinition, see Claude Lévi-Strauss, *The Savage Mind* (University of Chicago Press, 1966), pp. 40–42, 267–69; for a modern instance of the sterility of discussions of Thoreau's "primitivism" or lack thereof, see Roderick Nash, *Wilderness and the American Mind* (New Haven: Yale University Press, 1967), p. 92.

43. For Europeans and aborigines in "fragment cultures," see the excellent first three chapters of Louis Hartz, *The Founding of New Societies* (New York: Harcourt, Brace & World, 1964).

44. *Journal,* XII (October 21, 1859), 416–17.

Thoreau's determined opposition to the war against the Mexicans arose from a dawning sense of the international implications for a society that condoned the practice of hunting men at home as though they were deer. Had he been able to go back and study evidence on Hunter's last few months in Mexico, he could have seen it spelled out: the easy transition from domestic racism to imperial destiny was reflected in Joel R. Poinsett's assertion that "the United States are in a state of progressive aggrandizement, which has no example in the history of the world." With this proud claim in mind, along with knowledge of the fate of Hunter's Indians in Texas, Thoreau might even have sensed the full horror of the impending American Passage to Asia.

It was sad beyond words that Thoreau did not live to write his masterpiece on the Indians, the great work for which the *Week* and even *Walden* (1854) might have served as progress reports.[45] His whole life was in a sense a readying of himself to complete the study which might have meant so much to us all. I feel this all the more keenly because he was uniquely prepared to grasp the meaning of Hunter's life. As Emerson said of his friend, "Every fact lay in glory in his mind." Like John Donne and other seventeeth-century metaphysical poets, Thoreau knew a fact as something to be felt as well as thought about. His lifelong interest in the Indians equipped him to understand that Hunter put his captivity story before the world with precisely the hope that it would not only be thought about but felt as well. I have argued that its occasional awkwardness testified to the authenticity of its origins. It was the product of a mind which was still in some measure "mind in its untamed state," which happens to be Claude Lévi-Strauss's definition of *la pensée sauvage*, or the savage mind.[46] But long before the anthropologist, Thoreau knew that the poet in him made him one with the savage in his refusal to sever emotion from thought, knew that savage thought was human thought, knew that the savage mind was our mind before we cut it off from the rest of our body: "Inside the civilized man stands the savage still in the place of honor."

The wildness from which everyone but a savage like Hunter and a

45. In an essay on "Thoreau's Politics of the Upright Man," *Massachusetts Review*, IV (Autumn 1962), 136n, I expressed doubt that his untimely death at forty-four had robbed the world of a great work on the Indians, arguing "that The Civil War might have undone Thoreau along with so many others." A close study of his Indian Notebooks and related materials in his *Journal* has since persuaded me that, if anybody could have come through this nationalist bloodbath whole, it was Thoreau.

46. Lévi-Strauss, *Savage Mind*, p. 219.

poet like Thoreau and an artist like George Catlin fled was simply the "animal in us." Here Thoreau had broken through to the core of the mystery of why there was such horror over those captives who refused to return to the clearings: by electing to stay with their savage hosts, or identifying with them, as in Hunter's case, these "captives"—always an ambiguous term—presented the mind-reeling prospect of men and women choosing to throw themselves out of history. They had elected not to run any more from the animal within, which is to say from the mortal within, which is to say from the human within. To their compatriots, ever so willing to sacrifice their humanity on the altar of Progress and the American Empire, they seemed mad and threatening. But to Thoreau, who had reached the truth that mastery of the art of dying is a precondition for living, it was another story. He had no illusions about which side of the frontier real madness and ferocity came from.

Thoreau may easily have seen in Hunter, with his hauntingly allegorical name, a symbol of the meaning of America. Out of the encounter of the Old World with the New, white with red, was born a new man who sought a new heaven and a new earth where extermination was not one of the standing orders of providence. A new man no longer at war with the nature in himself or engaged in a frenzy of conquest of the nature without. A new man so a part of nature "that he is at home in her." A century later D. H. Lawrence wrote some famous lines which expressed the hope that the white man's spirit "can cease to be the opposite and the negative of the red man's spirit. It can open out a great new area of consciousness, in which there is room for the red spirit too." [47] Thoreau had already felt the old consciousness "a tight-fitting prison" and could have accepted Hunter as an accomplice in an attempt to light out for new territory.

3

Hunter was important to Thoreau, to the subversive side of Cooper, and to us for yet another reason. The Indians were "a rude and barbarous people," said Cass, "who had no governments to guide or control them, no laws to restrain them, no officers to punish them; who had no

47. Lawrence, *Studies in Classic American Literature* (Garden City, New York: Doubleday, 1953), p. 61.

permanent settled residence, where they could be found, nor any property to defend." What these barbarians lacked constituted the essentials of *civilization,* which was to say they lacked private property defended by government. Among civilized peoples the long arm of government reached out through law to find, to guide or control, to restrain or punish everyone, since everyone was a thief or a potential thief. John Neal arraigned Hunter for his ignorance of these elementary truths, for having no "knowledge of the first principles of political association. He would live without law; and he would have the Indians live without law, *after they have been civilized,*" which was to Neal a manifest absurdity. And Austin held it axiomatic that "no individuals have or ought to have the power of taking into their hands the authority vested by law in the competent tribunals": this was why the mad defiance of Hunter and Fields threatened to sweep everyone out "on the stormy ocean of anarchy." As he explained to his colonists, "The Mexican Govt is founded on the broad and Solid basis of rational freedom—it is modeled after that of the United States of the north." Rational freedom was remarkably similar to cowed subservience. But such perverse definitions of civilization and rationality had been seen for what they were a century earlier by the writer of our epigraph on page 231, "Of Tyranny, Anarchy, and Free Governments."

The definition of civilization as the power to coerce—find and control or punish—was of course in the interest of those with the most power. But there had always been grounds on which it could be challenged. Lord Moulton, the English statesman, once remarked that "the measure of civilization is the extent of obedience to the unenforceable." After a lifetime of studying neolithic communities in Central America, Sylvanus Griswold Morely quoted Lord Moulton's remark with the observation that, judged by this standard, the ancient "Maya must have measured high."[48] So too would have the North American Indians, who notably lacked repressive government and strong rulers, to the dismay of Cass and other whites, and who had finely woven networks of relationships into which individuals found their way freely and surely.

That was what Hunter brought to the English: he brought good news

---

48. Morely, *The Ancient Maya,* rev. by George W. Brainerd (Stanford, Calif.: Stanford University Press, 1956). Cf. Kenneth Boulding speaking to the same point: "I regard the lessening of coercion as one of the most fundamental long-run objectives of human organization and one of the most profound moral tests by which any social movement is to be judged," *The Organizational Revolution* (New York: Harper, 1953), p. 251.

from within tribal culture of the tenacious hold of the Indians on their close, voluntary community bonds. Uneasily aware that the times were sick and out of joint and rightly apprehensive that the Age of Machinery was ripping up the possibilities of community, intellectuals and reformers heard his message with intense longing. At exactly this point Hunter acted to link up the communalism of archaic man with the communitarian yearnings of modern man. With one hand he reached out to the Indian vision of a Pagan Paradise Retained and with the other to the dream of Villages of Cooperation and the Whole Earth a Garden. He introduced Tecumseh, so to speak, to Robert Owen.

Given their proud refusal to subject themselves to external or alien forces, the Indians were quite properly represented by Hunter at the birth of the modern libertarian tradition. Through him they were present as witnesses and perhaps to some degree as models. Hunter's association with and possible influence on "the father of English socialism" has already been discussed, along with the parallels between his and Owen's plan for establishing communities. Here I merely note in passing that the word "socialist" first appeared in 1827 and from the beginning meant someone like Owen or Hunter who was committed to work toward friendly, cooperative communities—Richard Fields, who gave his life trying "to setel a Poor orfan tribe of Red peopel" on lands held in common, would also have qualified. To be sure, the later rise of Marxism and modern state socialism left this tradition behind and disparagingly labeled as utopians and anarchists those radicals who turned to it in search of a usable past. But the important connections remain.

The links I have in mind were between Indian tribalism as depicted by Hunter and the libertarian tradition within which Peter Kropotkin, in *Mutual Aid* (1902), was to find in "the earliest tribal customs and habits" the mutual aid on which civilization depended. The gains of such free association and individual spontaneity had been blocked and dissipated by the state, he held, for the state "took possession, in the interest of minorities, of all the judicial, economical, and administrative functions which the village community already had exercised in the interest of all." Hunter's plan to help the Indians help themselves tied it across space and time to Kropotkin's belief that social organization had to be formed on freedom and nursed into being from the bottom up. The root principle of voluntarism committed the anarchists to work intentionally toward what the Indians already had: communities of the uncoerced. Hence Emma Goldman might have been describing tribal life when she stated at the Amsterdam Anarchist Congress of 1907 that her view of social organization was based on natural groupings, "on the harmony of organic growth which produces variety of color and form, the complete whole we admire in the flower."

Hunter also served as a link between the Indians and American radicals, who were fewer in number but not less significant for that reason than their English counterparts. He spoke to a native American tradition dating back to the Revolution which held government as at best a necessary evil and which gave some of our leading writers means to counterattack the onslaught against the Indians. Almost in spite of Cooper, Leatherstocking insistently posed the question: What if the United States government was in fact the primary vehicle of extermination and injustice? And he even outlined a reasonable response, based on considerations of natural justice: when laws "run a'gin the laws of God, they get to be onlawful, and ought not to be obeyed." Hunter could speak directly to Thoreau, who knew the Indian stood "free and unconstrained in Nature, is her inhabitant and not her guest, and wears her easily and gracefully. But the civilized man has the habits of the house. His house is a prison." [49] The author of "Civil Disobedience" and of the warm tributes to John Brown could readily have understood and sympathized with the anarchistic rebellion of Hunter and Fields.

Perhaps their attempt to establish a red and white republic was absurd. Perhaps after Hunter's death it was absurd for Robert Owen to take up the plan to build a community in Texas, on land owned by General Arthur G. Wavell and Benjamin R. Milam. In his extraordinary "Memorial to the Mexican Republic," Owen proposed to

> prepare the means to put an end to war, religious animosities, and commercial rivalries between nations, competition between individuals to enable the existing population of the world to relieve themselves from poverty or the fear of it; to create an entire new character. . . . This practice, so long promised to the human race, can never be obtained under any of the Governments, laws, or the institutions in any known part of the world.[50]

Nor can it yet . . . .

49. *Journal,* I (April 26, 1841), 253.
50. "Memorial of Robert Owen to the Mexican Republic," September 1828, reproduced in Wilbert H. Timmons, "Robert Owen's Texas Project," *Southwestern Historical Quarterly,* LII (1949), 289–93.

And we, standing as we do some hundred millions of exterminations later, can hardly dismiss out of hand Hunter's Edenic dream and his proposed reconciliation of the races. No longer can any thoughtful person turn to the United States government or any other as the embodiment of a progressive destiny. If it is absurd to hope that whites can live with nonwhites on the basis of friendship and respect for the other's autonomy, then we have pretty well run our string out anyway. In truth Hunter's proposal for an Indian country was no more absurd than the attempts of colonized peoples elsewhere to break free. It was no more absurd than George Catlin's pleas for a park where the Indians could roam free. It was no more absurd than the present-day attempts to save from slaughter some of the Indians in the Mato Grosso and Amazon basin. And it was something the United States might have afforded, especially on land belonging to Mexico. Hunter said it clearly in the beginning:

> The American community in particular, which has become great and powerful as it were on the destruction of the Indians, owes the accomplishment of this measure [of saving them], as far as is practicable, to its own character, to justice, and to moral right.

Bibliographical Essay

PERSONAL PAPERS AND PUBLIC RECORDS

Of course the "John Dunn Hunter Papers" do not exist. A student of his life cannot start out with a central body of materials to which he can add finds from other collections. The controverted narrative of his captivity is the sole source up to 1823. From then till 1827 he was almost always on the move, with little or no chance to accumulate letters and preserve memoranda or diaries. When he was murdered the few papers in his possession were destroyed or lost. Furthermore, other materials are not where one would hope to find them. One of Cass's heirs destroyed his papers. Hunter's letters to Elias Norgate have not survived. The Longman publishing house no longer has correspondence relating to his memoirs. The files of his American publisher have disappeared.

Happily the problem is less hopeless than it appears at first glance. Several items in Hunter's handwriting have been preserved. His letter to James Madison of October 15, 1824, is in the Madison Papers, Library of Congress. His letter to Robert Owen of January 2, 1825, along with the letter of introduction from J. Adams Smith, is in the Owen Papers, Holyoake House, Manchester. His letter to Thomas William Coke of February 15, 1824, reproduced in A. M. W. Stirling, *Coke of Norfolk and His Friends* (London: John Lane, 1908), II, 320–22, is at Holkham Hall, Ms. 747, Vol. III. His note of January 1, 1824, probably addressed to Dr. Petingale, the physician of the Duke of Sussex, is in the Autograph File, Houghton Library, Harvard. The holograph of his "Reflections on the Different States and Conditions of Society" is in the Chicago Newberry Library, Ayer Ms. No. 398.

A few of Hunter's letters were reproduced or quoted at length elsewhere. His communication on the meaning of his Indian names was published in the London *Literary Gazette*, May 3, 1823, p. 279. One of his letters to Neal, dated October 15, 1824, was reproduced in Irving T. Richards, "The Life and Works of John Neal" (unpubl. Ph.D. diss., Harvard, 1932, IV). Bessy Walker to Neal, April 10, 1825, *ibid.*, contains a long quotation from one of Hunter's letters to her. Hunter was also quoted extensively in Lady Dorothea Knighton, ed., *Memoirs of Sir William Knighton* (London: Richard Bentley, 1838), II, 56–63.

The Jared Sparks Manuscripts, Houghton Library, Harvard, are indispensable for understanding the origins of the attack on Hunter.

In the 1820s the Office of Indian Affairs (OIA), ancestor of the modern bureau, was appropriately lodged within the War Department: its files constitute Record Group 75, National Archives (NA). There are some relevant papers of Cass's in the Records of Superintendencies of Indian Affairs, Michigan, 1814–51, Microcopy (M) 1, Rolls (R) 16, 18, and 20. But the most valuable material on or relating to Hunter is in Letters Received by the OIA, 1824–80, M234. The letters of Cass and Clark to Colonel Thomas L. McKenney are in R247, R429, and, most important of all, R419. The files of the Department of State constitute Record Group 59. Hunter's presence in the City of Mexico is recorded in Despatches from US Ministers to Mexico, 1823–1906, M97, R1; Joel R. Poinsett's communications about him are in M97, R2 and R3.

Poinsett's important letter to President Samuel Quincy Adams of April 26, 1827, is in the Poinsett Papers, Historical Society of Pennsylvania (HSP). The Duponceau Papers, HSP, are crucial for understanding the attack on Hunter from this quarter. The American Philosophical Society holds Duponceau's letter to M. Jullien in Paris and also, in its Ord Papers, two valuable letters from George Ord to Waterton (October 20 and December 1, 1861).

The Austin Papers, published in the *Annual Report for the American Historical Association for the Year 1919,* II (Washington: Government Printing Office, 1924), contain a great deal of relevant evidence on Hunter and the events leading up to the Fredonian uprising.

Sir Henry George Ward's official correspondence is in the Public Record Office, Foreign Office Correspondence, Mexico, F. O. 50/3–32, especially 50/20, Nos. 18 and 20; 50/30; 50/31b, Nos. 34 and 49. See also Embassy and Consular Archives, Mexico, F. O. 204/1–15, especially 204/4, Part 2, No. 32.

HUNTER'S NARRATIVE AND PAMPHLET

The full title of the Philadelphia edition was *Manners and Customs of Several Indian Tribes Located West of the Mississippi; Including Some Account of the Soil, Climate, and Vegetable Productions, and the Indian Materia Medica: To Which Is Prefixed the History of the Author's Life During a Residence of Several Years among Them* (Philadelphia: J. Maxwell, 1823; Hunter applied to the clerk of the Eastern District of

Pennsylvania for a copyright on February 8). The work was out on or before March 7, 1823, which was the date the publisher presented a copy to the American Philosophical Society Library. The London editions were published under the title *Memoirs of a Captivity among the Indians of North America, from Childhood to the Age of Nineteen: With Anecdotes Descriptive of Their Manners and Customs. To Which Is Added, Some Account of the Soil, Climate, and Vegetable Productions of the Territory Westward of the Mississippi* (London: Longman, Hurst, Rees, Orme, Brown and Green; the first and second editions were published in 1823 and the third in 1824). The London editions contained three new chapters: "Observations on Civilizing the American Indians"; "Indian Anecdotes"; and "A Short Description of the Practice of Physic among Several Tribes . . ." The third edition had as well an afterword which set forth Hunter's further reflections on society: see the title of his pamphlet listed below. The German edition appeared under the title *Der Gefangene unter den Wilden in Nord Amerika; nach. J. D. Hunter's Denkwürdigkeiten seines Aufenthalts unter denselben und seiner Schilderung des Charakters und der Sitten der westlich vom Mississippi wohnenden Stämme,* edited by W. A. Lindau (Dresden: P. G. Hilscher, 1824). The Dutch edition was published the same year at Dordrecht and the Swedish in 1826 at Mariefred.

The first part of Hunter's narrative was reproduced in the *Book of American Indians* (Dayton, Ohio: B. F. Ellis [editor and publisher?], 1854). The entire Philadelphia edition was reproduced as *Manners and Customs of Indian Tribes* (Minneapolis, Minn.: Ross and Haines, 1957). This reprint lacks a great deal: it has no introduction and its title page does not list the original publisher or date of publication. Unfortunately the failure to select the fuller, more correct London edition of 1824 for reproduction was repeated by the Lost Cause Press (Louisville, Ky.) in its microcard publication of *Manners and Customs of Several Indian Tribes Located West of the Mississippi* (Catalogue [November 1969], p. 10). Finally, though in 1968 the Johnson Reprint Corporation of New York came closer by reproducing the second London edition (summer 1823), their volume still does not include Hunter's further reflections on society, available in the final edition and listed directly below.

Hunter's pamphlet, *Reflections on the Different States and Conditions of Society; with the Outlines of a Plan to Ameliorate the Circumstances of the Indians of North America,* which became an afterword to the

English edition of 1824, was originally published in 1823 by J. R. Lake of London, "for the *sole use* of the members of the New England Company."

SELECTED ARTICLES, PAMPHLETS, AND BOOKS

NOTE: The following sources are those which proved directly helpful and do not include many of tangential importance. For example, Cass's 1828 and 1830 essays in the *North American* are critical for understanding his views on the Indians but are not listed here. See the text and footnotes for citations to them, to other articles such as those of Neal in *Blackwood's Magazine*, to the indispensable reports of the Bureau of American Ethnology, and to relevant memoirs, biographies, monographs, and the like.

The article which led to the controversy was Anon. (George Procter), "The North American Indians," *Quarterly Review*, XXXI (December 1824), 76–111. Cass's attack was in "Indians of North America," *North American Review*, XXII (January 1826), 53–119. In response Elias Norgate wrote his pamphlet, *Mr. John Dunn Hunter Defended* (London: John Miller, 1826). Then John Neal entered the lists with "Mr. John Dunn Hunter," *London Magazine*, V (May–August 1826), 317–43.

Reviews of Hunter's narrative of course contained valuable evidence. The first discussion of it, along with lengthy extracts, appeared in the *Literary Gazette* of April 19, 1823, pp. 242–44; of April 26, pp. 260–62; and of May 3, pp. 278–79. See also the *Eclectic Review*, XX (July–December 1823), 173–81. A thoughtful analysis was published by Cyrus Redding's *New Monthly Magazine*, VIII (July–December 1824), 276–85; another by the *Monthly Review*, CII (November, December 1823), 243–56, 368–81. A French view appeared in *Révue encyclopédique*, XX (October 1823), 128. On the American side, editor John P. Foote probably wrote the perceptive critique which appeared in the first two numbers of the *Cincinnati Literary Gazette*, I (January 1 and 10, 1824). Disenchanted patron Robert Walsh unfavorably compared it with "[John] Tanner's Indian Narrative," *American Quarterly Review*, VIII (September 1830), 108–34. Finally, Mildred Mott Wedel reviewed the 1957 reproduction in *Nebraska History*, XXXIX (1958), 75–77.

In the relatively recent past several writers have had chance encounters with the narrative. In "The Education of John Hunter," *Social Science*,

XV (July 1940), 258–64, sociologist Brewton Berry discussed the phenomenon of acculturation. But, unaware of the charges of imposture and of what became of Hunter after 1824, Berry did not get very far with his topic. In 1915 W. J. Holland, the eminent entomologist, assumed in his *Butterfly Book* that the name of one of his insects commemorated "a most remarkable American, John Dunn Hunter. . . . He interested himself in securing natural history collections from America for certain of his acquaintances, and Fabricius named the beautiful insect shown on our plate in his honor. His *Memoirs of Captivity among the Indians* is well worth reading." Fabricius could not have so honored Hunter, alas, for he died in 1808 and therefore could not have known of the white savage. This curious misidentification is discussed by John Francis Kieran in his *Footnotes on Nature* (Garden City, N. Y.: Doubleday, 1947), pp. 204–8. The best of the recent articles dealing with Hunter is Erwin H. Ackerknecht's " 'White Indians': Psychological and Physiological Peculiarities of White Children Abducted and Reared by North American Indians," *Bulletin of the History of Medicine*, XV (January 1944), 15–36. Ackerknecht treated Cass's charges with some skepticism and even attempted to account for the peculiar fascination of Indian life for white "captives" generally. Though his attempt was less than successful, he is worth looking at for it alone. Finally, the narrative was competently placed within the history of the captivity chronicles by Dorothy M. F. Behen, "The Captivity Story in American Literature, 1577–1826" (unpubl. Ph.D. diss., University of Chicago, 1951).

Of the contemporary accounts, some of the most important were written by Hunter's English patrons: A. M. W. Stirling, *Coke of Norfolk and His Friends* (London: John Lane, 1908), II, 316–22; Lady Smith, ed., *Memoir . . . of the Late Sir James Edward Smith* (London: Longman, 1832), I, 513–15; Lady Dorothea Knighton, ed., *Memoirs of Sir William Knighton* (London: Richard Bentley, 1838), II, 56–63. Cyrus Redding wrote a sensitive, intelligent essay on Hunter in his *Personal Reminiscences of Eminent Men* (London: Saunders, Otley, 1867), III, 42–55.

Three English authors drew on Hunter and his narrative for their books on the United States and Indian–white relations: Isaac Candler, *Summary View of America* (London: T. Caldwell, 1824); James Buchanan, *Sketches of the History, Manners, and Customs of the North American Indians* (London: Black, Young, & Young, 1824); and, most valuable of all, John Halkett, *Historical Notes Respecting the Indians of North America* (Edinburgh: Archibald Constable, 1825).

Among Hunter's compatriots, Lewis Cass and Henry Rowe Schoolcraft were most fortunate in having biographers and editors who were all enthusiastic participants in the celebration of America; not one betrayed the possession of a critical intelligence. In the absence of perceptive biographies, then, the most revealing sources are Schoolcraft's own *Personal Memoirs of a Residence of Thirty Years with the Indian Tribes of the American Frontiers* (Philadelphia: Lippincott, Grambo, 1851), and his unsigned campaign biography, *Life of General Lewis Cass* (Philadelpia: G. B. Zieber, 1848). John Neal chose an apt title for his memoirs: *Wandering Recollections of a Somewhat Busy Life* (Boston: Roberts Brothers, 1869). Like Cass in this respect, Duponceau left the memorializing to friends: see Robley Dunglison, *A Public Discourse in Commemoration of Peter S. Duponceau* (Philadelphia: American Philosophical Society, 1844).

For Hunter's stay in Britain, the diary entries of Chester Harding are quite revealing: see Margaret E. White, ed., *A Sketch of Chester Harding, Artist* (Boston: Houghton, Mifflin, 1929). For Hunter's return to the West two other diaries are of critical importance: Caroline Dale Snedeker, "The Diaries of Donald Macdonald, 1824–1826," *Indiana Historical Society Publications*, XIV (1942), and Joel W. Hiatt, ed., "The Diary of William Owen from November 10, 1824, to April 20, 1825," *Indiana Historical Society Publications*, IV (1906). On Hunter in the City of Mexico, see Henry George Ward, *Mexico in 1827* (London: Henry Colburn, 1828) and Henry Stuart Foote, *Texas and the Texans* (Philadelphia: Thomas Cowperthwait, 1841), which contains valuable firsthand information, especially the testimony of Herman B. Mayo. Last but perhaps first in importance is George Catlin's *Notes of Eight Years' Travels and Residence in Europe, with His North American Indian Collection* (New York: George Catlin, 1848).

NEWSPAPERS

Elias Norgate's entire *Mr. John Dunn Hunter Defended* was republished, along with Robert Walsh's editorial notes, in the *National Gazette*, July 13 and 14, 1826. Major John Francis Hamtramck's letter charging Hunter with being a deserter appeared in the issue of January 10, 1827. Other relevant items appeared in the issues of January 25 and November

21, 1826, and, on the Fredonian rebellion, of February 16 and 27, March 13, April 10, and May 18, 1827.

Major Thomas Biddle's letter and collection of documents designed to prove Hunter's imposture were published in the *National Intelligencer* of November 8, 1826. Colonel Thomas L. McKenney was probably the author of the important denunciation of the *Quarterly Review* critic in the *National Intelligencer* of April 26, 1825.

The *Niles Weekly Register* of January 21, 1826, reported with satisfaction that Hunter had been conclusively proved "to be an arrant impostor."

In the *Saturday Evening Post* of August 16, 1823, there was a favorable notice of the narrative; the issue of November 13, 1824, carried a sizable extract from it.

Useful information on Hunter's movements and his plan to help the Indians surfaced in the *New York Religious Chronicle* of June 26, 1824, and August 6, 1825.

"Viator's" letter on Hunter was printed in the Natchitoches *Courier* of March 20, 1827. That newspaper carried items on the Fredonians and on Hunter's death in its issues of January 16, February 20, and March 20, 1827.

Obituaries also appeared in the Mobile *Commercial Register*, April 28, 1827; the Arkansas *Gazette,* May 20, 1827; and the Ohio *State Journal,* June 21, 1827. One obituary, delayed well over a century, was probably least deserved of them all: Hunter's colorful contributions to the history of the Lone Star State were exploited by columnist Frank X. Tolbert in "About White Chief of the Cherokees," Dallas *News,* December 24, 1959. Tolbert grandly depicted Hunter as "a fellow of Tarzan-like physique" and the holder of a doctor's degree from a European college. He concluded that, "with a little better luck, this brilliant white man might have become emperor of a nation of Indians." A lucky emperor?

Index

ing, 131; and Jefferson, 170–71; and Dwight Mission, 173; moved to former Osage lands, 174; Western, 177–78; Texas claims outlined, 181; and Hunter's speech, 196–97; adoption of Hunter and Basset, 204; and tribal separatism, 207–8; Hunter and warriors of, 211; Austin threat of extermination, 215–16; Austin on as savages, 226; betrayed by Bean, 226–27; expulsion from Texas, 228; mentioned, 19, 175, 208, 209, 214

Chickasaws, 161

Chippewas, 62

Chisholm, Jesse, 201

Choctaws, 19, 161, 178

Chouteau, Auguste (half-brother of Pierre), 75, 83, 85, 86, 87, 92, 94

Chouteau, Auguste Pierre (son of Pierre), 84

Chouteau, Pierre: on Hunter, 77; Gallatin on, 83; career of, 83–84; as Menard partner, 86; fear of Lisa, 92; and Jefferson, 115; and division of Osages, 138, 139; and Catlin, 149; mentioned, 85, 86, 87, 90, 93

Cincinnati Literary Gazette, 103

Civilization: Hunter on conditions of, 38; identified with agriculture by Hunter, 42–43; as industrial capitalism, 50; Byron on, 53; for Thoreau and Hunter, 249–52; real measure of, 253

Clark, Edward: as unnamed editor, 3–4; *Eclectic Review* questions about, 103–4; author of *Plan for Navigating the Rapids in Rivers,* 109–10; background and role of, 109–11; pledge to join Owen community, 161; mentioned, 107, 108, 128

Clark, George Rogers, 116

Clark, William: Harding portrait of, 33; at Prairie du Chien, 61–65

passim; on Tenskwatawa, 69–70; and Hunter's narrative, 77, 81, 82; as Chouteau and Lisa partner, 83, 93, 94; and Osage treaty of 1825, 84, 174; and Jefferson, 115, 116; and Indian-hating, 116; on source of Multnomah (Willamette), 142; and the Great American Desert, 145; and Catlin, 149; and Cooper, 233, 235; mentioned, 85, 86, 87, 90, 132, 140, 141, 142

Clavel, Marcel, 238

Clay, Henry, 168, 177, 187, 189, 191, 194, 201, 222

Clemson, Eli B., 88

Clermont, 137–39, 149

Clinton, DeWitt, 164

Cobbett, William, 54

Cody, William F. ("Buffalo Bill"), 39

Coke, Thomas William: life of, 21–25; Hunter letter to, 31–32; portrait of, 33; and Sussex, 34; and Owen's philanthropic society, 45; gifts to Hunter, 117, 159; mentioned, 48, 54, 55, 99, 110, 155–56

Colonialism. *See* Nationalism; Monroe Doctrine; Racism

Colter, John, 93

Comanches, 227

Communalism: Owen's views on, 45–47, 167–69; American receptiveness to, 167–68; archaic and modern, 253–55; and Owen's Texas project, 255; *See also* Anarchy

Communitarian. *See* Communalism; Anarchy

Conanchet, 236

Condorcet, Marie-Jean-Antoine-Nicolas Caritat, Comte de, 43

Confidence Man, 73, 244n

Conquering the Wilderness, 201

Conquest of Granada, 52

Cooper, James Fenimore: and "stages" of society, 43; Neal envy of, 96, 97; sources of, 233, 235,

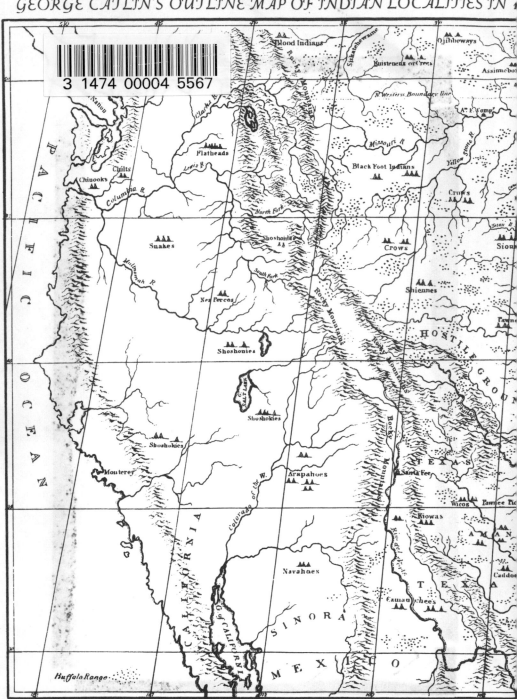